# INTRODUCTION TO FRENCH LAW

Cavendish
Publishing
Limited

# INTRODUCTION TO FRENCH LAW

**Walter Cairns**
Senior Lecturer in Law and Languages,
Manchester Metropolitan University

**Robert McKeon**
Senior Lecturer in Law and Languages,
Manchester Metropolitan University

Cavendish
Publishing
Limited

First published in Great Britain 1995 by Cavendish Publishing Limited, The Glass House, Wharton Street London WC1X 9PX.

Telephone: 071-278 8000   Facsimile: 071-278 8080

First Edition          1995

**British Library Cataloguing in Publication Data. A catalogue record for this book is available form the British Library.**

Cairns, W, McKeon R
Introduction to French Law

ISBN 1-85941-112-6

Printed and bound in Great Britain

# Foreword

The foreword traditionally provides the authors with an opportunity to express their gratitude towards those who have been of assistance in the realisation of their work. When we say we do not wish to thank anyone in particular, we are not doing so out of mean-mindedness, but because of a difficulty in identifying those whose contribution has outweighed that of any others. All our colleagues at the Manchester Metropolitan University have been most supportive and given the necessary amount of encouragement. The members of our families have displayed due forbearance when the work involved in preparing this book has sometimes been at the expense of participation in certain family occasions. In addition, our students have shown the necessary degree of equanimity and good humour in being 'used' as sounding boards for some of the more contentious parts of this work.

However, there are two institutions to whom due tribute must be paid. Mindful of the dictum that it is easier to write a book than to have it published, we must express our gratitude to the Cavendish publishing house for giving us the opportunity to give our writings the tangible form of this volume. In addition, we wish to thank the management and staff of the Institute for Advanced Legal Studies, for the ready access which they gave us to their excellent library facilities.

W.J.C.
R.C. McK.

# Contents

# 1 Introduction

It has been suggested that, when Rudyard Kipling made his famous remark that 'East is East, and West is West, and never the twain shall meet', he had in mind the English Channel and the two legal systems which prevail on either side. It is indeed extraordinary that the two countries in question, which share so many bonds of history and culture, have developed systems which regulate their everyday lives which are characterised by such a remarkable degree of mutual incomprehension. This does not necessarily imply that the two systems are totally dissimilar – in fact, it could be argued that it is this very lack of mutual understanding and knowledge which frequently obscures the fact that the differences between the French and English legal systems are often exaggerated. If this work can make even a modest contribution towards breaking down these barriers, this will give its authors a proper feeling of reward.

It has not, of course, escaped our attention that handbooks providing an introduction to the French legal system have become increasingly available over the past few years. Indeed, some works have boldly ventured beyond this general field and explored some very specific and sophisticated areas of French law. This work can make no pretence at any such in-depth exploration. What its authors can justifiably claim, however, is that it has added a distinct note of linguistic awareness to the general task of explaining the elements of a foreign legal system. Conscious of the fact that linguists and translators frequently turn to handbooks such as these for both general guidance and specific problem-solving, the authors have not only added an extensive glossary of legal terms, but also devoted an entire chapter to the problems associated with legal translation between French and English. This awareness of the linguistic dimension is the result of the many years in which the authors have been involved in the teaching of both law and legal translation. At a time when the inexorable process of European integration pursues its relentless course, it is more necessary than ever to provide every possible assistance in overcoming the 'great divide' which exists – or in many cases is thought to exist – on either side of *la Manche*. We sincerely trust it will prove useful to students, academics, practising lawyers and legal linguists alike.

Apart from the chapter on legal translation referred to above, we have endeavoured to cover as broad a range of topics in the practical area of the law as possible. Subsequent to this general introduction, we will provide an overview of the French court system and legal professions. This will be followed by two major subject areas in the field of private law, to wit the civil law and business law. Then our attention will focus on the area of public law, when

1

we consider, successively, constitutional and administrative law, as well as the criminal law. In conclusion, we will consider French court procedure and examine the main problems associated with the world of legal translation.

This general introduction is itself divided into several parts. Before focusing specifically on French law, it is appropriate to provide a word of explanation on the world of codified law, its principles, underlying philosophy as distinct from that of the Anglo-Saxon system, as well as its place among the major systems of law which prevail in the world. We will then provide a brief overview of the history of French law, in particular the major upheavals caused by the French revolution. This will be followed by a general introduction on French law, its major characteristics, its sources, and the place of some of these sources as compared to English law. Finally, we will examine and explain some of the basic concepts of French law which dominate and characterise its philosophy and practical application.

# I The world of codified law

## A General

The term 'codified law' denotes more than a legal system whose major legal topics are systematically grouped together into major compilations called 'codes'. It also describes a specific approach towards the law and the solving of legal problems. As such, the term 'codified law' is more often than not conflated with 'Napoleonic law', denoting the legal systems which underwent the influence of the major codes [which were] developed during the first decade of the 19th century on the initiative and under the direction of Napoleon Bonaparte.

In our view, this is a mistake. There is no such thing as a single codified law, since the notion of codification (a) did not originate in 19th century France but in 4th century Rome, and (b) because, in more recent times, there had occurred other codification movements which developed independently from, and in some cases prior to, the French model. The revival of codification in the 18th century was as much a product of the Enlightenment as of the practical need for legal reform, and therefore flourished in those countries where the Enlightenment took the firmest hold. Eloquent testimony of this proposition can be found in the Bavarian and Prussian codes of the 18th century,[1] which gave rise to their own codified tradition (with not a little global impact, as can be seen from those countries, like Greece and Turkey, whose codes are based mainly on the German model).

---

1    Robinson, O.F., Fergus, T.D., and Gordon, W.M., *An Introduction to European Legal History* (1985, Professional Books) p. 413 *et seq.*

Equally fallacious, in our view, is to use the term 'civil law' to the systems which are based on the Napoleonic model. Although it is true that the *code civil* was the first and most famous expression of the French codified school, it would be unwise to use the term 'civil law' to describe the legal system of this group of countries, fraught as it is with two potential misconceptions. The first is that the *code civil* was the only, or even the main, item of codified law to be adopted elsewhere. This is clearly not the case, since the other major Napoleonic codes (*code pénal, code de commerce, etc*) have been just as influential as the Civil Code. Secondly, it appears to imply that the countries having adopted other systems (*inter alia*, the common law system) have no 'civil law' themselves, which is obviously not the case. The term 'French codified law' or 'Napoleonic law' would therefore appear to be more appropriate.

## B Napoleonic law and the common law

Since many of the potential readers of this work will be English-trained lawyers, it is appropriate at this point to highlight some of the major differences between the common law and 'Napoleonic' codified law. These divergences spring not only from different historical developments, but also from a basic difference in philosophical approach, and they express themselves in various legal areas as well as having important linguistic implications. These aspects will be examined in turn.

### The philosophical dimension

The difference in the approach towards the law between the two systems can to a considerable extent be explained by different philosophical approaches. The French approach towards philosophical method is based on rationalism and is essentially deductive; it starts from broad principles which are then applied to individual cases. This was the method developed by René Descartes (1596-1650), the philosopher who altered an entire nation's way of thinking. Descartes assumed that the entire material universe could be explained on the basis of mathematical physics, and therefore all material phenomena were based on a number of *idées claires*,[2] ie basic principles. The British philosophical approach, on the other hand, is essentially inductive. It relies on empirical method, which was developed essentially by philosophers such as John Locke (1632-1704) in England and David Hume (1711-1776) in Scotland. Empiricism is sceptical of rationalism and its *a priori* positions which are accepted as being true regardless of the underlying experience. On the contrary, it believes that all knowledge is derived from experience, which means that broad principles can only be developed on the basis of inductive observation.

---

2    This thesis was developed in works such as *Discours de la méthode* (1637).

3

This divide is reflected in the legal thinking which prevails in both countries. Codified law is deemed to lay down a number of precepts which are deemed to be universally valid, irrespective of the time or place in which they apply. These rules govern the conduct of life in society, regardless of whether they will be applied or enforced in practice or not. The common law, on the other hand, seeks to provide solutions to individual disputes rather than lay down universal rules of conduct, and is expressed in court actions and legal remedies rather than in substantive rules. These are regarded as a generalised extrapolation of the solutions to individual disputes, whereas according to the lawyer trained in the Napoleonic tradition, rules must logically precede the solutions.[3]

### The historical dimension

Although a more detailed overview of the history of French law will be given elsewhere (cf. *infra*, p. 6), it is appropriate to point out in this respect two major differences between the development of the common law and that of the Napoleonic codified law.

First, there is the influence exerted by the Justinian Codes. When Justinian became emperor in 527 AD, he set about the task of consolidating into one set of instruments all the legislation which had accumulated over the centuries. The result was a systematic body of law consisting of six parts,[4] which together formed the *Corpus Juris Civilis*. For a long time these were only applied in parts of the Byzantine empire, until they were rediscovered by the scholars at Bologna University in the 11th century, where they were thoroughly studied and analysed. This set in motion a legal tradition which was to dominate most parts of Western Europe, except in England. In France, although it was not adopted throughout the entire country, they led directly to the first attempts at (unofficial) codification made by such jurists as Cujas, Godefroy and, later, Pothier. English law was also affected by Roman law, but that of an earlier period, ie that of the Praetorian decisions, which explains at least in part the leading role played by court decisions in the common law system.

Secondly, it is a historical fact that whereas the common law experienced an uninterrupted development from its beginnings in the 12th century, the Napoleonic law system came into existence as a result of one of the most dramatic upheavals in French and European history, ie the French Revolution. Although the pre-revolutionary law obviously continued to influence some of the new legal thinking, virtually all the legal institutions were swept away and gave rise to a new tradition in the law.

---

3   Nicholas, B., *French Law of Contract*, (1982, Butterworth), p. 4.

4   The Old Codex, the Fifty Decisions, the Pandects, the Institutes, the New Codex and the *Novellae*.

## The main practical differences

From a positive law point of view, the key difference between the common law and the Napoleonic law system resides in the order of priority as between the two major sources of law, which are the court decisions (the case law) and the rules laid down by parliamentary authority (legislation).

In the Napoleonic law system, legislation takes precedence over everything else, including the case law. As a result, no court decision may override legislation, every court decision must be based on legislation, and the courts are banned from issuing provisions by way of rules which are binding for the future.[5]

Under the common law, on the other hand, there is no clear hierarchy between court decisions and acts of the legislature. In those areas of the law covered by legislation, the latter takes precedence over court decisions. However, in spite of the exponential increase in state intervention by means of legislation which has affected many countries, including England, in the course of this century, some major areas of the law – eg the law of torts – are governed almost exclusively by the rules developed by the courts.

The difference between the two systems is also expressed in the hierarchy which exists within the case law itself. Under the Napoleonic law, no court decisions may take precedence over others, and in principle the decisions of the highest courts (the French *Cour de cassation* or the Spanish *Tribunal Supremo*) have no greater authority than those of the *Tribunal d'instance* (which is the lowest type of French court) or the *Juzgado de Paz* (which is the lowest type of Spanish court). Under the common law, on the other hand, there is a distinct hierarchy between court decisions. Thus in England, the decisions of the Court of Appeal take precedence over those of the county courts.[6]

Other major differences concern

- legislative techniques: the way in which laws are drafted also reveal differences between the two systems. In the Napoleonic law countries, the legislature normally contents itself with adopting the main outlines of a rule, leaving the executive to work out the details by means of secondary legislation. The common law tradition, however, is for the legislature to draft laws in a detailed manner, leaving as little as possible to be regulated by the executive (and as little scope for interpretation by the courts as possible).

- the structure of the courts: here, the main difference resides in the degree of specialisation. In the common law countries, the judiciary normally consists

---

5   Cf. Article 5 of the French *Code civil*, which is echoed in many other civil codes influenced by the French system.

6   Cairns, W.J., 'The Legal Environment', in Nugent, N. and O'Donnell, R., *The European Business Environment* (1994, Macmillan) p. 92.

of a uniform body of courts which settles all types of dispute. The Napoleonic law countries, on the other hand, have different sets of judicial organisation for different areas of the law; thus there are separate courts for disputes between the administration and the citizen (administrative courts) or for those which arise between traders amongst themselves or with ordinary citizens (commercial courts).[7]

• a different relationship between legislation and the courts. In the common law countries, and especially in England, there is a certain sense of rivalry between the statute law and the law of judicial precedent, which explains in part the more detailed manner in which English legislation is worded, and the stricter interpretation given by the English courts to legislation. This sense of conflict is almost completely absent in the Napoleonic law system, where the courts will always endeavour to find the *ratio legis* of a law in order to interpret it as faithfully as possible.

That being said, it must be conceded that there are trends at work which are evening out these differences. As will be explained in detail later in this work, the authority of the decisions of the higher French courts is almost as great as that of their counterparts in England; in addition, the pressures on the Parliamentary timetable in Britain, as well as the impact of EU directives, have resulted in the British Parliament increasingly adopting the 'continental' practice of issuing Acts which contain the main outlines of the matter to be regulated, leaving the Government to fill the gaps by means of regulations. It must also be admitted that the English courts have also of late been more prepared to establish the *ratio legis* of Acts of Parliament, rather than relying on the literal interpretation of the wording of legislative provisions.

# II An historical overview of French law

It is possible to discern four major periods in the history of French law: the pre-feudal period, feudal times, the period of absolutism, and the post-revolutionary period.

## A Pre-feudal law

In its earliest recognisable form, France was identified with ancient Gaul. This became part of the Roman empire in the course of the first century AD, during which time Roman law was obviously applied. As the Roman empire started to crumble under the invasions of the Germanic tribes, the legal situation became

---

7    There are exceptions to this; thus, for example, Italy does not have a separate system of commercial courts.

more diverse, mainly because of the system of *jus sanguinis* which was applied by these tribes. According to this system, each tribe was to be governed by its own legal system (eg the *Lex Salia* and the *Lex Ripuaria*) regardless of its location. As a result, both Roman law and the Germanic customs prevailed side by side for the next five centuries. Those governed by Roman law experienced a major restatement of the law in the shape of the *Lex Romana Visigothorum*, which was a collection of court decisions, decrees and legal opinions.

## B Feudal times

As France became a more identifiable state – particularly after the Capétiens assumed power in the Paris area and thereafter extended their control over the remainder of France through the vassal system – its legal system became more sophisticated. It was the vassal system which lay at the root of the feudal system, which abandoned the *jus sanguinis* and introduced the notion of territoriality into the law. However, although the law was defined on the basis of a locality and not on a person's tribal origins, not all the inhabitants of a particular location were subject to the same legal system. The population was divided into classes, ie the nobility, the clergy, the trading classes and the serfs, who were all subject to different legal rules.

However, this does not mean that the whole French territory became subject to the same class-based system. Two major legal zones emerged: the *pays de droit coutumier* and the *pays de droit écrit*. The former took root in the north, where the influence of the Germanic tribes was more marked and lasting. In the south, Roman rule had exerted a much more pronounced influence, and when the *Corpus juris civilis* (cf. *supra*, p. 4) was rediscovered, it was easily assimilated into the local legal system. However, this is not to say that Roman law had no influence whatsoever in the *pays de droit coutumier*, for on many matters, such as the law of obligations, the local customs were silent, which made recourse to the Justinian codes a matter of necessity.

Another factor which divided the two systems was the feudal law. Relations between feudal lords and their vassals were subject to a large set of complex rules. In the *pays de droit écrit*, the feudal law was contained in the decisions of the local courts (*les parlements*) whereas in the north, feudal law was governed by customary law. When in the middle of the 12th century, Obertus de Orto, a judge at the imperial court of Milan, made a compilation of the various feudal laws applying throughout Italy called the *Libri Feudorum*, it caught the attention of some parts of the *pays de droit écrit*. However, it never came to dominate the feudal law in other parts of France.

Nevertheless, there were some factors which had a unifying effect on these two areas. The French king made enactments (*capitularia*) which applied throughout the national territory, although their effect on the law was sometimes slight. In addition, matters which came within the scope of the ecclesiastical courts were governed by canon law, which applied both in the *pays de droit écrit* and in the *pays de droit coutumier*.

## C The absolutist period

The period of absolutist rule by the king can be said to have started with the accession of François I in 1494, and ended with the French Revolution in 1789. As the grip by the monarchy over the country became increasingly tight – to the extent of banning the French Parliament in 1614 – the stark differences between the *pays de droit écrit* and the *pays de droit coutumier*, whilst never completely abolished before the French Revolution, began to wither away. However, several other factors also played a part in this movement towards unification.

### Legislation enacted by the king

The right to issue legislation was an indispensable tool in the centralisation of power which took place during this period. François I issued the first major *ordonnance* in 1539 which required the registration of major events in a person's life which had legal implications (gifts, births, deaths and marriages), and reorganised criminal procedure. This was followed in 1566 by the *Ordonnance de Moulins*, which had important implications for civil procedure. However, it was mainly under the reign of that most absolute of absolutist monarchs, Louis XIV, that the *ordonnances* really came into their own. The king used to the full the services of a succession of excellent lawyers, especially Lamoignon and Daguesseau, and the driving force of his Chief Ministers Mazarin and, more importantly, Colbert, to issue many of these ordinances. Two such enactments, the *Code marchand* of 1673 and the *Ordonnance de la marine* of 1681, provided a great deal of the material for the post-revolutionary *Code de Commerce*.[8]

### The *coutume de Paris*

A number of customs had become codified in the course of the 16th century. Of these, the Paris *coutume* became the most influential, not only because of the position occupied by Paris as the capital city, but also because of the authority of some of the legal authors who produced extensive commentaries on it, in particular Dumoulin, who regarded the Paris *coutume* as being the *droit commun* of France. Such was its influence that, when other *coutumes* were revised, the changes were based on the Paris model, and that it was the latter which was introduced into the French colonies, in particular Canada.[9]

---

8  Robinson, O.F., Fergus, T.D. and Gordon, W.M., *op cit* p. 352.
9  Lawson, F.H., Anton, A.E. and Brown, L.N., *Amos & Walton's Introduction to French Law*, (3rd edn, 1967, Oxford University Press) p. 30.

**The influence of the leading commentators**

During the 16th and 17th centuries, a number of leading jurists had a decisive influence on the development of French law as a more harmonised system. The main authors of this type were:

- **Charles Dumoulin (1500-1566).** His first major contribution came in the shape of an influential commentary on the *coutume de Paris*, which encouraged him to think and write along the lines of a system of customary law which would apply throughout the *pays de droit coutumier*. His close relationship with the *parlement* ensured that the latter was influenced considerably by his writings.

- **Antoine Loysel (1536-1617).** He was both a scholar, particularly in legal history, and a practitioner, who for some years acted as the king's representative at the Protestant court of Guyenne. His main contribution towards the unification of French law was the publication of his *Institutes coutumières*, which contained a number of brief and useful legal maxims.

- **Robert Pothier (1699-1772).** He was a barrister who later became a judge and a professor of law. He was noted not so much as an original thinker on the law than as a writer with considerable organising ability, and as such was to exercise a considerable influence on many parts of the *code civil*.[10] In particular his *Traité des Obligations* affected the Napoleonic law of torts and contract law. For the first generation of lawyers after the Civil Code was enacted, Pothier's works were the authority most relied upon in order to fill any gaps or clarify any ambiguities inherent in the Code.[11]

# D The post-revolutionary period

Legal reform occupied a very prominent place on the agenda of the Revolutionaries, many of whom – including Danton – were lawyers. The first few years after the Revolution were a period of intense and sometimes chaotic activity, called the intermediary period, in which the fundamental assumptions underlying the entire legal system were changed.

The first legal reforms concerned basic civil liberties. The Declaration of Rights of Men and Citizens proclaimed all citizens to be equal before the law, which meant an end to the class-based justice system. The separation between Church and State was enforced, which meant that institutions such as marriage became secularised and the possibility of divorce introduced. The old court sys-

---

10  Robinson, O.F., Fergus, T.D., and Gordon, W.M., *op cit* p. 429.

11  Lawson, F.H., Anton, A.E., and Brown, L.N., *op cit* p. 31.

tem, based on the *parlements,* was abandoned and replaced by a judicial organisation which has largely survived to this day.

The initial attempts at adopting codes in the various individual areas of the substantive and procedural law were largely unsuccessful, until the period of the Consulate, when Napoleon Bonaparte set up a commission featuring the four best civil lawyers of the day,[12] whose brief it was to produce a draft Civil Code. Contemporary records show that Napoleon in fact took a very active part in the preparatory work for the new code. The *Code Civil des Français* was adopted in March 1804. This set off a wave of codification, in which the main areas of the law, ie commercial law, criminal law and procedure, and the law of civil procedure, were added to the list of codes to be introduced during the first decade of the 19th century.

## Development of post-codification law

It is perhaps useful to highlight a number of developments which have taken place in a number of individual areas of the law since the enactment of the original codes:

### Civil law

As will be explained later in the relevant chapter (*infra,* p. 51), the *code civil,* more than any of the other original codes, is a monument to legal durability. This is not only because its structure, and most of its provisions, have remained unaltered since their original enactment, but also because of its influence beyond the boundaries of France.

However a number of far-reaching changes were subsequently introduced. First of all, some of the provisions were changed, not least in the area of family law. These have tended to make divorce easier, and improved the position of the female spouse both in the family and in relation to the matrimonial property regime. Secondly, methods of interpretation have changed dramatically. Originally, the courts and lawyers were required to look upon the code as a self-sufficient document, which required no other aid to interpretation than the provisions themselves and the scheme of the code. This was the so-called exegetic school of interpretation.

However, in the course of the 19th century a reaction against this intellectual straitjacket was forthcoming, and demands grew for a greater freedom in interpreting the code. The catalyst for these demands arrived in the shape of François Gény. In his influential work *Méthode d'interpretation et sources en droit privé positif* (1892), he called for such factors as customary law, the case law and general principles of law to be allowed as aids to interpretation. This led indirectly to the method of interpretation which continues to apply today, to wit the

---

12   Portalis, Maleville, Bigot-Préameneau and Tronchet.

teleological method. This requires the courts to ascertain, when applying legislation, what was the intention of the legislature in enacting the rule in question. Initially, this had the courts and lawyers examining the *travaux préparatoires* of the legislation in question but later developed into a method of enquiry which sought to establish what would have been the attitude of the legislature if called upon to decide on the dispute at the time when it finds itself before the court.

*Criminal law and procedure*

In spite of the spirit of enlightenment which surrounded the French Revolution, the original Criminal Code of 1810 contained an extremely harsh and highly repressive set of rules. However, as the more liberal spirit of the 19th century began to make its influence felt, most of the provisions inflicting corporal punishment were repealed, the length of periods of imprisonment was reduced, and criminal policy began to move away from the purely repressive sphere towards other social objectives, such as crime prevention and the re-education and rehabilitation of the offender.

During the 20th century, this liberalising trend was continued in some areas, whereas in others a more repressive attitude was displayed. On the one hand, the abolition of the death penalty, the development of an increasingly sophisticated approach towards juvenile delinquency and the development of a new school in criminal policy which was headed by Marc Ancel, who introduced the notion of *la défence sociale* into the criminal law, all point towards an increasingly enlightened approach. On the other hand, it is a fact that more activities than before became criminalised, giving rise to new offences such as alcohol and drug abuse, business crime, and criminal negligence.

As will be explained in full later (*infra*, p. 145), both the criminal law and criminal procedure have very recently been the subject matter of comprehensive re-organisation.

*Judicial organisation*

As has already been mentioned, the confused and disparate system of justice administration was one of the first areas of major change following the Revolution. The laws of 16 and 24/8/1790 not only established a new judicial structure, but also introduced a number of principles which survive to this day, such as equality between all citizens before the courts, the administration of justice free of charge (*la gratuité*), and the appealable nature of all court decisions (*le double degré de juridiction*).

In addition, the basic court structure whose outlines survive to this day was introduced. The lowest court was the *Justice de paix* (Justice of the Peace), the forerunner of today's *Tribunaux d'instance*; at the next level were the *Tribunaux de district* (district courts), on which the current *Tribunaux de grande instance* are modelled, whereas the original courts of appeal were called *Tribunaux d'appel* (introduced by the Law of 27 *ventôse*, Year VIII). The court of final review, the *Tribunal de cassation*, was set up by the Laws of 27/11 and 1/12/1790, to become the *Cour de cassation* barely a few years later. In addition, the special courts dealing with commercial cases (*Tribunaux de commerce*) and with industrial disputes (*Conseils des prud'hommes*) were introduced.

The first major reform occurred barely two decades later, with the *Loi* of 20/4/1810. This law became a true charter of judicial organisation. The backbone of the system became the *Tribunal civil*, consisting of three judges appointed by the Government, and of which there was to be one for each *arrondissement;* at the instance of appeal there were the *Cours d'appel*, whose jurisdiction extended over several départements, and, at the review stage, the *Cour de cassation*.[13]

So durable was this structure to prove, that it was not until 1958 that the next major reform took place. Not that the intervening period was totally stagnant, since it established the *Conseil d'Etat* as a true judicial organ in administrative law (1872) and saw the birth and development of the *Conseils de préfecture*, later to become the *Tribunaux administratifs* in 1953. However, as the 20th century progressed, it became obvious that legal reform was badly needed. The main reason for a major overhaul was the fact that some courts no longer justified their existence in terms of the population they served.

This is why the system was changed by the law of 22/12/1958. The *Justices de paix* were replaced by the *Tribunaux d'instance*, of which there was to be one for each arrondissement. The *Tribunal civil* was replaced by the *Tribunal de grande instance*, of which there was to be one for every *département*. The *Cours d'appel* remained, but their jurisdiction was changed. This is the system which applies at the time of writing.

# III   The sources of French law

As is the case with any product, the law is the result of the processing of raw materials – in this case, the application of the various sources of law. These are:

• The constitution

• International treaties

---

13   Perrot, R., *Institutions judiciaires* (1993, Montchrestien) p. 11.

- Legislation

- Delegated legislation

- The decisions of the courts

- The *travaux préparatoires*

- *La doctrine*, ie the leading authorities, consisting not only of the major text-books and commentaries, but also of the annotations appended to court decisions

- The decisions of similar foreign courts

- Customary law

- General principles of law

Although there is a clear order of precedence between the first four sources, there is no distinct hierarchy between the remaining ones. A great deal will depend on the legal area in question, since there are some topics in which, for example, the case law is more highly developed than the *doctrine*, and others in which the reverse is the case.

Each of these sources will now be analysed in the light of their special characteristics and place in French law.

## A  The Constitution

The present Constitution is that of the Fifth Republic, which will be studied in detail in Chapter 6. For the purposes of this section, however, it should be pointed out that the Constitution is the supreme authority from which all other rules derive, since it organises and regulates the manner in which these rules are made. Its precedence in the hierarchy of sources is emphasised by the restricted constitutional review which can be exercised by the *Conseil constitutionnel* over the *lois organiques*, ordinary legislation and treaties (cf. *infra*, p. 43).

## B  International treaties

France belongs to the group of countries which adopt the 'monist' approach in relation to international treaties. This means not only that international treaties form part of the French legal system, but also that they take precedence over national legislation.[14] This rule has constitutional status, since Article 55 states:

---

14   The UK, on the other hand, adopts the 'dualist' approach, under which international law and domestic law constitute two separate legal orders, and the former may only become part of the latter by an express act of incorporation.

Treaties and (international) agreements which have been lawfully ratified or approved shall, as from the date on which they are published, take precedence over Laws, subject to the requirement that the other Contracting Parties apply the treaties or agreements in question.[15]

It therefore follows that the Constitution takes precedence over treaties as a source of law, since the treaties derive their superior status in relation to *lois* from the Constitution itself. If the latter were to be replaced by a new Constitution – a prospect which at the time of current writing seems less improbable than at any other time during the Fifth Republic – and the new Constitution were to stipulate a different kind of relationship between treaties and domestic French law, it would be the Constitution which would prevail.

A special position is occupied in this respect by the European Union treaties. This is not only because of the fact that the European Court of Justice has ruled that in principle their provisions also take precedence over domestic law. EU law also consists of the so-called 'derived legislation', being the binding instruments adopted under Article 189 of the Treaty of Rome (regulations, directives and decisions). Where these rules confer rights on individual EU citizens, and the latter plead them before the domestic courts of the EU member states, these rules of derived EU law will take precedence over domestic legislation. This rule is now accepted by all the French courts.[16]

## C Legislation

As will be reiterated later in greater detail, the Constitution of the Fifth Republic makes the Executive the dominant constitutional authority. One of the implications of this power relationship is that the term 'legislation', from the point of view of the hierarchy occupied by it among the sources of law, also includes certain rules which in the United Kingdom and other countries would be regarded as delegated legislation, ie regulations.

*Lois* are the generally binding instruments adopted by Parliament. The vast majority of these are ordinary laws which are adopted through the normal process of Parliamentary law-making. *Lois organiques* are laws which are based directly on the Constitution and enable the latter to be implemented. Although they are subject to special procedures, both in Parliament and before the *Conseil constitutionnel*, they do not have a higher hierarchical position than other laws.

In the main areas of the law, the *lois ordinaires* are grouped together in codes. These now include not only those which were adopted in the first decade of the

---

15  Translated by the authors from: *'Les traités ou accords régulièrement intervenus ont une autorité supérieure à celle des lois, sous réserve, pour chaque accord ou traité, de son application par l'autre partie'*.

16  For more details on the relationship between EU law and French law, cf. Lasok, D. and Bridge, J.W., *Introduction to the Law and Institutions of the European Communities* (1993, Butterworths) Chapter 11.

19th century. It must be pointed out, however, that these codes have been frequently amended, and even replaced wholesale (eg the new 1992 Criminal Code). In addition, new codes have materialised as certain areas of legislation have assumed such proportions as to require consolidation (eg the *code du travail* (industrial relations code) and the *code rural*). Administrative law, however, is a major area of the law which has not been affected by codification.

### The special case of *règlements autonomes*

It is arguable whether, under the present Constitution, the term 'legislation' must also include the regulations which the Government may make under Article 37. In a constitutional arrangement which would be anathema to the British system, with its accent on the principle of Parliamentary sovereignty, the areas which may be dealt with by ordinary *lois* are strictly defined in Article 34 of the Constitution.[17] The remainder is to be dealt with by regulations under Article 37 (the so-called *règlements autonomes*). In addition, where – under previous constitutional arrangements – the areas now falling within the scope of Article 37 were regulated by *lois* which continued to apply after 1958, the latter may be amended by *décrets*. Any such regulations which need to be incorporated into the various codes will be preceded by the initial R. in order to distinguish them from ordinary *lois*.

The quasi-legislative status of the *règlements autonomes* is, however, diminished by the fact that they are considered to be administrative actions and therefore subject to judicial review.

## D Delegated legislation

There are essentially two types of delegated legislation: those which have the same status as the *lois* and those which are subordinated to them.

As to the former, these are called *ordonnances*. Although they have the same status as *lois*, they are not 'legislation' in the same way as the *règlements autonomes*, since the latter, like the *lois*, derive their authority directly from the Constitution, whereas the *ordonnances* are only granted by authorisation given by Parliament, and therefore come within the scope of what can be termed as 'delegated legislation'. The relevant constitutional provision is Article 38, which states that, for the purpose of implementing its programme, the Government may request Parliament to grant it authorisation, for a limited period only, to adopt, by means of orders, measures which normally fall within the scope of

---

17 These areas are civil liberties, family law (including nationality and matrimonial property), successions, the *crimes* and *délits*, fiscal and monetary law, electoral law, the creation of public corporations, the status of civil and military officials, expropriation and privatisation law, defence, the status and powers of local authorities, education, property law, the law of obligations, industrial law, trade union law and social security law.

legislation. It should be remarked that these *ordonnances* are, in fact, a continuation of the old *décrets-lois* which applied under the Fourth Republic. The enabling law will fix the period for which the Government may exercise this power; during this period, Parliament forfeits the right to intervene in the areas concerned. Also, the ordonnances must be submitted to the *Conseil d'Etat* for an opinion and must be signed by the President of the Republic; in addition, they must be ratified by Parliament. Once ratified, they acquire the same status as laws, and may only be repealed or amended by another law. As long as *ordonnances* have not been ratified, however, they remain *actes administratifs* and are therefore capable of judicial review of administrative action. The first law enabling *ordonnances* to be made was passed on 4/7/1960; since then, more than 20 such *lois d'habilitation* and over 150 *ordonnances* have been adopted.

The other type of delegated legislation takes the form of *règlements*. One category of *règlement* (the *règlements autonomes*) has already been discussed. The other type is the *règlement subordonné*, which take the form of *décrets* (if adopted by the President or by the Prime Minister) or of *arrêtés* (if issued by individual Ministers, regional *Commissaires de la République* and mayors), and which are adopted in order to implement the *lois*. They have the status of administrative action and are therefore entirely subject to judicial review by the administrative courts.

# E Court decisions

It has already been stated that, in the Napoleonic conception, the courts have a subordinate role to play. Their duty is to interpret the law and to apply it to individual cases. The English system of judicial precedent is an anathema to this legal philosophy. There is no such thing as judge-made law; in fact, Article 5 of the Civil Code states that 'the courts shall be prohibited from issuing rules which take the form of general and binding decisions on those cases which are submitted to them'. The courts are therefore to be the servants, and not the masters, of the law. The authority of any decision of any court (*l'autorité de la chose jugée*) extends no further than the dispute for which the court in question was called upon to adjudicate. The only exception to this rule concerns the case where the *Cour de cassation* has for the second time been called upon to review a decision in the same dispute. Under Article 131(4) of the Code of Judicial Organisation, the *Cour de cassation* will then give a ruling which must be followed by the court to which the case is subsequently referred (*la seconde juridiction de renvoi*).

That, at least, is the theory. In practice, things have turned out very differently, for the following reasons:

- **The *Cour de cassation* was established in order to unify interpretation of the law**

  Although there is no hierarchy between the courts in France, the *Cour de cassation* was established in order to prevent the kind of divergences in interpretation between courts in various parts of the realm which occurred in the course of the *ancien régime*. Therefore a great deal of *de facto* authority attaches to the case law of the *Cour de cassation*, to the point that a consistent line of interpretation of a particular point of law has the official title of *la jurisprudence constante* (the established case law). It would be a bold *Tribunal d'instance* – or even a brave *Cour d'appel* – which presumed to contradict any such consistent body of case law.

- **The professionalism of the judges**

  It is a matter of professional pride for the courts to 'get it right'. Just as in England and Scotland, no court likes to have its decisions distinguished, so no lower court in France is particularly fond of having its decisions quashed on appeal, not only on the facts of the case, but also – and particularly – on a point of law. Therefore the courts will seek to give as professional a public service as possible by remaining abreast of the latest developments in the *jurisprudence* – not only of the *Cour de cassation*, but also of the other courts which are superior to them. In fact, there may be some areas which the Cour de cassation has not covered in its case law, and in respect of which therefore the decisions of the other courts – particularly the appeal courts – will need to be consulted.

- **The obligation to interpret legislation**

  It is slightly ironic that it is the obligation to interpret legislation that has led to the courts assuming an extremely important role in developing the law. Every decision by the courts must be based on an item of legislation, and the courts may not use gaps or lack of clarity in the law to avoid giving a decision in disputes submitted to them,[18] nor may they cite a previous court decision, even one of the *Cour de cassation*, as the sole authority for deciding a case. However, French legislation is worded in a very broad manner. This is particularly the case in relation to the provisions of the various codes. The basic provisions of the law of torts, for example (Articles 1382 *et seq* of the Civil Code), merely contain very general principles not unlike the common law principle laying down the 'duty to take care'. Therefore the French courts have had to be almost as inventive as their English counterparts in finding solutions to individual disputes.

---

18 Article 4 of the Civil Code.

To a certain extent, this enables the French courts to be more flexible than the English judiciary. Since the French courts are in principle not bound by the previous decisions of higher courts, they may, when they consider the moment to be ripe, ignore the latter and explore new avenues in legislative interpretation. Although in England the courts may in principle escape the strictures of binding precedent by applying the process of distinguishing cases, they are in many cases extremely reluctant to do so.

• **The availability of an abundant and well-organised body of case law**

As Lawson, Anton and Brown[19] point out, the sizeable and well-organised series of *recueils* of court decisions have a place in French libraries and in the minds of those professionally involved in the law which is almost as important as the position occupied by the Law Reports in this country. French lawyers frequently quote leading court decisions in their submissions and opinions, and ignorance of the *jurisprudence* would be as great a handicap for the French legal profession as it would be for their colleagues in England.

# F The *travaux préparatoires*

In Britain, *Hansard* and the other records of discussions taking place in the context of Parliament are very seldom prayed in aid of legislative interpretation. In France, on the other hand, the various debates and opinions which took place in the process of adopting a certain *loi* are frequently relied upon as a source of interpretation. It has to be conceded, however, that this is a source of law which has shed some of its prominence in recent years, for two reasons.

The first is a change in emphasis in legislative interpretation by the courts. There was a time when the courts endeavoured to ascertain what was the intention of the legislature when adopting the law in question, and to that end explored the *travaux préparatoires* for enlightenment. However, in recent years there has been a trend towards teleological interpretation, which seeks to establish how the legislature would have interpreted the law in the light of the circumstances prevailing at the time of the court case. For this purpose, the *travaux préparatoires*, whilst useful for the most recent legislation, are less relevant.

The second reason, closely related to the first, is the sheer age of some of the *travaux préparatoires*, particularly those which relate to the older codes. It is obvious that the debates and opinions which led up to the adoption of the *code civil* are less relevant now than at the beginning of the 19th century.

---

19  *Op cit*, p. 9.

# G *La doctrine*

The writings of the leading authorities on the law are more likely to be relied upon by French legal professionals than is the case in England. There was a good deal of resistance to the notion that the commentators could have a leading influence on the manner in which the law was to be interpreted and applied at the beginning of the 19th century, when, as will be explained later, the exegists ruled the roost: for them, the *lois* were the sole source of the law, because they were deemed to be self-sufficient and self-explanatory. This is why for some time, there developed an increasingly wide divide between the manner in which the leading commentators interpreted the law, and legislative interpretation as expressed in court decisions.

However, it soon became apparent to the leading authors that there was little point in allowing this gap to continue to prevail, and that it was for the commentators, rather than for the courts, to change their outlook. They therefore set about the task of commenting on the court decisions rather than devise the rather fanciful scenarios which they depicted in their major tomes. This was an extremely welcome development, since court decisions were often written in a very formalistic and terse manner, which required a good deal of clarification. This explains why the influence of the leading writers has increased considerably. It also explains why the profile of legal commentators is much higher than in Britain, not only among the members of the legal profession, but also amongst the general public.[20]

*La doctrine* is a very broad term, which covers a wide variety of legal commentary, which can assume various forms:

- **Treaties (*traités*)**

  These are major works on a major legal topic, such as the civil law, the criminal law, or administrative law, which often cover many tomes. They have no exact counterpart in England. The tradition of the major *traités* commenced in the early 19th century with such authors as Gény and Laurent, who were able to exploit to the full the fact that the new legal system developed after the French Revolution contained a great deal of unexplored territory. More recent exponents of this form of legal commentary have been de Page, Planiol and Ripert, and Mazeaud and Mazeaud (in relation to the civil law), Ancel, Bouzat and Pinatel (criminal law), Hamel and Lagarde (commercial law) and Vedel and Devolvé (administrative law).

---

20   Lawson, Anton and Brown, *op cit*, p. 13.

- **Handbooks (*manuels*)**

  These are shorter textbooks dealing either with more specialist topics or with general topics, but in a more concise and 'user-friendly' manner. They are as wide-ranging in their scope as is the case in this country.

- **Journals (*Revues*)**

  These too will be recognisable to the English lawyer, and consist of periodicals containing articles on specialist legal subjects with varying degrees of length, summaries of court decisions, and book reviews. Leading French law journals are *Revue trimestrielle de droit civil*, *Revue de droit pénal*, *Revue trimestrielle de droit commercial et de droit économique*, *Revue française de droit consitutionnel* and *Revue trimestrielle de droit européen*.

- **Annotations (*Notes*)**

  These are short commentaries contained in leading law reports such as the *Recueil Dalloz* and the *Recueil Sirey*. This is a phenomenon which is unknown in England, where law reports confine themselves to reporting the cases as they arise. These annotations serve the useful function of situating the decision in question in the context of the relevant case law.

- **Encyclopedias (*répertoires*)**

  These are topic-based commentaries not unlike *Halsbury's Laws of England*, and cover virtually every field of the law.

## H Foreign court decisions

In view of the considerable influence exerted by the French legal system worldwide, the French commentators – and even the French courts – have sometimes looked abroad for enlightenment on a particular legal topic. Particularly the decisions of the Belgian courts are sometimes cited, in view of not only the similarity between the two legal systems, but because the interpretation of the law (particularly the code civil) in the two countries shows a remarkable degree of similarity.

## I Customary law (*la coutume*)

As was the case with everything else which was even remotely connected with the *ancien régime*, customary law was strictly banned as a source of law during the early part of the 19th century. However, it started to reappear as gaps appeared in both the statute law and the case law, or as certain anomalous situations developed which could only be solved by referring to customary law, even where this meant going against a statute (eg Article 1154 of the Civil Code, which prohibits compound interest unless it has been expressly stipulated by the parties to an agreement, has been overruled in relation to banking accounts). In order to be accepted as a valid source of law, however, customs must fulfil some very stringent conditions:

- *they must be widely accepted in a certain field*, eg in a profession or certain commercial circles (or in commercial circles in a certain locality), in order to demonstrate their general applicability;

- *they must be considered as binding* by the people who apply them;

- *they must be consistent*, ie they must have been followed for some considerable time.[21]

## J General principles of law

These are fundamental rules which, whether stated in statutes or not, are deemed to underpin the entire legal system – principles such as the proportionality principle, the non-discrimination principle, etc. Here, a distinction must be drawn between two situations. Where the statute law expressly permits the courts to apply these general principles, the courts apply them by means of some kind of delegation conferred on them by the legislature. In the absence of such express delegation, however, the courts have still considered it necessary from time to time to apply them, because of the very nature of their activity and function. In most cases, these general principles of law have been applied in administrative law, more particularly in the field of judicial review. However, they have also been known to have been applied in the private law, for example the principle prohibiting misuse of the law.[22]

# IV Some essential concepts

## A General

To maintain that linguistic differences between two legal orders will present certain problems for the comparative student of these two systems could at first sight appear to be stating the obvious. Yet it should be pointed out that the degree of difficulty experienced by the English reader will be greater than, for example, those of the Dutch reader, regardless of the fluency in French which may be displayed by either. The main reason for this is that any person trained in the legal system of the Netherlands will find that the vast majority of the

---

21  Guéry, G., *Droit des affaires* (1993, Dunod) p. 73.

22  David, R., *Les grands systèmes de droit contemporains* (1982, Dalloz) p. 152.

legal terms which he or she may encounter when reading a French *loi*, court judgment or legal opinion have a direct one-to-one terminological equivalent in Dutch. This is the direct result of the fact that the law of the Netherlands is very strongly reminiscent of the French codified system; in fact, the Netherlands were one of the many countries which incorporated the main French codes wholesale into their domestic legal system in the early 19th century. Even the German reader will experience less difficulty, since German law, although it belongs to a different tradition, is based on codified law and has more in common with French law than with English law.

Nor are the terminological difficulties confined to mere linguistic differences. The professional legal language used in the common law and the codified law systems also reveals a divide of considerable proportions. This manifests itself in several ways:

## Abstract concepts

French legal language and thinking tends to be more abstract than is the case in English law. French legal texts constantly refer to such notions as *'le juge'* or *'le législateur'*, meaning the courts in general or the law-making authority respectively. Although the reader of French texts gradually becomes familiar with such means of expression, there are times when this gives rise to ambiguity. Thus where a French text may refer to 'le juge des saisies', it is sometimes unclear for all but those who are specialists in French law, even after having studied the context very carefully, whether the author is referring to (a) all the courts whose general powers include the ability to make decisions in distraints of property, (b) one particular court having this power, (c) all courts which have the specific power to order distraints, or (d) one such court.

## Conceptual language

As a general rule, it is safe to assert that French legal language is more conceptual than the language used in English law. French lawyers will attach a great deal more importance to the definition and scope of concepts than their English colleagues. For example, the English lawyer will tend to use the word 'agreement' and 'contract' at random and as alternatives to each other; French lawyers will draw a definite distinction between a *contrat* and a *convention*, and never use the two as being interchangeable. French legal philosophers will go to great pains to establish the difference between, and the definition of, concepts such as 'legal philosophy' and 'legal theory'– which is something which will not trouble the Anglo-Saxon legal philosopher in the slightest.[23] This is a direct consequence of the Cartesian approach to methodical thinking (cf. *supra*, p. 3).

---

23   For a good illustration of this way of thinking, see van Hoecke, M., *What is legal theory?* (1986 Akko).

## Formal nature of language

The language used in any French legal context is more formal than that used in English law. This is particularly the case in relation to court judgments, which allow much less scope for discursive treatment of problems than in England. The fact that court judgments consist of successive paragraphs introduced by the same formula (*'attendu que'* or *'considérant que'*), sometimes gives the impression of overlong and complex sentence structures which are an obstacle to their comprehension.

# B Some essential concepts

## *Acte juridique*

This is a fundamental concept of French law meaning any document or action which has definite legal implications (as opposed to *faits matériels*, which are mere facts; the latter do not normally have any legal implications, and if they do, this was purely unintentional). The former normally require a written document by way of evidence; the latter do not. Thus legacies, offers and acceptances of contracts, notifications of arrears of payment, etc, are *actes juridiques*, whereas the commission of negligence or of a crime, or making inquiries in response to an advertisement, constitute *faits matériels*. There is simply no English equivalent which comes anywhere near the meaning of this term.

## *Ordre public*

This is a term which, although it has a rough equivalent in the English term 'public policy', is much more widely used and of infinitely greater importance in French law. It is a concept based on general considerations of public order, public morality and the public interest, and it constitutes one of the major exceptions to the principle of liberal individualism which underlies the *code civil*. Thus Article 6 of the Civil Code issues the general principle that rules based on *ordre public* may not be departed from by private arrangement. In many cases, considerations of *ordre public* will be used to protect and promote the institution of the family.

## *Droit supplétif et droit impératif*

This is a notion which is closely related to the notion of *ordre public*. The *droit supplétif* consists of rules and precepts which are laid down for the guidance of the citizen engaging in a particular course of action, and which the latter is deemed to have complied with in the absence of any indication to the contrary. Thus, for example, where more than one person owes a civil debt towards a third party, these debtors are not deemed to be jointly and severally liable, unless an agreement to the contrary has been made by the parties involved. Rules of *droit impératif* on other hand, may not be departed from, in most cases for reasons of *ordre public*.

## Le patrimoine

This is an example of the tendency towards conceptual thought in French law which has been referred to earlier. Used mainly in the law of succession, it refers to the totality of the assets and liabilities of a person. Here again, it is almost impossible to find an equivalent in English law (the term 'estate' does not quite fit the bill, since the notion of *patrimoine* is also often used outside the context of wills and successions). Unfortunately, some French intellectuals tended to use this term in a somewhat loose and at times irrelevant manner outside the legal context (eg '*le patrimoine culturel*').

## Le principe du contradictoire

This is a term used widely in procedural law. It refers to any court proceedings in which there has been a fair hearing of both sides to a dispute. Here again, there is no English law equivalent.

## L'opposabilité

This is a term used to denote the ability to raise and plead against third parties certain rights acquired in relation to a thing, even though these rights were acquired under a private contract between two private parties. Again, although it is generally related to the notion of the privity of contracts, there is no exact English law equivalent.

## L'état civil

This refers to the whole range of attributes or qualities by which any person is characterised as a subject of rights and abilities – ie his age, nationality, parentage, adoption, premature majority (*émancipation*), etc.[24] All these details must be kept in a special and official register, kept by a special civil servant known as the *officier de l'état civil*. Here again, there is no English law equivalent.

## Le régistre du commerce et des sociétés (RCS)

In France, every trader, be he ever so humble, is obliged to register with the RCS, which has become a commercial institution in France – much more so than its rough equivalent in England, the Register of Companies.

---

24  Lawson, FH, Anton, AE, and Brown, LN, *op cit*, p. 37.

## Droit

At this stage already, it is useful to point that the term '*droit*' has several meanings. It can mean (a) a right, (b) the abstract term for 'the law' (as opposed to individual laws, which are called *lois*), and (c) a fee, duty or charge (eg *droit d'entrée*).

## D'office

This is a term which denotes the ability of a public authority to act by virtue of its powers, without requiring an application or request by a private party. It can be translated, depending on the context, as 'automatically', 'by virtue of his or her (or its in the case of an organ) office' or 'on his or her (or its) own initiative'.

## Juridiction

This is a tern which is fraught with danger for the English lawyer. It does *not* mean 'jurisdiction', but is the collective name for a court or judicial body. The term 'jurisdiction' is translated by *la compétence*.

## Sur le fond, sur la forme

Many French court judgments will be divided into the procedural issues (*sur la forme*) and the substantive issues (*sur le fond*). Such strict division of the issues is much less in evidence in England.

# 2 The French Courts

## I Introduction

The origins of the existing court structure in France can be traced back to the period immediately after the French Revolution in 1789. The Law of 16 and 24 August 1790,[1] encapsulating the principle of the separation of powers, gave rise to the two distinct legal systems currently operating in France – the 'ordinary' court system (*juridictions de l'ordre judiciaire*) and the 'administrative' court system (*juridictions de l'ordre administratif*). Both systems have, since that time, undergone substantial changes culminating in those introduced by the (current) Constitution of the Fifth Republic, adopted in October 1958. It is not intended in this chapter to discuss historical antecedents, but rather to concentrate on the role, composition and jurisdiction of existing courts.

Administratively, France is divided into 22 *régions* which, in turn, are divided into 96 *départements*. *Départements* are divided into *arrondissements*, *arrondissements* into *cantons* and *cantons* into *communes*. The French court system is hierarchical with the jurisdictional area of each court being loosely based on the administrative divisions. The French use the words *le Tribunal* and *la Cour* both to mean court, thereby also indicating a certain hierarchy between them. *Le Tribunal* should not be confused with the English 'tribunal'. A court referred to as a *Tribunal* is normally a court of first instance at the bottom of the hierarchical pyramid. A *Cour* is mostly a court of appeal (and sometimes a court of first instance), but is invariably found towards the apex of the pyramid. In addition, different words are used for the judgments of different courts. A *Tribunal* gives *un jugement*, whereas a *Cour* gives *un arrêt*. The word *Conseil* is also used for some courts and is a reflection of the historical background of such courts in that they were initially seen as advisory bodies.

All French courts render collegiate judgments and a dissenting opinion is never disclosed. The judgments themselves bear very little resemblance to those given by courts in common law countries. Most are extremely brief and reasons

---

1   In particular Article 13, which reads: *Les fonctions judiciaires sont distinctes et demeureront toujours séparées des fonctions administratives. Les juges ne pourront, à peine de forfaiture, troubler en quelque manière que ce soit les opérations des corps administratifs, ni citer devant eux les administrateurs pour raison de leur fonction.* (The functions of the courts shall be distinct, and shall at all times remain separate from the functions of the administration. The courts may not in any way, on penalty of committing an offence, disturb the functioning of the administrative authorities, nor may they summons any administrative official to appear before them by reason of the pursuance of their duties - translation by the authors.)

are only given in outline form. There are three main parts to a judgment, the first being the heading which identifies the court and gives the names of the parties. The second and major part is *la motivation* which sets out the court's reasons for arriving at its decision. These are given in a logical but brief series of developments each commencing with the formula *attendu que* or *considérant que* (for a more detailed examination of court judgments, cf. *infra*, p. 188; see also appendix).

The final principle to be borne in mind is that of the *double degré de juridiction*. The theory, which is not always adhered to in practice, is that there is a right of appeal to a higher court from the decision of any court of first instance. An appeal, unlike its counterpart in England, means a complete rehearing of the case, but it must be remembered that oral evidence is much less prominent in France and thus the appeal procedure is much less time consuming.

## II The civil courts

### A General

By reason of the diverse nature of the litigation which may come before the civil courts, the French system has a wide variety of courts. A distinction is to be drawn not only between courts of first instance and courts of appeal, but also between *juridictions de droit commun* and *juridictions d'exception*. The former are empowered to hear all cases unless a law has expressly granted jurisdiction to the latter, which are specialised courts.[2]

### B Courts of first instance (*juridictions du premier degré* or *juridictions de première instance*)

Courts of first instance comprise the *Tribunal d'instance*, the *Tribunal de grande instance*, the *Tribunal de commerce*, the *Conseil de prud'hommes* and the *Tribunal paritaire des baux ruraux*. It is intended to deal with each court in turn, setting out its structure, function and jurisdictional area.

#### The *Tribunaux d'instance*

There are 450 *Tribunaux d'instance* in France and the jurisdiction of each extends over several *cantons*, the precise number varying in accordance with the population size and the number of actions dealt with. Thus, generally, there is one in the chief town of every *département* as well as in other large cities and population centres. It is the court which deals with minor cases where the sum involved does not exceed FF 30,000.[3] There is an optional pre-trial conciliation service available and personal representation in court is allowed.

---

2  See diagram (overleaf).

3  Article R.321-1 of the *Code de l'organisation judiciaire*, as amended by *Décret* No. 85-422 of 10/4/1985.

## STRUCTURE OF FRENCH COURTS

**'Ordinary Courts'**     **Administrative Courts**

Tribunal des Conflits

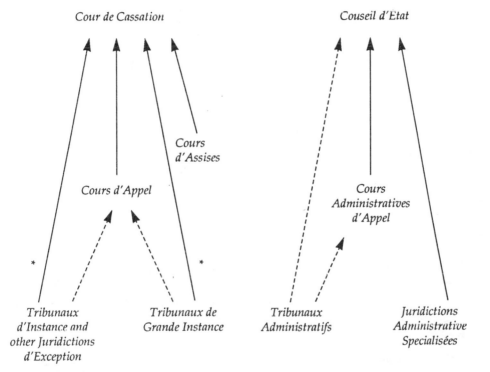

Cour de Cassation     Couseil d'Etat

Cours
d'Assises

Cours d'Appel

Cours
Administratives
d'Appel

*     *

Tribunaux
d'Instance and
other Juridictions
d'Exception

Tribunaux de
Grande Instance

Tribunaux
Administratifs

Juridictions
Administrative
Specialisées

\* – only for decisions given in first and last resort.
—— = Review on a point of law only.
- - - - = Appeal.

By way of exception to the norm, the *Tribunal d'instance* is not a collegiate court, but is presided over by a single judge. There is no appeal from a decision of the *Tribunal d'instance* (except for a review on a point of law to the *Cour de cassation*) where the sum involved is less than FF 13,000. Thus the principle of the *double degré de juridiction* is not considered relevant for such minor cases.

The *Tribunal d'instance* is a *juridiction d'exception*, but has had so many differing cases attributed to it that it has almost become a *juridiction de droit commun* in its own right.

The *Tribunal de grande instance* is perhaps the most important court of first instance and is the best example of a *juridiction de droit commun*. It has jurisdiction over all civil cases unless the value of the claim is less than FF 30,000 (except in the case of real property, where it has full jurisdiction irrespective of the value involved) or unless a law has allotted jurisdiction to a special court.

There are 175 *Tribunaux de grande instance* in 'metropolitan' France (ie mainland France and Corsica); one or more for each *département* depending on population. Each court is headed by a *Président* who has administrative as well as judicial functions. In an administrative capacity he is responsible for the internal operation of the court, allocating cases to the various *chambres* (chambers), supervising the issue of official documents relating to the status of persons (*actes de l'état civil*) and drawing up registers of those citizens within the *département* who are available for jury service. The most important judicial function of the *Président* is that of *juge des référés*. In this capacity the *Président* sits as a judge in chambers giving interim relief such as matrimonial injunctions. In addition to the *Président* there are the ordinary judges (*magistrats*). If, within the *Tribunal* there are more than five *magistrats*, the court is divided into specialist chambers (eg commercial, family etc) each of which is led by a *Vice-président*. A judgment given by any chamber is considered to be a judgment of the whole court. The court is collegiate, and there must be a minimum of three judges involved in each case.

### The *Tribunaux de commerce*

The *Tribunaux de commerce* are *juridictions d'exception* and have jurisdiction over commercial contracts, insolvencies and liquidations. There are approximately 200 such courts in 'metropolitan' France, additional courts being set up as and when warranted by the level of commercial activity in the area. Thus the jurisdictional area of each court does not necessarily correspond to an administrative area of France, nor to the jurisdictional area of any *Tribunal d'instance* or *Tribunal de grande instance.* If there is no *Tribunal de commerce* with jurisdiction in the area where the dispute arose, the relevant *Tribunal de grande instance* is empowered to act irrespective of the value of the claim.

The *Tribunaux de commerce* are composed, not of trained judges or lawyers, but exclusively of commercial traders elected to serve as judges. Judges are elected initially for a term of two years and thereafter for terms of four years. To be eligible, one must be over 30, have worked in commerce for a minimum period of five years and not have been declared bankrupt. A judge receives no remuneration for his services and after 14 years of service (ie four terms of office) becomes ineligible for re-election for a period of one year. Election is by way of an electoral college composed of current and former judges together with delegates (whose numbers vary in accordance with the size and population of the court's jurisdictional area) directly elected to the college by local commercial traders.

## The *Conseils de prud'hommes*

This type of court is a *juridiction d'exception* whose role it is to settle disputes arising out of contracts of employment. To fall within the jurisdiction of the court, such disputes must be between individual employees and employers, not collective disputes. There are almost 300 such courts in France, at least one within the jurisdictional area of such *Tribunal de grande instance*. As with the *Tribunal de commerce*, the court is staffed not by career lawyers, but by elected judges. Election is for a term of five years. It is known as a *juridiction paritaire* because half the judges are drawn from employers and half from employees. The presidency of the court rotates between employer and employee on a yearly basis. Each judgment of the court must be rendered by four judges (*conseillers*), two employers and two employees. With there being an even number of judges involved, there is an obvious possibility of the court being unable to reach a majority decision. In the event of this occurring the case is retried by the same judges with the addition of a professional judge drawn from the local *Tribunal d'instance*. This judge (known as a *juge départiteur*) has the casting vote in the event of a second stalemate.

In addition to being a court rendering judgments, the *Conseil de prud'hommes* plays an important role in conciliation. Procedural rules require that each case must first be submitted to the conciliation service (the *bureau de conciliation*) and only in the absence of agreement can the case then be heard by the full court. Two judges (one employer and one employee) are responsible for conciliation in each case. Approximately 15% of cases are resolved by the conciliation procedure.

## The *Tribunaux paritaires des baux ruraux*

This type of court, which is of relatively recent creation (1943), is a *juridiction d'exception* dealing with agricultural holdings. Each *Tribunal d'instance* includes a *Tribunal paritaire des baux ruraux* within its precincts and the jurisdictional area of the courts is identical. Unlike the other courts of first instance mentioned previously, the *Tribunal paritaire des baux ruraux* has no permanent sessions, only sitting as and when the need arises.

The *Président* of the court is a judge from the *Tribunal d'instance* who sits with four *assesseurs*, two representatives of the landlords (*bailleurs*) and two of the tenants (*preneurs*). Election to the position of *assesseur* is for a period of five years by way of electoral colleges for landlords and tenants.

**The *Tribunaux des affaires de sécurité sociale***

These courts (known as the *Commission des Affaires de Sécurité Sociale* until redesignated in 1985) deal with questions relating to social security benefits. The *Président* is a career judge who sits with two *assesseurs*, one drawn from employers and one from employees. The *assesseurs* are not elected but appointed for a five year term by the *premier Président* of the *Cour d'appel* from a list drawn up by the relevant regional director of social security having consulted relevant union representatives.

# III The criminal courts

## A General

Within the French criminal system crimes are divided into three distinct categories. This classification, based on the penalties which may be imposed, is important both as to the court with the appropriate jurisdiction and as to the requirements of the investigation procedure (*instruction*). The categories are:

(a) The *contravention* which is a minor offence, the penalty for which is a maximum of two months imprisonment and/or a fine not exceeding FF 10,000.

(b) The *délit* which is an offence of intermediate seriousness, where the fine or imprisonment exceeds that which may be given for a *contravention*.

(c) The *crime* which is the most serious offence for which a life sentence of imprisonment may be imposed.

Unlike the English system, the French adopt an inquisitorial rather than accusatorial approach to criminal litigation. This means that the court system comes into operation at an earlier stage in the proceedings and is intimately involved with the investigation and interrogation process, the police playing a less significant role than in England. Prosecutions are bought by the state in the form of the *Ministère Public*, represented by the *Procureur de la République*. Thus the French system involves two separate sets of courts, the courts responsible for the investigation (*les juridictions d'instruction*) and those responsible for the hearing of the case (*les juridictions de jugement*). To a greater or lesser extent both adhere to the principle of the *double degré de juridiction*. The procedure before these courts is described in detail in Chapter 9.

# B Courts responsible for investigation (*les juridictions d'instruction*)

## General

The investigation process (which also forms a part of civil procedure, but which, in that case, does not involve resort to a separate set of courts) lays on the relevant court the responsibility for obtaining evidence, examining witnesses and reaching a decision as to whether there is a *prima facie* case to answer. The investigating court does not give any judgment as to the guilt or innocence of the accused. This task is left to the *juridiction de jugement*. There are two courts responsible for the investigation process in criminal cases; the *juge d'instruction* and the *Chambre d'accusation*.

### The *juge d'instruction*

The *juge d'instruction* is a judge appointed to act as such by the *Tribunal de grande instance* and whose territorial jurisdiction is the same as that of the *Tribunal de grande instance*. As the name implies, this is not a collegiate court, all authority being vested in a single judge. A case is referred to the judge either by the *Procureur de la République* or by the victim, provided that the victim has properly applied for and obtained the status of the *partie civile*. (It is a further divergence of French and English law that the victim of an offence can be dealt with and receive compensation from a criminal court. In effect the victim has the choice of taking action before the civil or the criminal courts. In many cases the criminal courts are to be preferred as the victim will have easy access to all prosecution documentation and have his case dealt with rather more quickly. Further, the victim will be spared the expense of separate civil proceedings.)

The services of the *juge d'instruction* are, however, not required in every case. In the case of a *crime*, recourse to the *juge d'instruction* is mandatory. In the case of a *délit* it is optional and depends upon the complexity of the subject matter. In the more straightforward cases the investigation is done at the hearing by the *juridiction de jugement*. In the case of a *contravention* there is no recourse to the *juge d'instruction* save in the rare circumstances when one is requested by the prosecution.

The investigation of the case, including fact finding, investigation of documents as well as places, and the examination of witnesses may be undertaken by the *juge d'instruction* personally or he may delegate responsibility to the *police judiciaire* by way of a *commission rogatoire*, subject to being kept informed of progress at all times. At the conclusion of the investigation the *juge d'instruction* has the duty of deciding whether or not there is a *prima facie* case to answer. If it is considered that there is such a case, the *juge d'instruction* issues an *ordonnance de renvoi* and the papers are passed to the relevant *juridiction de jugement* for the case to be heard and the guilt or innocence of the accused established. If it is felt that there is no case to answer, the *juge d'instruction* issues an *ordonnance de non-lieu* and no further action is taken.

The main restriction on the powers of the *juge d'instruction* lies in his lack of jurisdiction to remand in custody pending trial (*détention provisoire*). Doubtless owing to the gravity of the consequences of a remand in custody, it was decided quite recently (Loi no. 87-1062, following *Loi* no. 85-1303) that applications to remand in custody should be heard before a collegiate court. This newly formed court is called the *Chambre des demandes de mise en détention provisoire* and consists of three judges from the *Tribunal de grande instance*. The *juge d'instruction* must pass all relevant file papers to this court along with his observations if a remand in custody is being considered. Exceptionally, the *juge d'instruction* may remand in custody for periods up to three (exceptionally four) days pending the sitting of the *Chambre*.

## The *Chambre d'accusation*

Appeal from an order of the *juge d'instruction* lies to the *Chambre d'accusation*. The court is part of the Court of Appeal (*Cour d'appel*) and is staffed by three appeal court judges. An accused may appeal against orders such as those for a remand in custody or on the grounds of procedural irregularity but there is no appeal against the finding of the *juge d'instruction* that there is a *prima facie* case to answer. The prosecution, on the other hand, have the right to appeal against any order including one of no case to answer.

In the case of a *crime*, every time the *juge d'instruction* finds that there is a case to answer the file must be transmitted to the *Chambre d'accusation* which acts not so much as an appeal court, but rather as a second court of investigation. On the conclusion of the second investigation, the court may make one of three possible orders. First, it may agree with the *juge d'instruction* and consider that there is a case to answer. In these circumstances it issues an *arrêt de mise en accusation* which transforms the accused into an *accusé* (formerly the accused was known as an *inculpé*) and passes the case to the relevant *juridiction de jugement* (the *Cour d'assises*). Secondly it may consider that there is no case to answer in which case it issues an *arrêt de non-lieu* and the affair is closed. Finally, it may consider that although there is a case to answer, there is not sufficient evidence for it to be classified as a *crime* but that there is sufficient for classification as a *délit* or *contravention* in which case it issues an *arrêt de renvoi* and transfers the case to the appropriate *juridiction de jugement*.

# C The trial courts (*les juridictions de jugement*)

The trial courts comprise the *Tribunal de police*, the *Tribunal correctionnel* and the *Cour d'assises*. It is intended to examine the function, structure and role of each court in turn.

### The *Tribunaux de police*

The *Tribunaux de police* are the courts which are appropriate in the case of a *contravention*. They are merely *Tribunaux d'instance* in a different guise. As with civil cases, judgment is given by a single judge (sometimes, in the smaller courts, the same one who is responsible for civil cases). There is no appeal (except for a review on a point of law to the *Cour de cassation*) from a conviction imposed by the *Tribunal de police* where the sentence involved was less than a fine of FF 1,300, or imprisonment for a period of five days unless civil damages were also awarded to the *partie civile*.

### The *Tribunaux correctionnels*

These are the appropriate courts for *délits* and is the criminal branch of the *Tribunal de grande instance*. They have the same territorial jurisdiction and the same collegiate nature as their civil counterpart. Appeal against any conviction by the *Tribunal correctionnel* lies to the *Cour d'appel*.

### The *Cour d'assises*

The *Cour d'assises* is the appropriate court for crimes and is a unique court within the French system. As the name implies, its origins are to be found in the English assize courts which were incorporated into the French system under the influence of Voltaire. It is a mixture of English features, in that there is a jury, and French features, in that it is a collegiate court.

There is a *Cour d'assises* in each *département* in France. It is situated in the chief town, bears the name of, and has jurisdiction over the *département*. It is composed of three judges – the *Président* (drawn from the *Cour d'appel*) and two *assesseurs* (drawn either from the *Cour d'appel* or the *Tribunal de grande instance*) – and nine jury members who sit on the bench with the three judges. The jury members are drawn by lot in three stages. At the first stage the *maire* (mayor) of each *canton* within the *département* draws names by lot from the annual electoral list. These names are communicated to the court. From them, 35 names are selected by lot and these form the list of possible jurors for the session of the *Cour d'assises*. Finally, nine names are drawn for the particular case, subject to challenge by the prosecution or defence. Originally the court operated in accordance with the English tradition of the judges alone being responsible for the application of the law to the facts as determined by the jury. This system fell into disfavour and both judges and jury now consider the facts and application

35

of the law, including the appropriate sentence in the event of the accused being found guilty. In an attempt to avoid the possibility of professional lawyers having undue influence on the lay jury, any decision unfavourable to the accused must be agreed by at least eight members of the court. This means that a majority of jurors (at least five) must agree with the professional judges and, further, that the judges can be outvoted by the jury on any matter.

There is no appeal (except for a review on a point of law to the *Cour de cassation*) from a decision of the *Cour d'assises*. It seems anomalous that the court responsible for the most serious offences within the French legal system departs from the principle of the *double degré de juridiction* in that there is no opportunity for the parties to have the case reviewed by the *Cour d'appel*. The reasons advanced for this are that, because a jury is involved, the decision of the court represents the sovereign will of the people whereas the Court of Appeal merely renders a decision of professional lawyers. Secondly, it is argued that an appeal is not necessary since the accused has had the benefit of a preliminary investigation both by the *juge d'instruction* and by the *Chambre d'accusation*.

## D Courts for young offenders

The main court for dealing with young offenders is the *Tribunal pour enfants*. This court is attached to the *Tribunal de grande instance* and has the same territorial jurisdiction. It may consist of a single judge (*juge des enfants*) who has full powers to hear all cases but not to impose a penalty which deprives the minor of his freedom. If it is felt that such deprivation may be necessary, the court must sit in collegiate form, the judge being joined by two lay *assesseurs*. The *Tribunal pour enfants* has jurisdiction over all *contraventions* and *délits* committed by persons under 18 years of age. In addition, it has juridication over *crimes* committed by persons under 16. In the case of *crimes* committed by persons in between the ages of 16 and 18, the relevant court is the *Cour d'assises des mineurs*. There is very little difference between this and the normal *Cour d'assises* save that the three judges are normally drawn from the ranks of the *juges des enfants*.

A preliminary investigation is mandatory for all cases of *crimes* and *délits* committed by minors. This may be undertaken either by the *juge d'instruction* or by the *juges des enfants*.

# IV The Courts of Appeal (*les Cours d'appel*)

Whether a decision emanates from a civil court or a criminal court, whether the court be a *juridiction de droit commun* or a *juridiction d'exception*, appeal lies to the *Cour d'appel* in all cases. There are 30 courts of appeal in 'metropolitan' France, each with territorial jurisdiction over (normally) two to four *départements*. For example, the *Cour d'appel* of Bordeaux has jurisdiction over the *départements* of Gironde, Dordogne and Charente.

The appeal procedure involves a rehearing of the entire case and the court of appeal is not bound by findings of fact or law in the lower courts. As has been mentioned previously, there is no right of appeal in minor civil cases (where the sum involved is less than FF 13,000) or minor criminal cases (*contraventions*) where the sentence involved is less than FF 1,300 or imprisonment for a period of five days. Given the great variety of subject matter dealt with by the courts of first instance, it is obvious that the courts of appeal have to incorporate specialist panels of judges. To this end, each court is divided into specialist *chambres*. In addition to the *chambres* dealing with general criminal and civil appeals, there is, within each court, a *chambre sociale* which deals with cases referred to the court from the *Conseil de Prud'hommes*, the *Tribunal paritaire des baux ruraux* and the *Tribunal des affaires de sécurité sociale*.

The head of the court is the *Premier Président* who has administrative duties (supervising the running of the court and first instance courts within the territorial jurisdiction of the *Cour d'appel*), as well as judicial functions. In this latter capacity, in addition to his general role of one of a given panel of judges, he may act alone in cases of urgency (eg where an injunction is required) or in non-contentious litigation. Each *chambre* of the court is under the juridiction of a *Président*.

Normally, the court sits with a panel of three judges (*conseillers*) but in certain important cases (such as a *renvoi après cassation*) the court sits in *audience solennelle*. This takes place before two *chambres* of the court and is presided over by the *Premier Président*.

# V The *Cour de cassation*

The *Cour de cassation* is at the apex of the ordinary (non administrative) French courts. It is situated in Paris and its role is to ensure that the law is interpreted in a uniform way throughout the country even though, in principle, it has no powers to ensure compliance with its rulings by the lower courts. Strictly speaking, it is not a court to which a further appeal may be made as it is only a judge of law and not of fact. It confines itself to ascertaining whether the law has been correctly applied by the lower courts to the facts as established by those lower courts. It is referred to as a *juge du droit* rather than a *juge du fait* or a *juge du fond*. Thus an applicant to the court must plead a breach of the law (*un moyen de cassation*) by the lower courts. The application itself is termed a *pourvoi* (rather than an *appel* or a *recours*) which indicates the declaratory nature of the judgment. It should be observed here that the *Cour de cassation* often takes a very broad view of what constitutes a point of law. Moreover, when it has reached its conclusion, the *Cour de cassation* does not substitute its own judgment for that of the lower court. It has in effect two choices. First, it may consider that the lower court has correctly applied the law. In this case the application for review is rejected and the decision of the lower court stands. No further appeal (within the French system) can be made.

Secondly, it may find that the lower court has not applied the law correctly. In this case its only option is to 'quash' (*casser* – hence the name of the court) the judgment referred to it. To repeat, it does not substitute its own judgment. This leaves an obvious difficulty as the litigation in question has now no definitive resolution. Let us suppose that the judgment of the *Cour d'appel de Bordeaux* has been quashed but the dispute between the parties is as yet unresolved as there is now no definitive judgment at all. In such cases, the *Cour de cassation* will refer the case to a neighbouring court of the same level as that from which the application for review was made (say the *Cour d'appel de Pau*).

This court is known as the *juridiction de renvoi* and it is its duty to hear the entire case again (*in audience solennelle*) both as to the facts and as to the law. The *juridiction de renvoi* is not bound to follow the interpretation of the law as given by the *Cour de cassation*. It has a completely free hand both as to law and as to fact.

If the *juridiction de renvoi* does not comply with the interpretation of the law as outlined by the *Cour de cassation* it is open to the disappointed litigant to appeal a second time. This *pourvoi* is heard by the court in *assemblée plenière* (full court) and once again its decision is based solely upon the interpretation given to the law by the *juridiction de renvoi*. Again it has the same two choices. It may take the unusual course of agreeing with the decision of the *juridiction de renvoi* thereby dissenting from its own previous opinion in which case it rejects the *pourvoi*.[4] Alternatively it may, as is the norm, agree with its own previous decision and quash the judgment. It still cannot substitute its own judgment so a second *juridiction de renvoi* is required. This will be a second court of the same rank as the original court and the original *juridiction de renvoi* (say the *Cour d'appel de Limoges*) This court rehears the case and has full jurisdiction as regards the facts. As to the law, however, it is bound by the interpretation given by the *Cour de cassation*. Finally, it must be recalled that the interpretation given by the *Cour de cassation* is only binding for the particular litigation in question. Were a similar case to arise shortly afterwards, all courts are, in principle, free to interpret the law in accordance with their own ideas. Of course, if they proceed to a different interpretation to the one previously given, they risk further *pourvois* to the *Cour de cassation*.

Administratively, the *Cour de cassation* is led by the *Premier Président* and is divided into six *chambres*, each headed by a *Président*. Each *chambre* comprises approximately 15 judges (*conseillers*) and the quorum for any case is five. Cases are allocated to a *chambre* in accordance with its specialisation. Thus the first

---

4    Cf. the case of *Franck: Cour d'appel* of Nancy of 1931, *Cour de cassation* 1936, *Cour d'appel* of Besançon 1937, *Cour de cassation* 1941.

*chambre civile* deals with contracts, the second with matrimonial affairs and the third with real property. The fourth is called the *chambre commerciale et financière* and the fifth the *chambre sociale*. The sixth *chambre* is the *chambre criminelle*. If a question arises which falls within the jurisdiction of two or more *chambres*, a special *chambre mixte* is constituted from judges drawn from the relevant *chambres*.

The *assemblée plenière* comprises the *Premier Président*, the *Président* of each *chambre* and at least two judges from each *chambre*. It meets to decide not only cases which are the subject of a second *pourvoi en cassation* but also those cases which involve an important principle of law and which require an immediate interpretation. Any interpretation given by the *assemblée plenière* is binding on other lower courts for the purposes of the litigation in question.

# VI  The administrative court system

## A General

It has already been observed that one of the basic principles on which the French legal system is based is that of the separation of powers. As a result, the administrative legal system in France is totally separate from the 'ordinary' legal system. The courts are termed the *juridictions administratives* as opposed to the 'ordinary' courts which are termed the *juridictions de l'ordre judiciaire*. Originally, the only court with jurisdiction to deal with administrative cases was the *Conseil d'Etat* (which, originally, was not even a court, but merely an advisory body issuing opinions on disputes). Pressure of cases necessitated the subsequent establishing of first instance and appeal courts, the *Conseil d'Etat* remaining as the final court of appeal in normal circumstances.

## B  The *Tribunaux Administratifs*

These are the courts of first instance within the administrative system. A *Tribunal administratif* is a court *de droit commun* in that it deals with all cases save those which are allocated by law to a different court (the *Conseil d'Etat*). There are 26 *Tribunaux administratifs* in 'metropolitan France' and they have territorial jurisdiction over several *départements*. This makes their field of jurisdiction far greater than that of a *Tribunal de grande instance*, for example the *Tribunal administratif* at Nantes has jurisdiction over the *départements* of Mayenne, Sarthe, Loire, Atlantique, Maine et Loire and Vendée, whereas there are two *Tribunaux de grande instance* (Nantes and St Nazaire) in the *département* of Loire Atlantique alone.

Each *Tribunal administratif* is led by a *Président* who, in addition to his administratives duties, has the position of *juge des référés administratifs* in that he may give rulings in urgent cases. Normally the court is collegiate and comprises three judges (*conseillers*), but in addition to the *juge des référés administratifs* the court can act by way of a single judge (*conseiller délégué*) in order to speed up the process of the court especially in fiscal and planning matters.

## C The *Cours administratives d'appel*

Until recently any appeal against the order of a *Tribunal administratif* lay only to the *Conseil d'Etat*. The proliferation of administrative litigation led, in 1987, to the creation of a second level of courts in the administrative system – the *Cours administratives d'appel*. Five such courts have been created in Nantes, Bordeaux, Lyon, Nancy and Paris. As can be seen, they have a large area of territorial jurisdiction extending over several *départements*. The *Cour administrative d'appel de Bordeaux*, for example, hears appeals from the *Tribunaux administratifs* in Bordeaux, Poitiers, Limoges, Pau, Toulouse and Montpellier, covering a total of 25 *départements* and five régions.

In general terms, the *Cours administratives d'appel* are *juridictions de droit commun* in that they have jurisdiction to hear appeals from the *Tribunaux administratifs* unless a law has provided that such appeals are to be heard by another court. In particular, cases relating to elections and appeals on a particular ground of *ultra vires* (*recours pour excès de pouvoir*) are subject to appeal only to the *Conseil d'Etat*. In addition, if the court finds itself dealing with a case which raises a novel and important point of law, it has the power to transfer the case to the *Conseil d'Etat* immediately.

The *Cour administrative d'appel* under the authority of a *Président* is a collegiate court comprising three judges (*conseillers*). It normally consists of the *Président* of the particular *chambre*, an ordinary *conseiller* and a *conseiller-rapporteur* who has the task of undertaking the preliminary investigation of the case (the instruction).

## D The *Conseil d'Etat*

As the name would suggest, the *Conseil d'Etat* was originally conceived as a consultative body to assist in the administration of the nation's affairs. Gradually it took on a legal function in addition to its administrative one. It is split into six *sections*. Five of these *sections* are purely administrative in nature in that they give advice to the government or civil service on proposed legislation and its possible legal implications. The sixth *section* – the *section contentieuse* (litigation section) is, in reality, a court and operates along the lines of any other administrative court. When a case reaches the court it is first submitted to the relevant *sous-section* which is then responsible for the *instruction* (investigation) process. On the conclusion of the *instruction*, judgment is normally given by that *sous-section*. Occasionally, depending on the subject matter of the case, judgment is given by two or more *sous-sections réunies*. In the most important cases judgment can be given by the *Section du contentieux en formation de jugement* or even the *Assemblé du contentieux* which is the most solemn form.

The *Conseil d'Etat* is the supreme court within the administrative hierarchy. It plays three distinct roles – a court of first instance, a court of appeal and a court of *cassation* (for review on a point of law).

### The *Conseil d'Etat* as a court of first instance

Some cases which come before a *Tribunal administratif* have implications which go beyond the territorial jurisdiction of that particular court and affect the whole of France. The disappointed party in such a case, having obtained a ruling from one *Tribunal administratif*, may be tempted to apply to a different *Tribunal administratif* in an attempt to obtain a different ruling as regards the jurisdictional area of the second court. This is, clearly, an unsatisfactory situation and thus the *Conseil d'Etat* takes immediate jurisdiction as a court of first and last resort. Its ruling is binding for the entire country. The *Conseil d'Etat* will also assume jurisdiction if the official document (*acte*) in question emanates from the national level. In this capacity, the *Conseil d'Etat* may also remove from an administrative court any case which raises an important issue and upon which a decision is thought necessary to be binding over the whole of France rather than merely limited to the jurisdictional area of one single *Tribunal administratif*. This is achieved by the procedure known as *l'évocation*.

### The *Conseil d'Etat* as a court of appeal

As has been explained earlier, the *Conseil d'Etat* retains the role of appeal court in the specific cases of elections and *recours pour excès de pouvoir* in place of the *Cour administrative d'appel*. As is the rule in the French legal system, an appeal is a complete rehearing of the case and the verdict reached by the *Conseil d'Etat* is not subject to further review.

### The *Conseil d'Etat* as a court of *cassation*

In a manner which is similar to the operation of the *Cour de cassation* within the 'ordinary' legal system, an appeal, based exclusively on a point of law, lies to the *Conseil d'Etat*. In order to prevent a proliferation of such cases and, probably to retain the status of the newly created administrative appeal courts, each application is subject to a 'filtering' process (*procédure préalable d'admission*). This procedure weeds out those appeals over which the *Conseil d'Etat* has no jurisdiction (eg those which do not plead an infringement of any law by the lower courts) or which do not raise any substantial (*sérieux*) grounds. It is interesting to note that a similar procedure existed in the *Cour de cassation* until 1981 when it was abolished owing, in part, to the adverse criticism as to the nature of the filtering process which served to prejudge all applications. It remains to be seen how the filtering process in the *Conseil d'Etat* will survive the test of time.

Given that the appeal to the *Conseil d'Etat* is on a point of law and that it is found that the lower courts have failed to apply the law in a correct manner, the options open to the *Conseil d'Etat* are wider than those available to the *Cour de Cassation* in similar circumstances.

First, as is the rule in the *Cour de cassation*, the *Conseil d'Etat* may refer the case back to a court of the same standing as that from which the appeal was made. Thus a decision of the *Cour d'appel administrative de Bordeaux* may be referred to the *Cour d'appel administrative de Nantes*.

Secondly, the court has the power to refer the case back to the same court (differently constituted) whence it came. This alternative is an obvious necessity when there is only one lower court with jurisdiction over the case within France. For example, there are many small administrative *juridictions d'exceptions*, such as the *Cour des comptes* which deals with the budgets and accounts of state offices. There is only one *Cour des comptes* situated in Paris, and the *Conseil d'Etat* must refer back to the same court if a successful appeal is made.

Thirdly, the *Conseil d'Etat* imposes its own decision on the litigation (*régler l'affaire au fond*) if it feels that this solution is in the interest of justice. This final option goes totally against the theory of the role to be played by a court of *cassation* – that it gives an interpretation of the law but not of the facts of a particular case. The paradox involved may partially be explained by the fact that, unlike the *Cour de cassation*, the *Conseil d'Etat* acts as a court of first instance in certain circumstances.

# VII The *Tribunal des conflits*

The strict adherence to the separation of powers as practised by the French legal system means that in order to obtain redress an applicant must petition the correct court within the correct set of courts. The administrative courts are forbidden by law from deciding cases which properly fall within the jurisdiction of the 'ordinary' courts and vice versa.[5] This poses obvious problems for a litigant in that it may not be immediately obvious which sets of courts have jurisdiction over the claim. Conflicts of jurisdiction can arise in a positive or negative way. Both the administrative and the 'ordinary' courts may claim jurisdiction or both may deny it. The *Tribunal des conflits*, based in Paris, is the court which resolves these difficulties. It makes no judgment on the substance of the case, it merely decides which court has jurisdiction to deal with the affair. It consists of nine judges, ie three from the *Cour de cassation* and three from the *Conseil d'Etat*: to these are added two further judges chosen by the first six who in practice will

---

5   Unless it is a question of a *voie de fait*, being an act by the administration which is so flagrantly wrong that it loses its quality of an administrative act and thus becomes triable by the 'ordinary' courts.

be one judge from the *Cour de cassation* and one from the *Conseil d'Etat*. The Minister of Justice chairs the court. The Tribunal also deals with conflicts of jurisdiction between the different 'ordinary' courts.

# VIII  The *Conseil constitutionnel*

The *Conseil constitutionnel* has two distinct roles. It has jurisdiction over any dispute arising from elections to both Houses of the French Parliament – the *Sénat* and the *Assemblée nationale* or from referenda. Any person on the electoral list for the disputed election or any candidate for that election may refer a case to the *Conseil constitutionnel*. There is no appeal against its decision.

Secondly, it has a duty to ascertain whether newly issued laws conform to the French Constitution or not. In this respect its powers are limited and it cannot proceed to examine the constitutionality of court decisions or individual administrative or state measures. Further, in relation to laws, it can only act before the official promulgation of such laws in the *Journal Officiel*. A distinction must be drawn between 'ordinary' laws and *lois organiques*, the latter being laws which affect in some way the Constitution itself or the operation of constitutional bodies and their relationship with each other. All such *lois organiques* must be referred to the *Conseil constitutionnel* prior to their promulgation.

As regards 'ordinary' laws, the French citizen has no power to refer any law about to be issued to the court. The only persons given such power by the Constitution are the President of France, the Prime Minister, the leaders of either of the Houses of the French Parliament or 60 members (*députés*) of either House who must make a collective application to that effect. Thus it may be seen that the supervision of the *Conseil constitutionnel* over the constitutionality of acts is much less extensive than (say) that of the *Bundesverfassungsgericht* in Germany to which, in principle, every citizen has access.

The *Conseil Constitutionnel* is composed of nine members, three appointed by the President of France, three by the leader of the *Assemblée nationale* and three by the leader of the *Sénat*. They hold office for a maximum period of nine years and, whilst in office, are prohibited from acting as a Government minister or as a member of either House of the French Parliament. Again, there is no appeal against the decision of the court.

# 3    The Legal Personnel

# I Judges

Within the French legal system the words *'le magistrat, le juge* and *le conseiller'* are all used to express the English concept of a judge. The term *le magistrat* is, by and large, confined to the 'ordinary' legal system – *les tribunaux de l'ordre judiciaire* – where there are two distinct types of *magistrat*. A distinction is drawn between, on the one hand, the *magistrature assise* (also known as the *magistrature du siège*) who are responsible for the actual hearing of the case and who correspond most closely to the English notion of a judge and, on the other hand, the *magistrature debout* who intervene on behalf of the *Ministère Public* (the *Parquet –* *infra*, p 47).

Within the administrative legal system – the *tribunaux de l'ordre administratif* – the terms *juge* and *conseiller* are used both for judges who try the case and those who intervene on behalf of the *Ministère public*.

It is intended to examine the recruitment, functions, and duties of each separate category of judge.

## A Recruitment

### General

In contrast to the situation in England where, for the most part, judges are taken from the ranks of practising barristers or solicitors, in France the majority of judges are civil servants (*fonctionnaires*) who choose as a career to become judges. For judges within the ordinary legal system the normal starting point is to gain entry to the *Ecole nationale de la magistrature* (ENM) at Bordeaux.

### Methods of recruitment

Entry to the ENM may be gained in three different ways.

- **Competitive examination:** There are two types of competitive examination. There are those which are open to students (under the age of 27) who hold a national qualification approved by the *Conseil d'Etat* which would allow them to proceed to post-graduate level studies. In addition to the obvious legal qualifications, a diploma from an *Institut d'études politiques* or one of the *Grandes écoles nationales* are included within the approved list. The intention here is to widen the base of recruitment by including those students whose background is not solely within the field of legal studies. The success rate at these examinations is approximately 10% and students admitted by this route account for about 75% of each yearly intake to the ENM.

The other type of competitive examination is for existing civil servants who have been in post for a minimum of four years. Here the success rate is about 15% and successful candidates form 20% of the total at the ENM each year.

- **Recruitment from the legal profession**: This method consists in the recruitment, without examination, of persons within the legal profession, such as existing *avocats*. Admissions by this route, which is something akin to the English route, amount to only 5% of total admissions.

Over the last decade there have been an increasing number of female applicants to the extent that the student population at the ENM has moved from parity to a 60/40 dominance of women. Following a period of tuition at Bordeaux and a work placement (*un stage*) in the courts, students take examinations according to the results of which they are classified and appointed (by decree of the President of France) either to sit in court or to the Parquet in accordance with the availability of places. Once an appointment has been made a career structure is in place allowing for promotion from the lower to the higher courts.

**Judges within the administrative legal system**

In this case a different mode of recruitment is used. The normal procedure involves obtaining a place at the *Ecole nationale d'administration* in Strasbourg. The ENA is not specifically established in order to train judges but exists to train potential civil servants generally for the exercise of public office.

Whether or not one becomes a judge following the three year training period under the auspices of the ENA depends both on the student's performance and classification in the final examination and on the availability of posts. Those who achieve the highest results may be offered posts directly in the *Conseil d'Etat* whilst those whose performance is not so good may go to the *Tribunaux administratifs*. As is the case for recruits to the 'ordinary' legal system, it is largely a matter of chance whether one is appointed to the bench or to the *Ministère public*.

There is also in place a system of direct recruitment to the administrative courts from current civil servants who, owing to their administrative experience, are considered to have the relevant ability. This form of recruitment is more widespread than in the 'ordinary' court system as the judges do not in any strict sense form a separate body from the administration in general and as the ENA cannot furnish a sufficient number of suitably qualified students to cope with the ever increasing volume of administrative litigation to be dealt with by the courts.

# II The *Ministère public*

The functions of the *magistrat du siège* within the 'ordinary' legal system and those of the *juge* or *conseiller* within the administrative system are similar to those normally encountered within the English legal system. What distinguishes the French system is the role of those persons who comprise the *magistrature debout* in both French court systems. They may be conveniently grouped under the heading of *Ministère public* but, although the *Ministère public* exists in all French courts, its role and functions differ according to whether it is a civil or criminal 'ordinary' court or an administrative court.

## A Before the 'ordinary' courts

Before the 'ordinary' courts the *Ministère public* operates on a hierarchical basis at the head of which is the Minister of Justice (*le Garde des Sceaux*). At each level of court he is represented by a *procureur* who is responsible for the working of the *Parquet* within that court. All *Tribunaux de droit commun*, ie the *Tribunaux de grande instance*, the *Cours d'appel* and the *Cour de cassation*, must have the services of the *Parquet*. Other courts (the *Tribunaux d'exception*) *may* call for such services though they are not obliged to do so.

In each *Tribunal de grande instance* the *Parquet* is headed by the *Procureur de la République* assisted, as the need arises, by *procureurs adjoints* and *substituts*.

In the *Cour d'appel* the head is the *Procureur général* assisted by *avocats généraux* and, for administrative duties, *substituts généraux*. In addition, the *Procureur général* has overall responsibility for the *Ministère public* within the jurisdictional area (*le ressort*) of the *Cour d'appel* in question.

In the *Cour de cassation* the head is the *Procureur général près de la Cour de cassation* assisted, once again, by *avocats généraux*. Before other courts not automatically provided with the services of the *Parquet*, the *Procureur de la République* may exercise the role of the *Ministère public* for all first instance courts established within his jurisdictional area.

The role of the *Ministère public* before the civil courts is to give the 'public interest point of view' by overseeing the proper and uniform application of all laws relevant to the case. This is achieved by making submissions (mostly in writing) to the court on the possible different interpretations of a given law and their consequences if applied to the instant case. These submissions (*conclusions*) are often closely reasoned with due attention paid not only to previous decisions but also to different academic interpretations. As has been seen earlier, trial judges are specifically prohibited from referring in their judgments to anything except the relevant law and case facts in order to arrive at their decision. Thus the *conclusions* of the *Ministère public* more closely resemble the judgments of an English court than do the judgments of their French counterparts.

In criminal courts the role of the *Ministère public* in overseeing the proper application of the law is exercised by taking responsibility for the prosecution of the case. In effect, they bring the case in the name of and on behalf of the public at large. In this respect their duties are somewhat akin to those of the Crown Prosecution Service in England.

## B Before the administrative courts

In front of the administrative courts the role of the *Ministère public* is exercised by the *Commissaire du Gouvernement* whose function is once again to inform the court of what is considered to be a proper application of the law.

# III The legal representatives

## A General

Prior to the reforms in 1971 (*Loi* no. 71-1130) and 1990 (*Lois* nos. 90-1258 and 90-1259), the right of legal representation of clients fell to a number of different categories of professional – *avocats, avoués, agréés, conseils juridiques* and *notaires*. The basic division of functions was as follows:

* *avocats* were, as the name suggests, principally advocates for a client before the courts. In addition, however, they had a role to play in giving advice on contentious issues prior to the hearing in much the same way as an English barrister operates today.

* *avoués* were responsible for procedural matters and paperwork in general prior to the court appearance. This division of duties is similar to the one subsisting in England between barristers and solicitors in so far as contentious matters are concerned.

* *agréés* were representatives before the *Tribunal de commerce* where, as is still the case, parties were free to choose their own representative rather than being forced to have recourse to the services of an *avocat*. Over the course of time the court established a list of recommended representatives (other than *avocats*) who were known as *agréés* and whose status was finally formalised in 1945.

* *conseils juridiques*. Certain areas of law were, historically, largely ignored by *avocats* – in particular company law and taxation. This gap was filled by persons calling themselves *conseils juridiques* who grew to have a specialism in these areas despite the lack of formal regulation of the profession – the term *conseil juridique* having no official status. They may be equated to some extent with 'in-house lawyers' or 'paralegals' within the system in England.

* *notaires* deal with non-contentious work and their major task is to draft, authenticate and preserve documents such as wills, conveyances and marriage settlements and to give clients general advice on those areas.

# B Reform

## The 1971 reforms

The first reforming law in 1971 sought to bring about a merger within the legal profession. It did so in two ways:

- The professions of *avocat* and *avoué* before the first instance courts were amalgamated and the functions of the former *avoué* before the first instance courts have now been subsumed within the profession of *avocat*.

- The profession of *agréé* at the *Tribunaux de Commerce* was abolished and, again, former *agréés* have become *avocats*.

Outside the scope of this merger remained the *conseils juridiques* and the *avoués d'appel*. It seems that the specialist nature of the work of the *avoués d'appel* before the higher courts in France has led the legislator to retain them as a separate body and it is they alone who continue to have the monopoly of representing clients before these higher courts.

## The 1990 reforms

The second reforming laws of 1990 achieved the merger of the professions of *avocat* and of *conseil juridique* who henceforth form a unified profession of *avocat*. The law also includes provisions as to eligibility to become an *avocat* especially in relation to the academic qualifications required.

It is to be noted that nothing in these reforms has in any way changed the nature of the profession of *notaire* which remains totally independent. The reasons are historical and rest now on the basis that alone amongst this class of legal representative they hold public office and are *officiers ministériels*.

Today the role of the *avocat* can be seen to be a dual one – a role of giving assistance and advice to clients and one of representing them before the courts – *la plaidoirie*. Although the *avocat* does not have a monopoly in the giving of professional legal advice (though those who are allowed to do so are limited by the Law of 1990 to persons fulfilling certain conditions – principally that the person concerned must hold a *licence en droit* or the equivalent) they do have a monopoly of appearing before the court as representatives subject only to certain exceptions for some *juridictions d'exception* and to the *avoués d'appel* in so far as some higher courts are concerned.

# C Regulation of the profession of *avocat*

Traditionally, to become an *avocat* one had to be of French nationality. The Law of 1990 has now extended this to include nationals of any of the EU member states along with reciprocal arrangements for nationals of countries outside the EU.

As well as being 'of good character', the aspiring avocat must have the required academic qualifications. Broadly these are that one must be the holder of (at least) a *maîtrise en droit* (or equivalent) and also the CAPA – *Certificat d'ap-*

*titude à la profession d'avocat* – which is awarded to candidates who have success-fully completed a one year training course at a regional training centre – CRFP (*Centre régional de formation professionnelle*). There are provisions for the recogni-tion of foreign qualifications and/or the taking of an examination on French law for non-French nationals who wish to establish themselves as *avocats* in France.

On completion of the professional course there follows a training period of two years' duration (*le stage*) with an *avocat* prior to the commencement of which one must be enrolled on the '*liste des avocats stagiaires*' at the local *barreau* (bar council). The *barreau* is headed by the *bâtonnier*, who deals with administra-tive and disciplinary matters. There is a separate *barreau* for the jurisdictional area of each *Tribunal de grande instance*. At the conclusion of the *stage* the *bâton-nier* delivers to the *avocat stagiaire* a certificate of due completion of the training period at which point the aspiring avocat becomes entitled to be enrolled as a full *avocat* and to have his name entered on the roll of *avocats* – the *grand tableau*.

The profession of *avocat* is 'liberal and independent' in the sense that an *avo-cat* is not an *officier ministériel*. It can be exercised in a number of ways – either as an individual or as an authorised group or association.

- **The** *association*, whereby *avocats*, whilst preserving their individual clients have common offices, secretaries, libraries etc. This resembles the way in which barristers' chambers operate in England.

- **The** *société civile professionnelle*, whereby the company (*la société*) is the client's representative but individual *avocats* remain jointly and severally liable for the company's debts.

- **The** *société pour l'exercice d'une profession libérale* was introduced by the Law of 1990 as a further opportunity for *avocats* to join forces. It functions in much the same way as a limited liability company and may be financed by non-lawyers.

# IV  Other legal personnel (*auxiliares de justice*)

As can be easily understood, the court system in France does not operate merely with *avocats* and judges. A complete infrastructure of legal or quasi legal personnel exists, to ensure its smooth operation. Of these, the most important is probably the *huissier de justice* who has much in common with the English bailiff or sheriff. It is the duty of the *huissier* officially to inform the parties to the case of its result (*la sig-nification*) and to enforce judgment by, for example, levying distress on a debtor's goods. Further the *huissier* acts as an independent process server.

Amongst the additional personnel mention can briefly be made of the *greffier* whose role can be equated with that of the clerk to the court in England and of the *expert comptable* whose expert evidence is heavily relied upon in cases of fraud and those in which accountancy related matters are at issue.

# 4 Civil Law

The *Code civil* is the very prototype of the codified law as it exists in many countries today. Even though, as has been mentioned earlier (cf. *supra*, p. 12), it was not the first example of a large body being incorporated into a systematic whole, it has come to symbolise the legal approach and policy which has become known as 'the civil law'. It encompasses such diverse areas as family law, the law of contracts, torts, the law of property and the law of succession.

## I Fundamental characteristics

Before describing the main topics as they are featured in the Code, it is essential to explain some of its fundamental characteristics.

### A Continuity

Although the *Code civil*, being a product of the French Revolution, was innovative in both its design and its approach, its contents showed a remarkable degree of continuity with the pre-revolutionary system. The law of contracts, for example, was drawn almost exclusively from the Justinian codes of Roman law, whereas the law of succession was largely based on the teachings of Domat and Pothier.[1]

### B Durability

The *Civil Code* can truly be described as a masterpiece of durability. In France, as in many countries, the *Code civil* remains applicable today in its original form, with hardly any structural alterations having taken place during the intervening years (although many of the original provisions have been entirely replaced – see, for example, the rules of matrimonial property law, cf. *infra* p. 69). There are two reasons for this durability:

- the original structure of the *Code civil* was so sound and comprehensive that the only changes made have concerned individual articles rather than entire chapters. Indeed, it has been possible to incorporate all the intervening legislation on civil matters within the existing structure of the *Code*;

---

1  Robinson, O.F., Fergus, T.D. and Gordon, W.M., *op cit*, pp. 428-432.

- the articles themselves were worded in such a flexible manner that it has been possible in many cases to change their substance without amending their wording. The best example of this is Article 1382 which deals with tort liability. This article contains the broad principle that anyone who causes damage to another person through his or her own fault is under an obligation to make good such damage. Subsequent articles deal in equally general terms with the principle of vicarious liability, ie the liability for persons or objects under one's control. The French law of torts has experienced the same development as that which took place in English law, to wit a shift in emphasis from individual and subjective liability to objective (or strict) liability. Such is the wording of the articles in question, however, that it has been possible to accommodate this development without requiring a change of text. Thus objective liability for damage caused by cars and other dangerous objects was able to be developed.

## C Deals only with substantive law

In principle, the *Code civil* deals only with the substantive issues, not the procedural (although some of its provisions have important procedural implications – eg Article 1328). This separation is typical of the French codified system and differs considerably from the Anglo-Saxon approach. Civil procedure is the subject matter of two separate *Codes* which were introduced relatively recently.[2]

## D Clarity

The style in which the *Code* is drafted is very clear; one of the objectives of its drafters was to achieve a simplicity of statement which would render the law accessible to all citizens.[3] The fact that it has required such a vast body of case law to interpret it is a function of the broad nature of its provisions rather than of its lack of clarity.

## E Individual liberalism

Although, as has been mentioned before (cf. *supra*, p. 10), French civil law has adapted itself to modern developments in society, its philosophy remains imbued with the notion of individual liberalism which inspired its creation. This is especially the case in the fields of contract law, which is marked by the principle of individual freedom to contract; tort liability, where the notion of individual responsibility remains the dominant philosophy; and the law of

---

2    The *Code de l'organisation judiciaire* (1978) and the *Nouveau code de procédure civile* (1975).
3    Lawson, F.H., Anton, A.E., and Brown, L.N., *op cit*, p. 32.

property, in which the absolute right of persons to have full use of their property remains the cornerstone.[4]

## F  Scheme of the *Code civil*

The Code is subdivided into books, titles, chapters, sections and articles. Normally, however, the Code is cited by article alone, since the latter are numbered successively regardless of the other subdivisions (eg Book III, Title III, Chapter V, Section II ends with Article 1281; Section III begins with Article 1282).[5]

Book I opens with six general articles which set out particulars of publication, effects and application of its provisions. Thus, for example, it lays down that laws cannot apply retroactively. The remainder of Book I concerns the status of persons and their capacity to act at law (*l'état et la capacité des personnes*). Book II, ie Articles 516-710, sets out the French law of property. Book III, which is more than twice as long as the other two put together, concerns the ways in which property may be acquired, starting with the law of succession and proceeding to the law of obligations.

# II  The civil code – an overview

## A  The law of persons

Logic dictates that the first book of the Code should deal with those without whose intervention no legal relations can come into being, to wit, persons. This concept covers not only physical (or natural) persons, but also entities which are created by natural persons and acquire for themselves the capacity to create legal relations. These are called 'legal persons' (*personnes morales*).

Book I deals with the situation which is deemed to be the norm, being natural persons having full legal capacity, then proceeds to describe the exceptions to this norm, being the cases in which certain physical persons are deemed to be incapable of creating normal legal relations (*les incapacités*) and the artificial type of person known as 'legal persons' (*personnes morales*).

---

4    Article 544 of the *Code*.

5    It is perhaps appropriate to point out at this stage that for the more recent French *Codes*, such as the new Criminal Code, a more modern numbering system has been devised (cf. *infra*, Chapter 9).

## Natural persons

### Nationality

Although all natural persons are, in principle, capable of creating legal relations, only a certain category of citizen enjoys full civil rights, the latter being reserved exclusively to persons of French nationality. Unlike Britain, which assumes that anyone born on its territory has British nationality, France applies the principle of *jus sanguinis*, under which anyone born of a French mother or father acquired French nationality, regardless of his or her place of birth. Some concessions are made to the *jus soli* principle, in that, for example, anyone who is born in France of a mother or father born in France (regardless of their nationality) is French.

French nationality can be acquired by means other than birth. Foreign women automatically become French on marrying a Frenchman, unless they expressly decline to do so before the marriage. Other foreigners may obtain French nationality through naturalisation.

### Official residence

Every person established in France has an official residence (*le domicile*), which shall be his or her main place of establishment unless he or she sets up a genuine home elsewhere in order to make that his or her main establishment. It is extremely important to establish a person's official residence, since it is there that he or she is deemed to be available for all civil purposes. Thus, for example, if a person is sued, the legal proceedings must in principle take place in the court of the defendant's official residence.

### Names

The birth certificate (*acte de naissance*) must state both the first name(s) (*prénoms*) and the family name (*nom de famille*, or *nom patronymique*, the latter being that of the father. Persons cannot lawfully change their names unless the President has issued a decree to that effect. Even a married woman does not, in principle, change her maiden name; nevertheless the law takes a broad view of the social habit whereby the married woman assumes the name of her husband for certain purposes.

### Missing persons

The *Code* makes provision for cases in which persons have disappeared for some time and about whom there is genuine uncertainty as to whether or not they are alive. In such circumstances, the person in question will be classified as 'missing' (*absent*). Special rules govern persons who are known with certainty to have died, but whose body has not yet been recovered, or persons having disappeared in conditions capable of endangering their life.

## Persons who are not capable of acting at law (*les incapables*)

### *Aliens*

In principle, the reciprocity rule applies to aliens, in the sense that they only enjoy such rights in France as those which are accorded to French citizens under treaties concluded with the alien's own country.[6] Subsequent legislation and case law has, however, mitigated the severity of this rule.

### *Married women*

Originally, the *Code* placed severe restrictions on the capacity of the married woman to act at law; more particularly she was not allowed to sign contracts or to be involved in any court action, whether as a plaintiff or as a defendant. Since those days, however, the status of the married woman has changed for the better, to the point where she now has practically the same legal capacities as her husband.[7]

### *Minors*

As from 1974, the age of majority has been fixed at 18 years. Persons under that age cannot, in principle, act at law, and must for this purpose be represented by a guardian. However, as is the case in England, a minor may perform such actions as concluding contracts for goods and services which are reasonably necessary. In fact, no contract signed by a minor may be cancelled merely on the grounds of his or her minority; the minor must also prove that the contract in question is improvident and imprudent.[8]

Not all minors are subject to these restrictions on their activities, since the Civil Code provides for the possibility of their being 'emancipated' (*émancipés*) as from the age of 16, which confers on them the capacity to perform a number of legally binding actions. It must be admitted that this mechanism has lost a great deal of its significance since 1974, when, as was mentioned earlier, the age of majority was reduced to 18. The original object of *l'émancipation* was to give the 'mature minor' (especially those aged around 18 and over) some control over his or her professional life. It is even of limited value in the world of commerce, since no minor may perform an *acte de commerce*[9] before having reached the age of 18, even if that minor has been *émancipé*.

---

6   Article 11 of the *Code*.

7   The main changes in the status of the married woman were introduced by a Law of 1938 and an *ordonnance* of 1945. See also the changes introduced by the legislation of 1965 and 1985 in relation to the applicable matrimonial property régime.

8   The *Code* provides no guidance or criteria in order to determine what constitutes improvident and imprudent contracts – and neither does the *Cour de cassation*, since this is purely a factual matter (cf. *supra*, p. 37)!

9   For the meaning of this term, cf. *infra*, p. 84.

Other categories of persons, such as those suffering various forms of mental deficiency, and criminals, may also be deprived of their capacity to act at law.

## Legal persons

Various theories have been developed to explain the legal fiction whereby entities other than natural persons acquire the right to act at law. Considerations of space prevent us from dealing with these in any length. Suffice it to say that the courts tend to confer legal personality on any group capable of 'collective expression for the defence of lawful interests'.[10]

Legal persons divide into three broad categories: (a) those governed by public law, (b) those governed by private law, and (c) those having a mixed character. It is those governed by private law which form the most substantial category, and which include:

- *Sociétés* (companies). These are not only the *sociétés commerciales* (commercial companies – cf. *infra*, Chapter 5), but also the *sociétés civiles*. Both have profit-making objectives, but the former achieves this by means of commercial operations, whereas the latter makes its profits in other ways (eg by lawyers forming a partnership).

- *Associations*. These are governed by the Law of 1/7/1901.[11] Associations other than religious congregations may be formed freely and without requiring prior permission or registration. However, they only acquire legal personality once certain particulars, such as their name and object, have been officially registered. Unlike the *sociétés civiles*, they lack full legal personality, in the sense that they may only engage in certain transactions; any others will be held to be illegal.

- *Fondations*. This is a property or a fund which is intended for a specific objective and has to this end its own administration or organisation.

## Marriage and divorce

Before 1789, French matrimonial law was governed by canon law, and the establishment of marriage as a civil, non-religious institution was one of the major demands of the revolutionaries. Henceforth, the only valid marriage ceremony was to be that which took place before the public authorities.

The legal capacity to marry is acquired by a man at the age of 18 and by a woman at the age of 15, marriages between persons not having reached this age being voidable unless special dispensation has been given. Another factor

---

10  Lawson, F.H., Anton, A.E. and Brown, L.N., *op cit*, p. 49.
11  Article 1 of this Law defines an association as a contract and not as a group formed by a contract.

which may render the marriage voidable is mistake or duress on the part of one of the spouses.

Apart from voidance and death, the only other factor which may discontinue a marriage is a divorce. The original Civil Code was far ahead of its time in allowing divorce, but this facility was temporarily abolished when, in 1816, Catholicism once again became the state religion, and it was not until 1884 that the original divorce provisions of the Code were restored, with the exception of the article which allowed divorce by mutual consent. It was not until 1975 that the latter was restored.[12]

The present grounds for divorce are: adultery, major offence (*injures graves*), cruelty (*excès, sévices*), the imposition of demeaning punishment, and consent.

The Code requires from both spouses a mutual obligation of faithfulness, support and assistance.[13] Originally, the Code demanded from the wife obedience to the husband, but this anachronism was abolished by a Law of 1938, which also conferred full legal capacity on the wife (even though the husband, who remains the head of the family, retains his dominant position in the marriage and household).

The institution of marriage inevitably has a number of financial implications, regarding which there is a comprehensive set of rules in the *Code civil*. On the one hand, there is the *obligation alimentaire* during the marriage, which obliges not only the spouses to provide each other and their children with the necessary means of subsistence, but also requires children to support their parents, and imposes a mutual obligation of maintenance owed by sons/daughters-in-law towards their fathers/mothers-in-law, and *vice versa*. The extent of the maintenance which must be provided is commensurate with the needs of the persons requiring the support and the means of those obliged to provide it.[14]

Secondly, the Code contains an extensive set of rules relating to marriage settlements – which, significantly, are placed in Book III (acquisition of property) rather than in Book I. This is in marked contrast with English law, where marriage settlements are relatively rare. Unless the spouses conclude a specific marriage contract, they are deemed to have adopted the system of *communauté*. This system, which was fundamentally altered in the mid-sixties, makes any personal and real property acquired after the marriage subject to joint ownership by the spouses. Any property acquired prior to the marriage remains the property of the individual spouses. The law of marriage settlements is explained more fully later (cf. *infra*, p. 69).

French family law still stops a long way short of giving legal recognition to unmarried couples living together. However, recent legislative changes have

---

12  This procedure now accounts for one-third of all divorces in France.

13  Article 212 of the Code.

14  Article 208 of the Code.

made it possible for such persons to assert certain financial rights (for example in landlord and tenant law, where the cohabitee now has the same rights as a married partner of having the tenancy transferred to him/her after the death of the other partner). The relevant case law has also recently shown itself to be more flexible in this regard.

## Parent and child

In principle, any child conceived during marriage has the husband as its father.[15] One of the basic assumptions made by the Code is that the time difference between conception and birth is a minimum of 180 days and a maximum of 300 days; therefore it is only if the presumed father can prove that he could not have cohabited with the mother during that period that he may disavow the child.

The Code places children under 'paternal authority'. This is not strictly speaking correct, since this authority is now exercised by both parents – even though the father, in his capacity of head of the family, will have the upper hand. Thus Article 373 makes it clear that paternal authority 'shall be exercised during the marriage by the father in his capacity of head of the family'. This authority is matched by a number of rights and obligations towards the child.

The position of illegitimate children has improved considerably from the original provisions of the Code, under which illegitimate children had hardly any means of enforcing recognition of paternity. This position improved after the Law of 16/12/1912. This gives the illegitimate child claims to recognition by the natural father, not only in extreme cases such as rape or abduction, but also if there has occurred an unequivocal admission of paternity, or if the natural father has contributed towards the maintenance and education of the child.

### Adoption

There are three types of adoption: the ordinary adoption, *the adoption simple* and the *légitimation adoptive*. The requirements for ordinary adoption are that (a) the adopting parent has no legitimate children, (b) that he or she be at least 30 years old, or has been married for a minimum period of five years, and (c) that he or she be a minimum of 15 years older than the adoptee. The adoptee becomes a member of the natural family of the adopter, with all the attendant rights and obligations. In addition to the adoption described above, which is called the *adoption plénière*, there is also the *adoption simple*, which does not break the link with the natural parents, but gives the adopted child additional succession rights. The *légitimation adoptive*, on the other hand, is only possible for children under seven years of age, whose natural parents are dead, unknown or have abandoned them.

---

15   Article 312 of the *Code*.

Adoption is an activity which falls within the decision-making powers of the courts, more particularly the *Tribunal de grande instance*.

*Guardianship*

Every minor who has lost one of his parents must have a *tuteur* (guardian) and a *subrogé tuteur* (supervising guardian). The guardian shall be the surviving parent, who will also exercise parental authority. Where both parents have died, guardianship belongs to the person appointed by the will of the last surviving parent. If no such appointment has been made, it will belong to the next ascendant of the ward, and if none have survived, the guardian shall be the person appointed by the *conseil de famille* (family council) which must also appoint the appropriate guardian. The obligations of the guardian are not confined to custody and education: he or she also administers the ward's property and represents him/her in court actions. Persons who have reached the age of majority may be placed under guardianship if they are judged to be permanently of unsound mind.

# B The law of property

## General

The law of property is contained in Book II of the Code. Like its English counterpart, French property law is weighted heavily in favour of real property or land. This has started to attract a great deal of criticism on the grounds that this bias is very much a reflection of 19th century economic priorities rather than those of our present age, where moveable assets have become as important – in some cases, more so – than real property.

## Three major distinctions

Book II starts by making two important distinctions: one is between moveable property (known in English law as 'personalty') and real property; the other is between private property and property owned by the state. Property owned by the state is in turn divided into the private domain and the public domain. The public domain consists of what would now be referred to as 'the public infrastructure', ie property intended for use by the general public, such as roads, rivers, harbours, etc. In principle, goods in the public domain cannot be disposed of. The private domain, on the other hand, covers all other State-owned property which does not have this special status, and therefore can be disposed of.

Another key distinction to be made in the French law of property is that between ownership and possession.

- **Ownership** (*propriété*); this forms the subject matter of the second title in Book II, and is defined in Article 544 as 'the right to have the benefit of, and dispose of, property in the most absolute manner, provided that no use be made thereof which is prohibited by law or regulation'.[16] The status of ownership protects its holder against confiscation, and also covers the 'accessories' of the main item of property, such as its income and products. Any new object formed from materials not belonging to the maker is treated as an accessory.

  Book II also deals with rights which fall short of full ownership, ie usufruct (*l'usufruit*) and easements (*les servitudes*), as well as other burdens on the property, such as pledges (*nantissement* for real property – *gage* for moveable property). The holder of a usufruct has no 'ownership for life' (as is the case with 'life tenancies' in English law), but merely title to use and enjoy the benefit of the object owned by another person, regardless of the period involved.

- **Possession**, on the other hand, is a factual situation rather than a right, but which has important implications in French law. To have possession of a physical object is to exercise over it such control as the owner would have.[17] To possess an insubstantial item of property, such as an easement, is to have enjoyment over it as if one were lawfully entitled to exercise it. In addition to enjoyment, however, there must exist a mental element, ie the *animus domini*: the possessor must intend to exercise control over the item on his own behalf. This is why a lessee cannot have true possession but only *détention précaire*. For practical reasons, there is always a presumption that the possessor of the object is also its owner, which can only be rebutted by a better title to property.

### Transfers of ownership

The ownership of personal (moveable) property is transferred to the purchaser merely by the agreement between the parties, even where the object in question has not actually been delivered. If goods are only described in general terms, ownership will only be transferred once they have been specified. The ownership over real property, on the other hand, is transferred by an ordinary contract, but can only be invoked by third parties once the title deeds have been officially registered. Other transactions affecting real property, such as usufructs, easements and mortgages, are also subject to official registration.

---

16  Translated by the authors from: '*La propriété est le droit de jouir et disposer des choses de la manière la plus absolue, pourvu qu'on n'en fasse pas un usage prohibé par les lois ou par les règlements*'.

17  Lawson, F.H., Anton, A.E. and Brown, L.N., *op cit*.

## *Hypothèques* and other charges on property

As to their object and general character, *hypothèques* resemble mortgages (or, perhaps more accurately, remortgages) in that they are real rights created by way of security for the payment of money. The advantage conferred on the creditor by holding a *hypothèque* consists in the last resort in the right to seize the property on which the charge rests and to sell it by auction under the supervision of the court, with the right to preferential payment from the proceeds.[18]

*Hypothèques* are, in principle, only allowed on real property; however, recent legislation has allowed this type of charge to rest on certain types of moveable property, such as commercial undertakings, patents and copyrights, ships, aircraft, etc.

*Privilèges* (whose closest equivalent in English law are liens) are also preferential rights to the debtor's assets, which is why the Code deals with them under the same title as *hypothèques*. *Privilèges* take precedence over all other claims to the debtor's property, even *hypothèques*. They can be either special or general according to whether they affect the debtor's entire assets, or only certain items of property. Legal expenses incurred in preserving or realising the debtor's assets, expenses of a person's last illness, wages and salaries are examples of general *privilèges*; the debt owed to the unpaid seller of real property, or to architects, contractors or other workers employed to construct or repair buildings, are examples of special *privilèges*.

## Mines

Mines belong to the owner of the surface area; however, their operation requires a concession from the State. This will give the grantee 'permanent ownership' of the mine. He or she may sell or mortgage it, though a partitioning of the mine is only allowed with the consent of the government.

## *Biens de famille*

The tying-up of land was abolished in France following the Revolution, because of the stultifying effect exercised by this practice on trade generally. However, legislation was introduced in 1909 which allowed, and gave protection to, family homesteads (*biens de famille*). These are plots of land with a house, not exceeding a certain amount in value, which cannot then be seized to pay any debts, even if the owner thereof becomes bankrupt. The owner may dispose of his or her *bien de famille*, but only with the consent of his or her spouse and, if he or she has minor children, of the *conseil de famille* (cf. *supra*, p. 59).

---

18  However, he or she shall not have the right to enter into possession of the property.

**Intellectual and industrial property**

- **General**. The notion of 'property' concerns not only concrete objects, but also intangible matters such as copyright, trade marks and patents. This is known as intellectual property. As its importance has increased, so specific legislation has been introduced in France to regulate its implications. This legislation has not, however, been incorporated into the *Code civil*, but now constitutes a Code in its own right (*Code de la propriété intellectuelle*).

- **Literary and artistic property**. This is governed by the Law of 11/3/1957, and contains two types of protection for the holder of the intellectual right in question: the *droits patrimoniaux* (which protects the financial implications) and the *droits moraux* (which protects the purely intellectual aspects of the artistic or literary creation in question). The former are transferable, whereas the latter cannot be disposed of.

- **Patents (*brevets*)**. These are regulated by the Law of 2/1/1968, which has subsequently been amended on several occasions to take account of international treaties on this subject to which France is a signatory. The two rights which are conferred on the patent holder are:
  (a) the exclusive right to the commercial utilisation of the invention in question for 20 years. However, where a *certificat d'utilité* has been issued, the protection only lasts six years, since the reason for issuing such certificates is to indicate that the area in which the invention took place would suffer from excessive restrictions on subsequent improvements to the invention in question;
  (b) the right to trade the patent: this confers on the patent holder the right to transfer the patent, or to licence others to utilise it commercially.

- **Trade marks**: these are governed by the Law of 4/1/1991, which implemented an EU directive on this subject. Here again, the protection granted takes the form of the exclusive right to the commercial utilisation of the trade mark, and the right to trade it.

## C The law of obligations

Under French law, the law of contracts and the law of torts are not, as they are in English law, two separate, self-contained legal subjects. The authors of the *Code civil*, following the example of the Justinian codes on which the latter was based, regarded both contracts and torts as sources of legal obligations on private parties. Therefore the manner in which these obligations are discharged will be subject to the same general rules, regardless of the events or circumstances which caused these obligations to come into being.

To be more precise, the Civil Code lists four sources of legal obligations for private parties: contracts, quasi-contracts, delicts, and quasi-delicts.[19] However, one discerns a fundamental divide between contractual and non-contractual obligations. The former are left much more to the law-creating initiative of the parties concerned, in that the parties are free, in principle, to enter into any obligations they may choose, and are only restricted in this endeavour by considerations of *ordre public* (public policy) and *bonnes moeurs* (public morality). Non-contractual obligations, however, are normally incurred involuntarily by the parties concerned, and are therefore subject to closer regulation by the law.

## General rules relating to obligations

An obligation is a legal bond between two persons under which one of them is bound to give, do or abstain from doing something for the benefit of the other. The latter's right is a personal right, ie one which is valid only against the person on whom the obligation rests.

Obligations are redeemed by performance, voluntary release, the substitution of one obligation by another (*la novation*), identity between the debtor and creditor (*confusion*), loss of the thing due, limitation in time (*prescription*) and set-off (*compensation*).

It is possible to assign (ie transfer) debts (*cessation*) by means of a formal agreement between the former and the new creditor. It will then be necessary to notify the debtor of this development in order to transfer ownership of the debt to the new creditor. If the debtor pays the former creditor before notification of the change, the obligation will have been fulfilled, regardless of whether the debtor was aware of this assignment.

Another legal aspect of obligations, regardless of their source, is that they are necessarily limited in time. Since the ultimate aim of the obligation is its performance, it must terminate at some time. This performance may be instant (payment in cash), successive (repayment of a loan by instalments) or continuous (the obligation to allow the lessee of an item undisturbed enjoyment of an object). As a result, no-one may be bound by an indefinite obligation: any obligation stipulated in such terms is cancellable, subject to adequate notice being given.

## Contracts

Normally, no formalities need to be completed in order to make a valid contract. Only certain special contracts, such as gifts, marriage contracts and transfers of land, require a deed passed before a Notary Public (*notaire*). It is possible to conclude valid contracts by word of mouth; however, only written contracts

---

19   The term '*delict*' is also used in Scots law to designate the law of torts.

will constitute valid evidence for any agreements other than those involving a trifling sum.[20]

The Civil Code requires contracts to fulfil certain fundamental criteria. The first is that of consent, which presupposes the existence of an offer and an acceptance. The offer may be withdrawn until the moment of acceptance. One of the more controversial issues among the French courts and authors is that of the precise moment at which the contract is regarded as having been legally concluded. Some consider that the contract is complete at the moment of despatch – ie when the letter of acceptance is being posted. Others maintain that the contract is only validly concluded as from the moment of reception, that is to say as soon as the letter reached the offeror. This question has yet to be settled conclusively.

Certain factors may distort this consent, namely mistake, fraud, duress and lesion. As to mistake (*dol*), the Code draws a distinction between (a) errors which are so fundamental as to exclude the possibility of consent and to prevent the formation of the contract (*erreur-obstacle*), (b) mistakes as to the substance, (c) mistakes as to the person, (d) errors of law and (e) arithmetical errors. Duress includes both actual and threatened violence on the person[21]; however, merely to threaten the exercise of one's legal rights will not constitute duress. The notion of fraud is also defined in a very general manner, and includes all such fraudulent manipulations as are designed to deceive or surprise the other party.[22] Lesion (*lésion*) occurs where certain types of contract, eg those involving persons requiring special protection such as minors, cause serious prejudice to that party.

- **Simulated contracts**. Where contracts are countered by a covert agreement (*contre-lettres*) that their contents are not really intended, the latter shall void if its cause is unlawful. However, this voidance cannot be relied upon against third parties.

- **Cause of the contract**. The second element required of a valid contract is, in accordance with Article 1108 of the Code, that it should have a lawful cause. This is a concept which is unknown in English law. Strictly speaking, we are not dealing here with the cause of a valid contract, but with the cause of a contractual obligation. Thus in sales agreements, there is one cause for the obligation of the seller and one cause for that of the purchaser, whereas in relation to gifts by promise there is only one cause because there is only one obligation.

---

20  Article 1341 of the Civil Code.

21  However, contracts cannot be challenged on grounds of duress if, after the duress has ceased, the contract has been approved expressly or implicitly, or where the time fixed by law for bringing the challenge – ie 10 years – has expired.

22  Article 1116 of the Civil Code.

The term 'cause' is not defined in the Code, and there have been several theories to explain its meaning. According to the classical theory,[23] the cause of an obligation of one party is the obligation of the other. Thus the cause of the purchaser's obligation to pay the stipulated price is the vendor's obligation to deliver the article in question, whereas the cause of the vendor's obligation is the purchaser's obligation to pay the stipulated price. In contracts such as loans and pledges, the cause of the obligation of the borrower and of the pledgee is the delivery of the article in question. According to this theory, the cause was identical in every contract of a particular type. The main criticism levelled at this approach was that it made the concept of cause superfluous, since it became identical with the object of the obligation in contracts which impose obligations on both parties (*contrats onéreux*).

Other authors developed a different explanation. Some sought to abandon the objective element in the cause; instead, they saw the cause as the individual motive for the promisor, being the *cause impulsive*,[24] which is not always the same for contracts of a particular type. It is, of course, not necessary for the parties to agree on such motives; however, motives can be important where the question arises whether a contract infringes public policy or is immoral, and therefore voidable. Others, like Capitant, assimilated the cause with the conclusive purpose of the parties which was to be objectively deduced from the contract itself, being to obtain the performance from the other parties in the *contrats onéreux* or to confer a benefit on someone in contracts bestowing gifts.

The reason why the cause of a contract is so important in French law is found in Article 1131 of the Civil Code, which stipulates that an obligation which is based on an unlawful cause can have no effect. Article 1133 of the Code explains that a cause is unlawful where it is prohibited by law and where it is contrary to public policy and morality. The courts have wide discretion in determining whether or not a contract infringes these criteria or not.

It should perhaps be pointed out at this stage that under French law, a contract could have a lawful *object* but nevertheless be void because the cause was illegal. Thus a contract to hire a room is valid as to its object; it becomes invalid as to its cause where the reason for concluding the contract was to use the room as a place for hiding stolen goods.

*Effects of contracts*

The general legal effect of contracts is explained in Article 1134, which states that lawfully formed contracts have force of law as between contracting parties. According to an early decision of the *Cour de cassation*, this means that it is not

---

23  These found their inspiration in Domat's work *Des lois civiles dans leur ordre naturel*.

24  This was the theory developed by, *inter alia*, Josserand in his *Cours de droit positif français* (3rd edn, 1940).

permissible for the courts to modify, for reasons of equity or on any other grounds, any contract which has been freely concluded between the parties. This principle has not invariably been upheld by the courts, which have intervened to take into account various circumstances when, for example, reducing doctors' or lawyers' fees. In most cases, the courts have intervened in order to redress an unequal relationship between the two parties, or, in the case of the *imprévision* doctrine, in order to re-establish the contractual balance between the obligations of both parties where this equilibrium has been destroyed by unforeseen extra-contractual events.

The same desire to redress the balance in contractual relationships has motivated the legislature also to intervene in order to limit the contractual freedom of the parties. In France, as elsewhere, legislation has been passed imposing moratoria for certain debts, restricting the right to give notice of withdrawal from the contract, or fixing prices at a certain level.

### Breach of contract

Various remedies are available in case of breach of contract. Normally, the remedy will consist of an action for compensation, with the creditor also being entitled to have the contract rescinded. For compensation to be claimable in the event of delays in performance, it is a requirement that the creditor should serve notice of this fact to the defaulting debtor. This will be done by arranging for a bailiff and process server (*huissier*) to serve a document which contains such notification (*la sommation*). This notice is even required where the contract in question has fixed a certain date by which performance is to be completed. It is possible to obtain specific performance from a defaulting debtor, but this tends to be an exceptional remedy in French law.

It is also open to the innocent party to rely upon the so-called *exception non adempleti contractus*. This is the right of the party to refuse performance of his or her part of the bargain if the other party has failed to carry out his or her part without a valid excuse.

In assessing the amount of the compensation, the courts may only take account of such loss as is an immediate and direct consequence of the breach of contract,[25] and then only to the extent to which this could have been within the contemplation of the parties at the time of concluding the contract. However, such foreseeability is not required where a wilful breach of the contract by the debtor has occurred. The terms of reference of the claim for compensation are not restricted to material losses, and may include 'moral damages' (*dommage moral*) – for example, where persons have been scarred for life as a result of a fault committed in the course of a contract.

---

25 The creditor may recover both the loss suffered (*damnum emergens*) and the gains lost (ie loss of earnings – *lucrum cessans*).

*Specific contracts*

Apart from these general rules relating to contracts, the Civil Code also makes provision for certain types of contract, such as contracts of sale, which, although they are also governed by the basic rules of contract law as stated above, nevertheless require certain additional rules in order to accommodate their special nature. Special legislation has also been introduced for certain other specific forms of contract where the traditional balance between the parties is tilted in favour of one of them in order to protect the weaker party – eg contracts of employment. These contracts will be discussed in full in the chapter dealing with business law (cf. *infra*, p. 76).

## Quasi-contracts

This is an area which has outgrown the original provisions of the Civil Code. Initially, the Code only made provision for two cases of quasi-contract: (a) the *gestion d'affaires*: this deals with the implications of an agency by necessity, which arises where, as a result of various circumstances, someone manages another person's affairs without having a mandate to that effect, and (b) the *action en répétition de l'indu*, which is the right of a person to the recovery of articles transferred by him to another person under the mistaken impression that he or she was performing a valid obligation. Other quasi-contracts have been added by the courts and by the leading authors under the general title of *enrichissement sans cause* (unjustified enrichment). A classic case is that of a foreign national who performs a service under a contract of employment without, however, being in the possession of a legal work permit. Although the contract itself is unlawful, the foreign citizen in question may claim restitution from the employer of the agreed remuneration for services rendered; otherwise the employer would have enjoyed extra benefits without having any cause for such enjoyment.

## Torts

On this subject, the Code draws a distinction between torts (*délits*) and quasi-torts (*quasi-délits*), according to whether the tortfeasor intended to cause damage or not. This distinction was inspired by the Justinian codes, and is of no importance here.

*Fundamental principle: Article 1382*

The basic principle which governs the entire law of torts in France is contained in Article 1382 of the Civil Code, which states that 'any act committed by a person which causes damage to another obliges that person by whose fault it occurred to make reparation'.[26] This is unlike English law, which recognises a large number of specially designated torts such as trespass, negligence, nuisance and defamation.

Article 1382 of the Code has been widely criticised as being too vague, and for failing to give the courts even an indication of the manner in which they are to interpret the concept of 'fault'. As a result, the case law of the courts and the writings of the leading authors are not free from ambiguity, controversy and mutual contradiction in the manner in which this notion is interpreted. Normally, the term *faute* is interpreted as meaning the infringement of a specific right of the victim, on condition that the tortfeasor acted intentionally or negligently, or an intentional misuse of the tortfeasor's own right.

Before a plaintiff can successfully claim damages in tort, it must be proved that damage has been suffered, and that the damage was caused by an act or omission for which the defendant was responsible. This liability may have been incurred because the defendant was personally at fault, or was vicariously liable for another person's fault, or because the damage was caused by an object in his or her care. These three elements, ie damage, fault and the causal link between them, form a necessary precondition for any successful action in tort.

*Vicarious liability*

French law also applies the principle of vicarious liability, which is imposed on parents for damage caused by their minor children, and on principals and employers for damage caused by their agents or employees respectively (*responsabilité du fait d'autrui*). There is also liability for objects placed under one's care (*responsabilité du fait des choses* – Article 1384). Strict liability is imposed on the person who makes professional use of an animal or, in the absence of such a person, on its owner, regardless of whether it is under someone's care or not.

*Strict liability*

As has been mentioned earlier, the French courts have been able to construe Article 1382 in such a way as to accommodate the principle of no-fault liability (*la responsabilité objective*). The major breakthrough in recognising this principle was achieved by the *Cour de cassation* in 1930.[27] In this case – probably the equivalent, in terms of its impact on the law of torts generally, of the House of Lords decision in *Rylands v Fletcher* (1868)[28] – the Court held that the presumption of liability imposed by Article 1384 for damage caused by objects in one's care was not limited to dangerous things, and that the defendant could not

---

26  Translated by the authors from: '*Tout fait quelconque de l'homme, qui cause à autrui un dommage, oblige celui par la faute duquel il est arrivé, à le réparer*'.

27  Decision of 13/2/1930 in *Jand'heur* case (*Jand'heur v Les galeries belfortaises*) (1930) D 1.57.

28  LR 3 HL 330.

exclude liability by proving that he or she had not committed any fault or that the cause of the tortious event remained unknown. The defendant had to prove an external cause for which he or she was not to blame, ie to demonstrate that there had been a case of *cas fortuit* or *force majeure*.

*Liability for damage caused by buildings*

Under Article 1386, the owner of a building is liable for any damage caused by its collapse where the latter occurred as a result of a maintenance fault or by a construction fault.[29] The lack of repair or construction defect constitute objective elements which, once they have been proved, render proof of fault unnecessary. Often the lack of repair will simply be concluded from the fact that the building collapsed, and therefore virtually constitutes a rule of strict liability: the owner will only be able to rebut this presumption of liability by proving *force majeure*.[30]

Tort liability is, however, no longer the exclusive preserve of the Civil Code. As has been the case in other countries, legislation has been introduced as a result of social and economic developments, particularly in the field of workers' compensation.[31]

# D Matrimonial property law

## General

The system of rules which will govern the property of the spouses after marriage is taken considerably more seriously in France than in England. This is one of the consequences of the spirit of individual liberalism which characterises the *Code civil*, and which attached a great deal of importance to the financial implications of all human activity. It is significant in this regard that the law of matrimonial property is contained, not in the chapter devoted to persons and the family, but in that which is entitled 'different methods of acquiring property'.

When two people marry in France, they opt for a particular method of settling the financial implications of their marriage, regardless of whether they have consciously chosen to do so or not. If the spouses give no intimation as to what matrimonial system they wish to have applied to their possessions, they are deemed to have opted for the *régime légal*, meaning the system laid down in Article 1400 *et seq* of the Code. If the spouses wish to depart from this system, they have a choice: they can either devise their own 'customised', original settle-

---

29  Translated by the authors from: '*Le propriétaire d'un bâtiment est responsable du dommage causé par sa ruine, lorsqu'elle est arrivée par une suite du défaut d'entretien ou par le vice de sa construction*'.

30  Lawson, F.H., Anton, A.E. and Brown, L.N., *op cit*, p. 232.

31  Thus, for example, the *Loi sur les accidents de travail* of 9/4/1898, which has been amended on several subsequent occasions.

ment, or adopt one of the systems which are contained in the Civil Code for the spouses' guidance and information.

Major changes were made around 30 years ago in the articles of the Civil Code dealing with the *régime légal*. Formerly, the official system imposed the principle of joint ownership which affected all goods belonging to the spouses (with the exceptions of the real property owned by the spouses at the time of concluding the marriage). In the administration of the jointly-held property, it was the husband who used to have the upper hand. In addition, once a particular régime had been chosen (or had been imposed on the spouses in the absence of a conscious settlement), it was impossible to change it subsequently. This too changed in 1965.[32]

## The *régime légal*

### The current system

Before 1965, all the goods owned by the spouses became subject to joint ownership with the exception of such real property as was owned by the spouses separately at the time of the marriage, or as was acquired during the marriage by gift or succession. The new official régime restricts the joint ownership principle to goods acquired by the spouses during the marriage. The jointly-held property forms a *patrimoine*,[33] called *la communauté*, which is composed of an assets side (*l'actif de la communauté*) and of a liabilities side (*le passif de la communauté*).

### Assets of the *communauté*

The assets consist of all such goods as are acquired by the spouses, either together or separately, in the course of their marriage, and which are the fruits of their efforts, as well as the income derived from their separately-owned goods.[34]

Each of the spouses has the right to manage the jointly-held property by himself or herself, and has the right of disposal over them, but will be accountable to the other spouse for any errors committed in the course of managing the property. Those actions which have been made without any misrepresentation can be relied upon against the other spouse.[35] However, where either of the spouses exercises a profession separately from the other, that spouse has the sole right to take all such measures of management as are necessary for the performance of his or her professional activity.

---

32  Law of 13/7/1965.

33  For an explanation of this term, cf. *supra*, p. 24.

34  Article 1401 of the Civil Code.

35  Article 1421 of the Civil Code.

*The liabilities*

The liabilities of the *communauté* consist of all those debts which each of the spouses has incurred, for whatever reason, in the course of their marriage. These debts may be claimed against the jointly-held property by the creditor, unless there has been fraud on the part of the spouse owing the debt, and bad faith on the part of the creditor; in addition, all this is subject to compensation which is payable to *la communauté* where appropriate.[36] However, the household of the spouses is protected against the worst rigours of this principle by Article 1414(1) of the Code, which stipulates that the income and salary of the spouses will only be able to be impounded by the creditors once all the legal obligations to provide the household with the necessary means for its subsistence and to make provision for the children's education have been fulfilled.

## Contractual régimes

Since the reforms of 1965 have swept away the old *régime dotal* as a possible contractual option, the only practicable alternative to the legal régime is either the system of *séparation des biens* (separation of property) or that of *participation aux acquêts* (participation in goods acquired during the marriage). Under the former system, each of the spouses continues to have the free disposal over his or her property, whether he or she owned the property on entering the marriage, or acquired it subsequently. On the other hand, each partner remains solely liable for the debts incurred by him or her, regardless of whether these were contracted prior or subsequent to the marriage.

Under the second system, that of participation in the goods acquired during the marriage, each of the spouses retains the power to administer, enjoy and have the free disposal over his or her own property, regardless of whether that property was owned by them at the time when the marriage was contracted or whether it was acquired subsequently by succession, gift or purchase. In fact, in the course of the marriage, this system operates as if the spouses were married under the separation of goods régime. However, once the régime is dissolved, each of the spouses becomes entitled to half the value of the net acquisitions which have accrued to the assets of the other spouse.[37]

# E  The law of succession

## General

The general scheme of the law of succession is similar to that which applies under the law of matrimonial property, in that (a) in spite of (relatively) recent changes in the law, the relevant provisions of the Civil Code continue to be

---

36  Article 1413 of the Civil Code.

37  Article 1569 of the Civil Code.

characterised by the 19th century notion of emphasising the property aspects of all human activity and events (in this case, death!) – in fact, wills and successions are also viewed as a means of acquiring property – and (b) the law in principle gives the person involved (here, the testators) a choice in the system which they wish to adopt; however, in the absence of any legally recognised statement as to the manner in which they wish to see their goods disposed of, the Civil Code will assume that a certain system of dividing the property among the surviving relatives – if any – will apply.

Nevertheless the parties involved do not enjoy complete freedom in the manner in which they wish to divide their property after their death. One of the interesting features of the French law of succession is known as *la réserve héréditaire*. This is the part of the estate of the deceased which may not be disposed of in accordance with the wishes of the testator. Unlike the position in English law, which is characterised by the complete freedom of the testator, the French civil law has some concern for the fate of the surviving relatives (though not, strangely enough, of the surviving spouse). In order to avoid a situation whereby the surviving relatives in the ascending and descending line could find themselves without any means of support following the death of the testator, it is stipulated that, whatever may be the latter's last will and testament, the relatives will obtain at least part of the estate.

## The legal régime

### Who may inherit

One of the striking features of the system of heirs under the Civil Code is the precedence given to blood relatives over the surviving spouse. In fact, the spouse is still quite literally the poor relation of the French law of succession. This has been mitigated slightly by (a) a legislative change which occurred in 1972, and (b) the fact that the matrimonial property system of the spouses is automatically terminated and dissolved on the death of one of them. This lowly status of the spouse is already apparent from the basic distinction which is made between 'lawful heirs' on the one hand, and *successeurs irréguliers* (which we will charitably translate as 'secondary heirs') on the other hand. The descendants and ascendants are found amongst the former category; the surviving spouse finds himself or herself among the latter category, alongside illegitimate children and the State!

Before the order of precedence is established between the various heirs, the latter must satisfy two conditions: they must actually exist at the time when the succession opens (which also includes children conceived but not yet born) and they may not have proved themselves unworthy of the inheritance (eg by having killed, or attempted to kill, the testator).

When it comes to establishing the order of precedence between the heirs, a distinction must be made between categories (*ordres*) and degrees (*degrés*) of heirs. The most basic order of precedence is that between the various categories, of which there are four: (1) the descendants, (2) the privileged ascendants (parents) and collateral relatives (brothers and sisters), (3) the ascendants other than parents, and (4) the collateral relatives other than brothers and sisters. Within each category, there are several degrees, each taking precedence over each other. Thus within Category 1 (descendants), the children will take precedence over grandchildren, who in turn will take precedence over great-grandchildren. However, the Civil Code allows the practice of what is known as 'inheritance by substitution' (*représentation*). This means that, where a child of the testator dies before the latter, that child's children will take the place of their deceased parent in the order of precedence; they will inherit in equal proportions that part which the testator's child would have inherited had he or she lived to survive the testator (allocation *per stirpes* – cf. 739 *et seq* of the Civil Code).

*The options available to the heir*

It must not be glibly assumed that whoever is legally the heir will necessarily want to inherit. The estate of the deceased forms a *patrimoine*, with not only assets, but also liabilities. This is why the Civil Code gives the heir a number of options: (a) he or she may accept the inheritance without reservation, in which case he or she will be liable for all the debts as well as enjoying the benefit of all the assets; (b) he or she may accept 'with benefit of inventory' (*sous bénéfice d'inventaire*); in this case the heir is given a period of three months in which to compile an inventory of all the personalty belonging to the estate, and a further 40 days in which to accept or reject; and (c) he or she may reject the inheritance, in which case he or she will not only receive nothing and not be liable for anything from the estate, but will be considered as never having been an heir.[38]

*The position of joint heirs*

If there is more than one heir they will become the joint owners of the estate. However, because it is a fundamental principle of the Civil Code that no-one may be compelled to remain in a state of joint ownership[39] – which presents many obvious disadvantages – any of the heirs may at any time demand partition of the estate.

## Wills

Subject to the restriction inherent in the *réserve héréditaire* (cf. *supra*, p. 72), the testator enjoys complete freedom to dispose of his or her property by means of will (*testaments*). There are four types of will:

---

38  Article 785 of the Civil Code.
39  Article 815 of the Civil Code.

Holograph wills *(testament holographe)*

These are the most straightforward type, and require no particular form. All that is needed is a statement written by the hand of the testator and dated and signed likewise.[40] Very often they will be entrusted to a Notary Public for the sake of security.

Authentic wills *(testament authentique)*

These must be made before a Notary Public and in the presence of two witnesses. They are drawn up by the *notaire* in accordance with the instructions supplied by the testator.[41] This is a much safer form of will, in that the fact of being an *acte notarial* puts its authenticity beyond doubt, and the *notaire* will make every possible effort to avoid any ambiguities when drafting the will. It is naturally more expensive.

Secret wills *(testament mystique)*

This is a combination of the holograph and the authentic will. The testator will write or type his or her will (or have this done by someone else), hand it to the Notary Public under sealed envelope in the presence of two witnesses, and make the statement that the envelope contains his last will and testament. This is recorded in a written statement by the Notary Public, which is then signed by the *notaire*, the witnesses and the testator.[42]

Privileged wills *(testaments privilégiés)*

Special circumstances may make it impossible or very difficult/expensive to choose one of the forms stated above. This is why the Civil Code makes it possible for certain wills to be made to public authorities. This happens, for example, where a will needs to be made at sea or by a member of the Army on active service.[43] Within six months of the special circumstances ceasing to apply however, a will must be made in one of the ordinary forms stated above.

---

40   Article 970 of the Civil Code.
41   Article 971 of the Civil Code.
42   Article 976 of the Civil Code.
43   Articles 981 *et seq* of the Civil Code.

# 5    Business Law

## I Introduction

In any legal system, the term 'business law' is very broad and flexible, and it is rare indeed to encounter two works on the subject with the same material on this topic. At its narrowest, business law is restricted to company law and the sale of goods; at its broadest, it has been known to comprise such areas as taxation and land law.

For the purpose of this work, the interpretation adopted of this term will be restrictive rather than wide, on the grounds that it is better to deal with a few topics in depth rather than a very superficial exploration of a dozen topics. The areas which will be discussed under this chapter heading have been selected on the basis of their practical interest (company law and special contracts) and for considerations of comparative interest (which is why a section is devoted to the notion of *le fonds de commerce*, which has no counterpart whatsoever in English law).

At this stage, it is appropriate to set the general legal framework in which French business law operates. First of all, it must be pointed out that, unlike the position in England, the world of business has always occupied a special niche in French law. As Brice Dickson points out,[1] this is a phenomenon which long pre-dates the French Revolution. This special position is highlighted by two factors: (a) the fact that, as has already been seen (*supra*, p. 30), disputes between traders are settled by special courts called *Tribunaux de commerce*, and (b) the fact that a special code, called the *Code de commerce*, governs major parts of French business law.

French business law has often been accused of being excessively legalistic and formal, to the point of sometimes impeding business efficiency. It is true that, at first sight at least, French business law appears to be more regulated than that of England; however, France has in many respects succeeded in updating and modernising its business law in a way which makes English business law look sluggish by comparison. In addition, a comparison between the health of the business sector in both countries hardly substantiates the criticism that French business law is a millstone round the neck of French commerce.

There are three main parts to this chapter. In the first, we will consider the area of 'special business contracts', meaning those contracts whose provisions

---

1   *Introduction to French Law* (1994, Pitman) p. 168.

depart from the general rules of contract law covered in an earlier chapter (cf. *supra*, p. 63) and which are the most relevant to the conduct of everyday business – contracts of sale, contracts of *intermédiaire* and contracts of employment. Secondly, we will examine two concepts which are specific to French law and go a long way towards explaining the difference between French and English business cultures, ie *les actes de commerce* and *le fonds de commerce*. Thirdly, the main forms of business organisation will be covered in Section IV.

# II  Special business contracts

## A  General

As is the case in England, it is recognised by French law that there are certain types of contract for which the general rules of contract law as stated in Articles 1128 *et seq* of the Civil Code are inadequate. In fact in relation to contracts of sale, the *Code civil* had already in its 1804 text included a separate section devoted to special rules on the sale of goods. However, many of the special contracts which derogate in part from the general rules governing contracts have developed outside the context of the Civil Code. For the two other types of contract under discussion in this section, ie contracts of *intermédiaire* and contracts of employment, it is mainly the *Code du travail* which will be of relevance here.

## B  Contracts of sale

### General

In French law, contracts of sale form part of the general category of commercial transactions (*actes de commerce*), being those transactions which are designated by law as falling within this category. The question of what constitutes *actes de commerce* will be explored more fully under Section II of this chapter (cf. *infra*, p. 84). These transactions already present a number of general derogations from the ordinary rules of contract law:

- **Burden of proof**. In the ordinary law of obligations, the only evidence admitted in respect of any contract worth more than FF 5,000 is a written document,[2] an admission by the debtor[3] or affidavit.[4] For commercial contracts however, the rules of proof are much more flexible, and oral evidence is admitted for any contract where the court considers this to be appropriate (except for a few major contracts, such as marine insurance).

---

2   Article 1341 of the Civil Code.
3   Article 1356 of the Civil Code.
4   Article 1358 of the Civil Code.

- **Interest rates.** Under the ordinary French law of obligations, whenever an amount becomes legally payable, there is a general presumption that this sum attracts interest as from the moment when it should have been paid. In commercial contracts, the applicable interest rate is 1% higher than is the case with ordinary contracts. In addition, the interest becomes payable as from the moment that the person to whom the sum is owed communicates his desire for payment to the debtor: no official notice (*mise en demeure*) is required, as is the case under the ordinary law of obligations.

- **Debt settlement.** For ordinary contracts, the limitation period for claiming debts is 30 years; in commercial contracts, debts are time-barred after 10 years. In the ordinary law of obligations, where a debt is owed by more than one person, the latter will only be jointly and severally liable for the sum owed if this is expressly stipulated. In commercial contracts, however, there is a legal presumption that co-debtors are always jointly and severally liable.

There are, however, a number of rules which derogate from the ordinary law of obligations and which are specific to the sale of goods. These are discussed below in relation to both general and specific contracts of sale.

### General contracts of sale

*Concluding contracts of sale*

Here, the major differences with the ordinary law of contracts concern the nature of the items sold and the price payable. As to the former, the same distinction is drawn as that which applies in England, which is that between specific goods (*corps certains*), being goods which can be clearly identified at the moment of sale (eg a car, a watch), and unascertained goods (*corps de genre*) which by their very nature are hardly ever identified at the time of sale (eg rice, coffee, coal). This has two closely inter-connected legal implications.

The first of these concerns the transfer of ownership. On the one hand, the ownership over specific goods which are sold is transferred at the moment at which the contract is concluded, which is the time at which mutual consent was reached.[5] The ownership over unascertained goods, on the other hand, is transferred as soon as they are identified (subject to provisions to the contrary in the contract of sale).

The second, closely related, consequence concerns the risk of any economic loss. It is the person who has become the owner of the item sold who will have to bear the risk of economic loss in the event of the item being destroyed, spoilt or causing damage to others – even if the item in question had not yet been delivered into his or her hands. Therefore the risk of economic loss is, in princi-

---

5    Article 1583 of the Civil Code.

ple, particularly high in respect of unascertained goods. However, this rule may be departed from by express agreement between the parties, which is quite often the case.

As to the price payable, the main issue concerns the obligation to fix a price. Under Article 1591 of the Civil Code, the price *must* be stipulated and fixed by the parties. The courts have interpreted this rule as implying that any contract of sale which does not fix a price is null and void. However, the harshness of this stance has been mitigated in recent years by the requirement that the price be capable of being fixed on the basis of the terms of the contract.

*Obligations of the seller*

In principle, the seller has two obligations: to supply the item or items sold, and to provide a guarantee that the latter will be free from hidden defects. As to the first, called *la délivrance* (often inaccurately translated as 'the delivery'), the goods sold must be supplied at the place where the item is located at the time of the sale. This will in most cases be the seller's premises. As to the date on which the goods must be supplied, this will in most cases be stipulated in the contract itself. However, this is not compulsory, and in the absence of any such clause, the item should be supplied 'within a reasonable period'.

If the seller, after having served notice in the normal manner (*mise en demeure*), still fails to meet his obligation to supply, the buyer will have a choice of three remedies. First, he may apply to the court for an injunction ordering the seller to supply (more often than not subject to the payment of a financial penalty (*une astreinte*)). Secondly, he may obtain a replacement item from a third party, at the seller's expense, and thirdly, he may apply to the court to have the contract set aside.

As to the obligation to provide a guarantee against hidden defects, Article 1643 of the Civil Code stipulates that the seller is answerable for any hidden defects, even those which were unknown to him or her. However, both parties may contract out of this requirement, subject to the proviso that if the hidden defects were known to the seller, any such exclusion clause will be null and void.

*Obligations of the buyer*

The buyer has essentially two obligations to fulfil: to pay the stipulated price, and to withdraw the item purchased. As to the first, payment must in principle be made in cash and at the place where the item was supplied; however, in most cases this rule is departed from by common consent. In the absence of payment, the seller may use all the remedies available under the ordinary law of obligations, as well as the right to have the sale annulled. The latter will be possible even where only a fraction of the price remained to be paid (although in most cases the court will grant extra time in order to enable the buyer to pay the amount outstanding).

As far as the obligation to withdraw the item sold is concerned, the rule in principle is that the item sold must be withdrawn by the seller from the place where it is located at the moment of sale, unless delivery by the seller has been expressly stipulated. If the buyer fails to do this, the seller may apply either for a specific performance injunction (*exécution forcée*), or for the contract of sale to be set aside.

### Specific contracts of sale

Here, a distinction is normally made between prohibited sales, and sales which are closely regulated by law.[6]

#### Prohibited sales

As is the case in English law, there are certain types of sale which are expressly prohibited as contravening public policy. The first such category is that of sales subject to unacceptable conditions (*ventes subordonnées*). These are sales which are concluded subject to such conditions as the purchase of a certain quantity, or the purchase of another item or service. The fine imposed for infringing this rule varies between FF 3,000 and 6,000. The second category to be prohibited is that of 'snowball' sales (*ventes à boule de neige*), which consist in offering goods for sale to the general public which hold out the prospect for the latter of obtaining the goods free of charge or at a reduced price on condition that the customer renders such services as issuing order forms to third parties or collects a certain number of subscriptions or membership applications. Here, the penalties are even more severe, since not only the fine is higher (FF 3,000 to 40,000) but also any infringement could give rise to fraud charges.

Thirdly, a Decree of 1961 prohibits 'forced sales' (*ventes forcées*), being operations whereby sellers send goods to potential customers, informing the latter of the price of that item (or a subscription to this item), and stipulating that, should the 'customer' not wish to avail himself of the offer, the goods should be returned. Any such practice attracts a fine of FF 3,000 to 6,000 and/or a possible prison sentence of 10 days to one month. Fourthly, a recent *ordonnance* of 1986 prohibits all 'bonus sales' (*ventes avec primes*), being sales, or offers of sales, which entitle the purchaser to a bonus consisting of goods or services, unless these are identical to the goods or services sold. Infringements are punishable by a fine of FF 3,000 to 6,000.

6    Guéry, G., *op cit*, p. 191 *et seq*.

*Regulated sales*

Several categories of contracts of sale are regulated more strictly than others. The first such category is constituted by various 'occasional' sales, such as the *ventes en solde* (seasonal sales, such as 'summer' sales or 'January' sales). Not only must these be genuinely occasional, but they must also be accompanied by appropriate advertising, and are subject to prior permission by the authorities. Similar conditions are attached to the 'closing down sales' (*les liquidations*) and to the *ventes au déballage* (sales of surplus stock transacted on non-commercial premises).

The second category consists of canvassed and door-to-door sales (*ventes à démarche et ventes à domicile*). For these, the relevant legislation seeks particularly to protect the consumer, by insisting not only that such contracts are written, but also that they contain a certain minimum number of particulars, on penalty of being declared null and void. Infringements of this legislation can give rise to very heavy penalties, including imprisonment for a maximum of five years.

Other categories of regulated sales are telephone sales and sales subject to credit and security (hire-purchase, conditional sale, etc).

# C Contracts of employment

## General

In the overwhelming majority of Western countries, the provisions of the ordinary law of contracts were made inapplicable to industrial relations as soon as it became clear that the equality in principle which is supposed to govern relations between contracting parties was a myth which could not be maintained and which had all manner of undesirable social consequences. France being one of the oldest industrialised nations in Europe, special legislation governing conditions of work was adopted already during the early part of the 19th century (eg a Law of 1812 prohibiting the employment of children under 10 in mines).

The special rules which govern contracts of employment are contained mainly in the *Code du travail*. The relevant legislation is based on the same definition of a contract of employment as that which applies in England: it is an agreement by which a person, called the employee (*le salarié*) undertakes to work for another person, called the employer (*l'employeur*), under the latter's direction, in consideration of a remuneration (*le salaire*). As a general rule, however, it can be stated that contracts of employment are more closely regulated in France than in England.

## Conclusion of the contract

As is the case under the ordinary law of contracts, it is not necessary for a contract of employment to take the form of a written document. However, the employee must be issued with a written contract no later than two months following the moment of employment. It must be worded in French, but any foreign worker may demand a translation of the contract into his mother tongue.

For a contract of employment to be valid, it must have been entered into freely by both the employer and the employee, it may not involve any illegal work, and, if the employee is a minor, he or she must be of school-leaving age (16).

As to the duration of the contract, the assumption is that it will have been concluded for an indefinite period, subject to express provision to the contrary. Although the duration has not been specified, the contract may, subject to the appropriate periods of notice, be terminated at any time on both sides. Any temporary contract must from the outset take the form of a written document, which must contain such elementary conditions of work as the nature of the employment, the salary paid, etc. Temporary contracts which concern a specific task may be renewed on two occasions, but the duration of such a renewal may not exceed that of the first contract; the maximum duration of any such task-related temporary contract is 18 months. Employees working under a temporary contract enjoy the same contractual rights and advantages as employees whose conditions are governed by a permanent contract.

## Obligations of the parties

The employee must be capable of performing the work which forms the subject-matter of the contract. He or she must observe the internal rules of the business which employs him or her (which is understood to include the safety instructions and work instructions). The employee must in addition take care of any equipment entrusted to his or her care, observe strict confidentiality as to the firm's production secret (even after his or her employment with that firm has terminated), and refrain from working for his or her own account during working hours.

As for the employer, he or she must provide the employee with the work as agreed, pay the stipulated salary, and comply with a number of rules: those contained in industrial legislation, in collective bargaining agreements, internal rules of the firm, health and safety regulations, etc.

## Terminating the contract

Contracts of employment may be terminated by either the employee or the employer. For temporary contracts, the date of termination will be that of the expiry of the contract, subject to a serious error or *force majeure* forcing an earlier termination. Permanent contracts, on the other hand, may be terminated at any time subject to the appropriate period of notice having been observed. The period of notice required of the employee is generally determined by the relevant collective bargaining agreement, and is normally eight days. The notice which needs to be observed by the employer, on the other hand, depends on whether the employee is being dismissed for economic reasons or not.

If the dismissal is for non-economic reasons, it will only be justified on truly serious grounds, such as the refusal to comply with working hours, theft, disruptive behaviour, etc. The employee will need to be summoned by registered letter, and have the opportunity to defend his or her position during a preliminary interview. If the employer persists in his desire to dismiss the employee, he must communicate to the latter an official notification of dismissal (*notification du licenciement*).

Where the dismissal is caused by economic circumstances – in other words, redundancy – the same formalities of summoning, interviewing and notifying the employee will need to be completed, but, in addition, the employer will need to inform the local employment office. Special procedures apply in the case of collective redundancies.

**Working hours**

Contracts of employment are limited in what they can stipulate by way of working hours. In principle, industrial legislation fixes the maximum hours to be worked per week at 39 hours, subject to a daily maximum of 10 hours. The weekly hours may be spread over 6, 5.5, 5, 4.5 or 4 days.

However, there are certain circumstances in which the weekly maximum may exceed 39 hours. For certain occupations, work is not continuous and interrupted by rest periods (for example in the case of firefighters or kitchen cooks). For these professions, longer working hours, as stipulated by collective bargaining agreements, may be worked (up to 52 hours for night watchmen). For high-risk occupations, such as miners or long-distance pilots, the maximum working week will be shorter.

# D *Intermédiaire* contracts

**General**

In England, the general law of agency governs a wide variety of contractual situations, including those under which persons act as commercial middlemen and travelling sales representatives. In France, however, the situation is a great deal more differentiated. In addition to the ordinary law governing general situations of agency (*le mandat*), there are special rules which govern *les intermédiaires*, whose status is much more clearly defined than is the case in England. This explains why there are several distinct types of sales representative in France. These can be broken down into two main categories. On the one hand, there are the *intermédiaires dépendants*, consisting of those who operate as employees in relation to their principal, and whose status is therefore governed by the provisions of the *Code du travail* (Industrial Relations Code). Except for a few derogations for travelling salesmen (*VRP – Voyageurs, représentants et placiers*) their contracts are subject to the same regulatory provisions as ordinary employees (cf. *supra*, p. 80).

The second category is composed of *les intermédiaires indépendants*, being those who operate on a much more independent basis in relation to their principal. Their status is governed by individual pieces of legislation. They break down into three categories:

## Commercial agents (agents commerciaux)

These are agents who have a continuous assignment to negotiate and, where appropriate, conclude contracts of sale, leases, or contracts for the provision of services on behalf of their principal, without, however, being bound by any contract of service, but by a contract of agency. Their status is governed by the Law of 25/6/1991 on commercial agents.

The relevant contract must be written whenever the agent so wishes, and any commercial agent entering into it must be entered on a special register held for this purpose with the *Tribunal de commerce*.

If the contract is concluded on a permanent basis, it may nevertheless be terminated, but subject to periods of notice, starting from one month as from the first year of completion, and increasing by one month for each subsequent year. Termination will give rise to payment of compensation which, according to a well-established case law, amounts to an average of two years' commissions.[7]

In most cases, the remuneration of the commercial agent will be fixed by contract. However, in the absence of any such stipulation, the relevant legislation, more particularly Article 5(3) of the Law of 25/6/1991, provides that his commission will be determined by that which is custom and practice in the commercial area in which the agent operates. If no such custom exists, the remuneration must be reasonable.

## Commissionnaires

These are agents who manage the commercial affairs of another business, but in so doing act in their own name and for their own account. They do not have total freedom of action, however, since they must comply with the instructions issued by their principal. The main difference from a legal point of view with the commercial agents lies in their liability towards third parties.

## Courtiers

These are commercial agents who, acting under the instructions of their principal, merely negotiate contracts between third parties and the principal, without

---

7    Guéry, G., *op cit*, p. 331.

ever concluding them. Their status is the closest to that of the agent under English law. Their obligation is therefore to take all such measures as are appropriate to enable the contract to be concluded. Subject to agreement to the contrary, the principal will owe the agreed commission as soon as the contract is concluded, even though it may subsequently not be performed.

Apart from this distinguishing feature, the terms and conditions which apply to *courtiers* are very much the same as those which apply to the *agents commerciaux*.

# III *Actes de commerce, commerçants* and *fonds de commerce*

## A General

It has already been stated that the French commercial trader has a special status which will enable him or her to enjoy certain rights and privileges, such as the right to have disputes with other traders settled by a court consisting of fellow-traders (the *Tribunaux de commerce*). There are two elements which are specific to the trader under French law: the *actes de commerce*, which relate to the trader's activities, and the *fonds de commerce*, which relates to the trader's assets and property rights.

## B *Actes de commerce* and *commerçants*

### Activities qualifying as *actes de commerce*

In order to qualify as a 'trader' (*commerçant*), and thus fall within the scope of commercial law, the person in question must meet certain requirements. These are set out in Article 1 of the Commercial Code, which defines a trader as anyone who 'carries out commercial activities (*actes de commerce*) and makes these activities his or her habitual professional activity'. These *actes de commerce* are listed in Article 632 of the Commercial Code, the most important of which are the following:

- any purchase of moveable goods in order to resell them, either in their original state or after having processed them and put them into operation;

- any purchase of real property in order to resell the latter, unless the acquirer thereof has purchased them in order to improve one or more buildings and to sell them as a block or as individual premises;

- any business activity consisting in the hiring of moveable property;

- any operations engaged in as *intermédiaire* which involve the purchase, underwriting or sale of real property, of *fonds de commerce*, or shares in estate agency companies;

- any business involved in manufacturing goods, in commission agency activity, or in transport by land, water or sea;

- any business involved in the provision of equipment, agency, in marketing, in auctioneering, and in public entertainment;

- all exchange operations, banking operations and any brokerage;

- all operations involving public banks;

- all obligations between commercial agents, traders and bankers;

- all bills of exchange, regardless of which persons are involved in them.

This means that certain activities will, by exclusion, not be considered to be *actes de commerce*. The main categories of activities which, in spite of involving important financial transactions, are not considered to be commercial by nature are:

Agriculture

The main reason why agricultural activity does not fall within the scope of commercial activity is that the farmer does not normally buy in order to resell: he sells mainly the products of the earth or of the livestock which he has reared. In addition, farming is not formally organised on a commercial basis: very little accounting and very few economic calculations are involved. Even if the farmers process their own products, the courts tend to deny them commercial status. However, if the farmer processes products bought from others as well as his own products, he will be deemed to be acting commercially.

Crafts

The activities of craftsmen are excluded from the scope of *actes de commerce*. A large body of case law has developed a number of criteria for deciding which type of operation can qualify as craft activity. These criteria concern mainly the size and scale of the operations involved. Thus occupations such as that of hairdresser, cobbler, tailor, locksmith, electrician, mechanic etc, have been excluded from the scope of commercial activity.

The 'liberal profession'

These are activities which are exempted from the commercial sphere more by tradition than by current practice. They concern occupations such as the medical professions, lawyers, architects, surveyors and accountants. The fact that their remuneration has the status of *honoraires* (a term somewhat more exclusive than the English 'fee') and that the service provided by them is linked to their personal capacity and expertise are deemed sufficient to place them firmly within the scope of *activités civiles*.

Although the list contained in Article 632 of the Commercial Code includes a number of operations, such as bills of exchange, which will be commercial by nature regardless of the persons involved in the transaction, there are a number of transactions which will have a mixed status by virtue of being concluded between a trader and a civilian. This situation arises quite regularly, and has required a number of rules to regulate it. As to the question of court jurisdiction, the rule is that where the plaintiff is a trader, he or she must bring the dispute before the commercial court; where the plaintiff is a civilian, he or she will have the option of taking it to the civil or the commercial courts. On the question of limitation in time, Article 189 stipulates that the 10-year limitation rule will apply in the case of 'mixed' activities.

### The status of *commerçant*

As has already been mentioned, Article 1 of the Commercial Code qualifies as *commerçant* those who engage in the activities designated as *actes de commerce*. However, this is not sufficient to determine with precision those who do and those who do not qualify as *commerçant*. A number of explanatory observations must be added.

First, the said Article 1 requires the person engaging in these activities to have made the latter their 'habitual occupation'. This postulates a degree of regularity, consistency and durability in the manner in which these activities are pursued.

Secondly, the person in question must engage in these activities in an independent capacity. Although this requirement is not expressly stipulated by Article 1, it nevertheless is a logical outcome of the very nature of trading activity. Therefore salaried workers cannot have the status of *commerçant*; nor can the members of company boards of directors, since they represent not themselves but the company; nor indeed can shareholders in large companies (an exception is made for the smaller companies such as *sociétés en nom collectif* or *sociétes en commandite*).

Thirdly, the spouse of the trader can only be deemed to be a trader where he or she operates a commercial activity which is separate from that of his or her spouse.[8]

Fourthly, four types of company (*sociétés anonymes, sociétés à responsabilité limitée, sociétés en nom collectif* and *sociétés en commandite*) are invariably deemed to act as traders, regardless of the nature of the activity in which they are engaged.

---

8    Article 4 of the Commercial Code.

It must also be stressed that there are certain categories of person who are barred from being regarded as *commerçants*. These include both persons who are barred by their very nature, such as minors (even those who have become *émancipés*, according to a relatively recent change in the applicable legislation), and those who have been declared incapable of managing their own affairs (*les incapables majeurs*). However, there are also those who are barred because of certain measures taken against them; either because they exercise certain activities (eg public offices) which preclude them from acting as traders, or because they have been sentenced by the criminal courts for certain types of misdemeanour.

The legal implications of *actes de commerce* as distinct from ordinary 'civilian' activities have already been explained earlier. The status of *commerçant* also has certain legal consequences:

* **Trading name**. The trader will invariably trade under a certain name – which may or may not be his or her own. Unlike the 'civil' name, the commercial name is transferable to others.

* **Commercial address (*le domicile commercial*)**. This will be the main place where the trader operates his or her commercial activity. This address will be kept strictly separate from the trader's civil residence (*le domicile*), even though, as is quite often the case, the actual location of the commercial address is the same as that of the civil residence.

* **The trader's spouse**. Very often the trader's husband or wife takes part in the operation of the business without any specific remuneration. As this often led to an unacceptable situation whereby the spouse became a well and truly exploited figure, the Law of 10/7/1982 was adopted in order to improve the rights of these working spouses. In the first place, the latter now have a right of veto in relation to the most important transactions which affect the very essence of the business. Secondly, on the death of the spouse operating the business, the other spouse will have priority rights from the point of view of inheriting the business.

## C The *Fonds de commerce*

### General

Another element which gives French commercial law its special profile is the legal status which it confers on the business assets themselves, which is the *fonds de commerce*. This notion, which is virtually untranslatable into English, denotes all the moveable goods, whether tangible or intangible, which are used by the trader in operating a commercial activity, and which have the purpose of attracting his customers. The *fonds de commerce* is therefore more than a collective name for property. It is greater than the sum of its parts, since it is not only the goods, but the use made of them which determine its true value.

## Tangible elements

The tangible element will consist first of all in the actual equipment used. However, this will only be the case where the trader rents his business premises, for if he or she owns the latter, the equipment will become real property by destination. The other component will be the merchandise, being the stock of moveable objects intended for sale.

## Intangible elements

The intangible elements will be the most difficult to assess. They normally include the following:

- *La clientèle*. This too is a term which is greater than the sum of its parts, and refers to the customer base acquired by the trader.

- *Les droits de clientèle*. These are all the aspects which enable the trader to retain his or her existing *clientèle*. These consist of (a) distinctive signs such as the company logo, the firm name, etc, which are all legally protected; (b) business monopolies such as patented inventions, drawings and designs, trade marks, production processes, as well as literary and artistic intellectual property rights; and (c) administrative permits, such as market stalls, stands in public areas, drinks licences, transport licences, and certain authorisations issued from a public health point of view.

- **Commercial leasing rights**. This is by far the most controversial aspect of the *fonds de commerce*. Until relatively recently, leases, including commercial leases, were regulated entirely by the Civil Code, which meant that, when the lease expired, nothing obliged the owner to renew the lease, which obviously had dire consequences for the trader. It was in order to avoid these circumstances that the Decree of 30/9/1953 was adopted, which protected the status of commercial leases (*baux commerciaux*).

A number of conditions must be fulfilled before a trader can enjoy the benefit of the legislative protection. The object leased must be a building or other permanent premises, and a lease agreement must have been concluded. the latter must have a certain degree of permanence, which appears to exclude the category of insubstantial agreements known as *conventions d'occupation précaire*. In addition, the trader must operate a *fonds de commerce* on these premises, and have his own customer base. The legislation on protecting commercial leases was in fact enacted with a view to protecting the trader's *clientèle*. This problem has arisen in connection with petrol stations, which could not be said to have a client base which was specific to the operator.[9] In addition, the lease may not be for a period of less than nine years.

---

9   Guéry, G. *op cit*, at p. 552.

The protection given to the commercial leaseholder concerns both the amount of the lease payable and the renewal of the agreement. In France, rent agreements are normally concluded on a '3-6-9' basis, which means that the lease is concluded in principle for nine years, but subject to the possibility of review at the end of each three-year period; this review can concern the amount payable under the lease, and even termination of the entire agreement.

As to the former, the 1953 decree stipulates that, where no provision for any increase in rent is made in the lease agreement, the payments under the lease will increase every three years by a set percentage aimed at retaining the *valeur locative* (value of location as leased premises). Where a special clause has been inserted in the agreement stipulating the increases in payments under the lease, the latter will obviously take precedence, subject, however, to certain restrictions contained in the 1953 decree.

Regarding the termination of the agreement, the lessor may only enforce this at the end of each three-year period for a number of limited reasons stated in the 1953 Decree (eg in order to erect buildings, or rebuild the existing premises). When the lease itself expires, the trader does not have an automatic right of renewal; however, where the lessor wishes to terminate the lease, he or she must pay to the lessee a sum by way of eviction damages (*indemnité d'éviction*).

Since the commercial lease forms part of the *fonds de commerce*, the trader may transfer the lease as part of the *fonds de commerce* to a third party (Article 35-1 of the 1953 Decree). This rule is a public policy rule, and therefore cannot be departed from by agreement between the parties. However, where the person to whom the *fonds de commerce* would be transferred does not intend to continue operating the business, the agreement of the lessor to such a transfer will be required.

### Using the fonds de commerce as security (*nantissement du fonds de commerce*)

The *fonds de commerce*, being an item of property in its own right, may be used as security against loans – the closest English law comes to this phenomenon is the floating or fixed charge which companies may use on their assets by way of security. This can be done in two ways: by contract and by court order.

If agreed by contract, the latter will be concluded between the owner of the *fonds* and the credit-awarding institution. Any such agreement requires some publicity, as is the case with mortgages: the Registrar of the commercial court will enter the transaction in the *Régistre des nantissements*. As to the *nantissement* granted by court order, this will occur where the creditor of a *fonds de commerce* has reason to fear that his debts will not be met, he may apply to the President of the *Tribunal de grande instance* or of the *Tribunal d'instance* (depending on the amount involved) for a *nantissement* to be registered against the *fonds de commerce* in question.

The security in question may concern either the entire *fonds de commerce*, or parts thereof. The Law of 17/3/1909 on *nantissements de fonds de commerce* specifies those elements of the *fonds* which may be used by way of security, and may concern the equipment, the logo or the trade name, the intellectual property rights, etc. There is one major exception: the actual stock of merchandise may never be used as security, since it is unsuited to any long-term credit.

In many respects, the practical effects of the *nantissement* are similar to those of *hypothèques*, in that the claims of the holder of the charge are given precedence over those of the ordinary creditors, and that the rights of the holder of the charge follow the *fonds de commerce* regardless of those in whose hands they fall. However, there are some differences. The value of a *fonds de commerce* is less stable than that of an item of real property which is subject to a *hypothèque*, because it depends on the manner in which the *fonds* is managed and operated. The Law of 17/3/1909 provides the holder of the charge with a number of safeguards against events such as the moving of the location of the *fonds de commerce*, or the termination of the commercial lease, which are capable of affecting its value.

# IV Companies

## A General

Although there continues to be a flourishing sector of French business life which is based on businesses operated by single *commerçants*, the proportion of the French Gross National Product assumed by larger business associations continues to grow apace. The term 'companies' will be used here in the broadest sense of the term, as encapsulated by the definition given in Article 1832 of the *Code civil*: 'A company is an organisation established by two or more persons who agree, by contract, to use certain goods, or their industry, in the pursuit of a joint economic activity, with a view to sharing the profits or the economic benefits which may result from this endeavour'.[10] Therefore, the profit motive is not necessarily the decisive criterion, since some types of company, such as the *société civile*, may be set up simply in order to share expenses and enjoy other benefits of economic co-operation (eg a law firm).

In principle, there is a good deal which English and French company law have in common, if only because the major types of company, such as the limit-

---

10  Translated by the authors from: '*La société est instituée par deux ou plusieurs personnes qui conviennent par un contrat d'affecter à une entreprise commune des biens ou leur industrie en vue de partager le bénéfice ou de profiter de l'économie qui pourra en résulter*'.

ed liability and public limited companies, were inspired by English companies which came into existence in the course of the 19th century. However, since these common origins, a number of divergences have occurred between the two systems, even though, interestingly enough, there is now once again a tendency for the two systems to come closer to each other under the influence of EU company law legislation.

Although companies account for a large proportion of French commercial activity, there are hardly any provisions in the *Code de Commerce* which regulate them. Most of French company law is contained in the *Code civil* and in specific legislation. Generally speaking, companies can be divided into three categories: (a) those which are based on persons (*sociétés de personnes*) (b) those which are based on shares (*sociétés de capital*) and (c) those which are based on a specific activity. Each of these categories will be studied in turn, following a section describing those features which are common to all companies under French law.

Two major upheavals have taken place in recent times in the field of company law. The first occurred in 1966, and had implications mainly for the limited liability companies (which now undisputedly became *sociétés de capital*) and for the *sociétés anonymes*, which underwent – at least in part – major changes as regards their management structures. The second occurred in 1985, when the one-man limited liability company became authorised (cf. *infra*, p. 95).

# B Rules which are common to all companies

Three features are shared by all French companies. The first, which clearly emerges from the definition given in Article 1832 of the Civil Code, is the fact that they must be established by means of a contract. The second, which is inherent in the very purpose of any business organisation on any scale, is their legal personality. The third, which is stated in each individual item of legislation governing the company in question, is the adoption of *les statuts*, which is as it were the company's 'charter'.

### The *contrat de société*

In order to form a valid company of whatever type, the founder members will need to draw up a contract before a Notary Public, setting out the basic features of the company to be set up, which are:

* **the contributions by the members**: every company needs resources to commence and sustain its operations. These can be made not only in cash, but also in kind (buildings, inventions, even amounts owing by third parties, etc), and even in a person's industry. However, this type of contribution is not allowed in the *sociétés à responsabilité limitée* and the *sociétés anonymes*. The contract will need to contain a valuation of all contributions.

- **the allocation of profits**: the parties to the contract are free to stipulate the manner in which the profits will be shared. However, any clause which allocates all the profits to one person only, or which excludes a member totally from them, will be deemed not to exist.[11]

- **the allocation of losses**: here again, the parties are free to enter into the arrangement of their choice, but the same limitation as that which applies to the allocation of profits applies *mutatis mutandis*.

- **the *affectio societatis***: this is a statement by the founder members that the object of the exercise is actually to associate for the purpose of furthering the interests of the company.

## Legal personality

Unlike the situation in England, where it was left to the courts, in *Salomon v Salomon* (1897)[12] to confer legal personality on companies, French company legislation recognised this inevitable aspect of company activity from the outset. As a result, companies exist as a legal entity which is totally separate from those natural persons who constitute them. Like natural persons, therefore, companies begin, conduct and end their lives, and each of these three stages has legal implications.

- **Birth of the company**: the company must satisfy a number of conditions before it can be officially 'born'. Some of these are formal requirements: thus a company must have business premises, constitute the resources with which the company will need to operate, draw up and register the *statuts* (cf. *infra*, p. 193), publish the birth of the company, expressly state that it complies with all the applicable laws and regulations, keep certain documents, and present these to the Registrar of the *Tribunal de commerce*, as well as being registered with the latter. Other conditions are substantive: thus there must be a minimum number of members (seven for the *sociétés anonymes*, two for the others) and these members must be aged at least 18. Any shortcomings in the light of these conditions will cause the company to be declared null and void (without retrospective effect).

- **Normal life of the company**: in the course of the existence of the company, the latter will, like any other person, acquire rights and incur obligations. For this purpose, the company will need to have an identity, which will be expressed in the form of a name (*le dénomination sociale*), a registered office (*le siège social*) and a nationality (*la nationalité*). As to the rights which may be

---

11   Article 1844(1) of the Civil Code.

12   (1897) AC 22.

conferred in the company, these can be limited only by legislation and by the nature of the company. As to the ability to pursue these rights at law, the *statuts* must lay down the identity of a natural person who will represent the company for this purpose.

- **Dissolution of companies**: there are two types of conditions in which a company can be dissolved: one type is common to all companies, concerns (a) the conditions laid down by law (expiry of the maximum 99 year term for which all companies are in principle constituted, the loss of the company's objects, one member acquiring all the shares, and the annulment of the company), (b) the conditions laid down by *statut*, and (c) the conditions in which a court decision may dissolve a company, namely for 'good cause' (*juste motif*).[13]

### The *statuts*

French company law does not make the distinction, made in English law, between the articles of association and the memorandum of association. The 'charter' of the company is one single document, called the *statuts* (often inaccurately translated into English as 'the statutes'). Article 1835 of the Civil Code lays down that the *statuts* must be in written form, and must specify the form of the company, its duration, its objects (*la raison sociale*) or name (*dénomination sociale*), its registered office (*siège social*), and the amount of the authorised capital (*capital social*). These *statuts* must be presented not only to the Registrar of the Commercial Court, but also (in four copies) to the fiscal authorities.

## C The *sociétés de personnes*

### The *société en nom collectif*

This is the most basic of all companies, and is formed by two or more *commerçants* with a view to engaging in a commercial operation. Its status is regulated by Law No. 66-537 of 24/7/1966 and by Decree No. 67-236 of 23/3/1967 (which govern all the other types of company). The main characteristic of this *société* is the fact that all its members will be jointly and severally liable for all the debts incurred by the company. It is also a company to whom the law leaves a great deal of freedom in the manner in which it operates, except where the law or the articles of association impose limits to this freedom.

One such restriction, imposed by law, concerns the management of the company. The aforementioned Law of 24/7/1966 stipulates that the *société en nom collectif* must have at least one manager, being the only permanent organ of the

---

13  Article 1844(7) of the Civil Code.

company. These may be freely chosen by the company (the only exception being the company's auditors, who are banned from acting as their manager for at least five years after having supervised its accounts). Their brief is a very wide one: to take all such management actions as are in the company's interest.

**The *société en commandite simple***

This is the equivalent of the English limited partnership. It is used comparatively rarely. Its salient characteristic is the dual nature of its membership: the active partners (*les commandités*) and the silent partners (*les commanditaires*). The former are those who actually perform the trading activity of the company, and must have the status of *commerçants*. They are jointly and severally liable for the company's debts. The latter are the providers of the company capital. They cannot take part in the major management decisions of the company, and their liability is restricted to their capital contribution.

## D The *sociétés de capital*

### The limited liability company (*société à responsabilité limitée* – SARL)

Before the reforms which took place in 1966, the limited liability company was essentially regarded as a person-related company; since then, however, it has moved decisively into the *société de capital* camp. It is a company whose members do not have the status of *commerçants* and whose liability is restricted by their shares (*les parts sociales*). The main difference with the *société anonyme* is one of scale, its minimum authorised capital being FF 50,000.

The SARL must have a minimum of two and a maximum of 50 members. Its capital is divided into *parts sociales* which must have a minimum value of FF 100. These must be entirely underwritten and paid up as from the moment at which the company is established.

As to its management organs, the SARL must have at least one *gérant*, who are either designated by the articles of association (*gérants statutaires*) or by a subsequent decision (*gérants non statutaires*). Their mandate may be terminated either by the members or by a court decision. In the absence of any specific provisions to that effect in the *statuts*, the managers may perform all such actions as are in the interest of the company. In relation to third parties, the managers have the widest possible powers to act on behalf of the company; any clause in the *statuts* which restricts these powers cannot be relied upon against third parties. Their liability can be incurred both at the civil and at the criminal level.

At the civil level, they are liable towards the company or towards third parties for any infringements which they commit against the law or against the *statuts*, and for any errors committed in the course of performing their duties. In addition, any company member may sue the managers for any personal damage which they may have incurred through the fault of the *gérants*. At the criminal level, they have a general liability for any irregularity which assumes a certain degree of seriousness.

The shareholders exercise their powers through meetings (*les assemblées*), which can be either general or special. In principle, decisions at these meetings are taken by a simple majority, except for such circumstances as a change in the *statuts*, the dismissal of managers, etc, which requires a qualified majority. They have two types of right:

- a right to information: at all times, the shareholder has a right to receive from the company a copy of the *statuts*, and to consult at the registered office various documents such as the balance sheet and profit and loss account. Prior to the general meeting, the shareholder must have certain accounting documents sent to him, whereas prior to the special meetings they have a right to have sent to them copies of the proposed resolutions as well as the reports of the manager and, where appropriate, of the auditor.

- his rights in relation to the shares: the shareholder does not have an automatic right to a share in the profits. As regards the transfer of shares: as between shareholders, there is no limit to the number of transfers which may be carried out (subject to limitation by the *statuts*), whereas any transfer to third parties must be approved by the majority of shareholders representing at least 75% of the shares. They are freely transferable between relatives and by way of succession rights.

As to the dissolution of the SARL: in addition to those grounds for dissolution which are common to all companies (cf. *supra*, p. 000), there are certain grounds which are specific to the SARL: where the number of shareholders exceeds 50 or the amount of the authorised capital drops below FF 50,000, and the loss of at least 50% of the authorised capital.

It should also be mentioned that in 1985, the law was changed to allow a limited liability company to operate even if it involved only one person (*entreprise unipersonnelle à responsabilité limitée*). The reason for this was the reality that in fact several SARLs had been operating as no more than shells with only one active member and several mere figureheads. This enabled individual traders to separate their commercial assets from their private property.[14]

## The *société anonyme*

For the largest commercial operations, the *sociétés anonymes* (SA) were created. Since the 1966 reforms, there are now two types of SA: those who call on public money and those who do not. There are some differences in the legal rules applicable, although the scope of this work does not allow us to go into any detail.

---

14  Dickson, B., *op cit*, p. 175.

As to the setting up of SAs, the requirements are that there be at least seven shareholders, that the *statuts* be already drafted; that the authorised capital be fully subscribed, and that they be paid up for at least 25%.

The SA has essentially three organs. One is the decision-making body, which is constituted by the meetings of shareholders; the second is the management organ, and the third the supervisory body.

- **The general meetings**: there are two types of general meeting: the annual general meetings and the extraordinary general meetings. The former can only be held where at least 25% of all vote-carrying shares are represented. It has the general power to take all decisions except for alterations in the *statuts*, which is the prerogative of the extraordinary general meetings.

- **The management organs**. It is here that the reforms of 1966 had their greatest impact on the SAs. However, the 1966 Law did not eliminate the old system: it merely added a new one, inspired by European directives, to the existing traditional structures; companies can now choose which system to adopt. As from that date, the SA retained in principle the traditional structure whereby the main management body was the *conseil d'administration* (Board of Directors), one of whom has to be appointed as Managing Director (*Président directeur général* – PDG).

- **The supervisory body**. The general meeting may also decide to opt for the 'European' model, which provides for a board of directors (*le directoire*) and a supervisory organ (*le conseil de surveillance*). Whereas the *conseil d'administration* has a maximum of 14 members (who must all be shareholders in the company in question), the *directoire* is a good deal more streamlined, and has a maximum of seven members, who must be appointed by the supervisory organ. The latter is a body consisting of a maximum of 12 members, who must all be shareholders. The civil and criminal liability of the directors is largely the same as that which applies in the case of SARLs (cf. *supra*, p. 94).

Special rules apply in relation to those contracts which directors are authorised to conclude with the company. In the first place, there are some transactions, such as loans or overdraft facilities, which are strictly prohibited between the company and its directors. Others are automatically authorised, such as 'agreements which concern everyday operations and which are concluded in normal conditions'.[15] Any other contracts are authorised but regulated.

---

15   Article 102 of the 1966 Law.

# E  Other companies

*Sociétés civiles*

These are companies which cannot be classed as commercial companies because either their nature or their object is not recognised by law (mainly Article 632 of the Commercial Code) as being 'commercial' in the strict sense of the term. However, they need to be given some attention in the context of this chapter, because the nature of their activity is financial and involves trading in the broadest sense of the term (eg agricultural co-operatives).

The *sociétés civiles* are governed entirely by the provisions of the *Code civil* (Articles 1845 *et seq*). One of the chief characteristics of this type of company is the considerable amount of freedom enjoyed by the partners in the company, especially in relation to its management organs: these may be one or more persons, natural or legal, members of the company or not. In addition, the *statuts* of the civil company are left as much freedom as possible to regulate the period of office, remuneration and conditions of dismissal of the manager (although it is possible to have a manager dismissed by a successful application to the court).

However, the rules are somewhat more mandatory as regards the powers and obligations of the managers. As to their powers, Article 1849 of the Civil Code stipulates that the manager shall bind the company towards third parties by any of his or her actions which fall within the scope of the company objects clause. Where there is more than one manager, these powers are to be exercised separately, and any objection raised by one of the managers against the actions engaged in by another do not affect third parties in any way. Any clause in the *statuts* which restricts these powers of the managers cannot be relied upon against third parties.

As to their obligations, the managers have a wide range of duties to provide the members of the company with frequent and relevant information, in particular as regards the financial position of the company. For any shortcomings in the discharge of their office, or for any infringements of the law or of the *statuts*, the managers shall be jointly and severally liable towards both the members of the company and towards third parties. However – unusually – where the liability of more than one manager has been incurred by their participating in the same event, the court will also determine the allocation of the liability amongst the managers in their mutual relations.

The relations between the ordinary members (shareholders) is also much looser than is the case with commercial companies. Thus the convening of a General Meeting is not compulsory, even for the purpose of approving the company accounts. The decision-making process may take the form of a written consultation instead.[16]

Auditors must be appointed to supervise the financial management of the *sociétés civiles*.

### The *sociétés en participation*

This is a very exceptional type of company, in the sense that it has no legal personality as such, and therefore is not obliged to register with the RCS. In fact, this type of company was strictly speaking illegal, since any such company could be classified as a *société irrégulière* (unlawful company). It was given legal status in 1978 because of the large number of recondite companies of this type in existence, living at the margins of illegality, but constituting no threat to *l'ordre public*. The Law of 4/1/1978, which gave these companies the benefit of legality, was incorporated into the *Code civil*, more particularly under Articles 1872 *et seq*.

Like the *société civile*, the *société en participation* is organised on a less formal basis than the commercial companies. This is especially the case in relation to the constitution of the company, since it is not even necessary for the founder members to agree to a written *contrat de société*.

The fact that the *société en participation* has no legal personality obviously has a number of consequences. This is why the Civil Code divide the assets of the company into two parts:

- **The goods which continue to be the private property of the members (*les biens privatifs*).** As far as third parties are concerned, these are the goods which the members placed at the disposal of the company at the moment of its establishment.[17] This serves to protect the interests of the members' creditors.

- **The goods over which the members become the joint owners (*les biens indivis*).** Quite apart from the case of a *contrat d'indivision*, which gives the status of joint property to any goods belonging to the members personally, these are the goods which have been acquired as a result of the use or re-use of goods which were jointly owned in the course of the company's existence, and those which were jointly owned before being placed at the disposal of the company.[18]

---

16   Article 1854 of the Civil Code.
17   Article 1872(1) of the Civil Code.
18   Article 1872(2) of the Civil Code.

The management of these jointly-owned goods will be subject to the ordinary rules of the Civil Code on jointly-held property. Therefore, in the absence of any *contrat d'indivision*, the management of such goods will require the consent of all the joint owners, although the latter may confer general powers of management on one of these members.[19] Where there is a *contrat d'indivision*, on the other hand, every member will be deemed to be managing the jointly-owned property, and will have general powers of representation and management.[20]

## The *groupements d'intérêt économique*

This too is a relatively recent form of business organisation to be given legal status in France, and has been considerably influenced by EU legislation in the shape of Directive 2137/85. The current legislation governing it is ordonnance No. 68-821, as amended by the Law of 13/6/1989.

The *groupements d'intérêt économique* (GIE) are a form of business organisation which enables firms to combine forces without losing their legal identity, in order to perform certain joint activities (such as research and development, production, and marketing). The *groupement* itself has a legal personality which is separate from the legal persons who set it up. It is even capable of issuing bonds where it is made up exclusively of companies which meet the conditions required for issuing bonds.

Here again, the main characteristic of this type of business association is flexibility, in the sense that most of the legal provisions governing it are *droit supplétif* (from which it is possible to depart by private arrangement). However, it is also a condition for its lawful existence that it has a purely auxiliary function, in the sense that its main object is to facilitate or develop the economic activity of its members.

The *groupement d'intérêt économique* may be established by natural or legal persons, or by a mixture of both. It may be set up without any capital, or even without any commercial objective. Its object must, however, be lawful.

The GIE may be managed by one or more persons, who may be legal persons (which was prohibited until the amending Law of 13/6/1989). The managers may be selected from among the members of the GIE or outside its ranks. The manner of appointment and dismissal are normally stated in the *contrat constitutif*; if not, by the General Meeting of its members.

Every manager is capable of binding the GIE in its relations with third parties. Managers are liable, both towards the GIE and towards third parties, for

---

19   Article 815(3) of the Civil Code.
20   Article 1872(1)(4) of the Civil Code.

any infringements of the law and of the *statuts*, and for any mistakes committed in the course of managing the GIE.

The GIEs are subject to a system of dual supervision: both as to its management and as to its finances. Supervision of the manner in which it is managed must be carried out by natural persons, in accordance with the relevant provisions of the *contrat de société*. As to its financial supervision, this must be entrusted to registered auditors only where the GIE is one which issues bonds and which has 100 salaried employees or more. In that case, the auditors are appointed by the general meeting of its members for a duration of six financial years.

# 6    Constitutional Law

## I Introduction

Unlike the UK, France has a codified constitution,[1] with precise terms of reference. It is deemed to be the origin of all legal rules, and there is a general requirement that any law, regulation or court decision should be based on one of its articles. However, unlike some other countries such as Germany or the USA, there is no right of action to a constitutional court for the citizen who considers that a law or regulation infringes a constitutional provision. The only scope for constitutional review of legislation consists in a challenge which may be brought before the *Conseil constitutionnel*, *before* the law in question is truly enforceable, and only by a relatively small number of highly-placed individuals (cf. *infra* p. 113).

The present-day French constitutional model was inspired by what is generally regarded as the first modern constitution ever, ie that of the USA, which was enacted in 1787. Unlike the USA, however, France has brought about constitutional change, not by amending the original document, but by replacing it entirely on no fewer than 17 occasions. In fact, as can be seen from the historical overview, the leading French authors on public law prefer to view French constitutional development in terms of cycles rather than on the basis of individual constitutions (cf. *infra* p. 103). The present Constitution is that of the Fifth Republic and was adopted in 1958; however, constitutional change may very well once again be imminent, given the general public dissatisfaction with the way in which it is felt that the present constitution, with its pronounced bias towards the executive, has led to an overbearing and remote administration.

However, it needs to be stated that there is a greater degree of continuity between successive French constitutions than is generally admitted. Three basic principles have always guided French constitutional thought, ie the notion of national sovereignty, the separation of powers, and the separation between Church and State (not to mention the civil liberties clauses). The former is a

---

1    The term 'codified constitution' is preferred here to the term 'written constitution', since it expresses more accurately the difference between the British and French Constitutions. The former is *written*, in the sense that all the sources of British constitutional law have been reduced to writing in some document or other (court decisions, key Acts of Parliament, Parliamentary procedure in Erskine May, etc). The latter is *codified*, in the sense that all its provisions are contained and systematically ordered in a single document.

notion originally developed by Jean-Jacques Rousseau in *Le contrat social* (1762); however, whereas Rousseau saw sovereignty as being essentially an attribute of the people, French constitutional practice considers sovereignty to belong to the nation, since it cannot be allocated to each individual separately, but constitutes a unique and indivisible notion.

The separation of powers, on the other hand, was the brainchild of Montesquieu, who considered that to enforce a total separation between the legislature, the executive and the judiciary was one of the most essential checks and balances necessary in order to prevent too much power from being concentrated in too few hands. In practice, however, this principle needed to be mitigated, at least in relation to the executive and the legislature, since it is generally recognised that no modern system of government could operate effectively without a close and continuous co-operation between these two organs. However, as between the judiciary and the executive, this rule has been rigorously adhered to throughout the history of French constitutional law, and explains, *inter alia*, why to this very day the administration is subject to a totally separate system of judicial control which has been removed from the jurisdiction of the ordinary courts (cf. *infra* p. 22).

The separation between Church and State represented a reaction against the old confessional state which existed under the *Ancien Régime*. It is a principle which has been pursued to a much greater extent in France than in other 'non-confessional' states. Indeed, at one time, the Vatican broke off diplomatic relations following the enactment of a Law of 1905 which discontinued any assistance by the State with the remuneration paid to the clergy of the main religions.

The remainder of this chapter is divided into three main parts: Section II covers the historical development of French constitutional law; Section III covers the constitutional institutions; and Section IV deals with civil liberties. The organisation of the central and the local administration, as well as the law relating to public finances, will be dealt with in the chapter devoted to administrative law.

# II The historical development of French constitutional law

## A General

It has already been mentioned that France has known a succession of constitutions ever since the French Revolution, which ushered in the first modern statement setting out the relationship between the State and the citizen. Virtually every French author on public law has discerned a series of cycles among these successive constitutions, each of which runs to the same pattern comprising three stages: the first is marked by the predominance of the legislature; during the second, it is the executive which dominates, whereas the third stage witnesses a balance being struck between these two. We will therefore examine the successive constitutional cycles in that light – allowing for an initial period of instability and fermentation immediately following the Revolution.

## B The constitutional monarchy: 1789-1792

Immediately after the Revolution, the constitutional organisation of France greatly resembled that of Great Britain, which had inspired many of those who laid the intellectual foundations for the new constitutional order. The King represented the executive, and his powers extended to the appointment and dismissal of ministers, the leadership of the army and exercising a right of veto over the decrees passed by the legislature, ie the National Assembly. The latter proposed and enacted legislation and had control of the state finances. The powers of the State were laid down by the first French Constitution, which was the Universal Declaration of the Rights of Man. However, following the constant attempts by Louis XVI to subvert the new order with outside assistance, the monarchy was abolished on 10 August 1792, paving the way for the First Republic.

## C The first constitutional cycle: 1792-1848

This period saw a succession of very different political systems, in that it included a republic, a monarchy, and a consulate. However, it established a pattern which was to reappear during each successive constitutional cycle.

- **Preponderance of the legislature**: this was very much the case under the *Convention* (1792-1795). It was elected by indirect universal suffrage, ie by a special electoral college, and constituted the most radical rule-making body France has ever known. It acted both as legislature and as executive.

- **Re-assertion of the executive**: once the *Convention* had collapsed in acrimony and confusion, the authority of the state was shared by two organs: (a) the legislature, which for the first time was divided over two bodies, ie the *Conseil des 500* (which initiated legislation) and the *Anciens* (which adopted it), and (b) the executive, which was represented by the *Directoire*, a body of five leaders proposed by the *Conseil des 500* and appointed by the *Anciens*. The executive received a further boost under the Consulate (which also witnessed a weakening of the powers of the legislature) and acquired absolute supremacy under the Empire (1804-1815).

- **Striking of balance: introduction of the parliamentary system**. Following Napoleon's defeat at Waterloo in 1815, France for the first time experienced a system of direct elections to a Parliamentary assembly (the *Chambre des* *députés*), even though only citizens able to meet a very high personal property requirement were eligible to vote. The other chamber, the *Chambre des pairs*, consisted of members appointed by the king. The powers of the Parliamentary chambers were further increased under the *Monarchie de juillet* which followed the 1830 revolution.

## D The second constitutional cycle: 1848-1870

- **Preponderance of the legislature**: the *Assemblée nationale constituante* which was instituted following the 1848 revolution was the first to be elected by direct universal suffrage, without any property requirement.

- **Re-assertion of the executive**: this was particularly the case following the *coup d'état* of 2 December 1851, under which the future Napoleon III acquired extensive powers and the Parliament was reduced to a *Corps législatif*, whose authority was considerably reduced. The powers of the executive were enhanced even further under the *Empire autoritaire* of 1852-1860.

- **Striking a balance: reassertion of the parliamentary system**. Under the Empire libéral (1860-1870), the *Corps législatif* was strengthened and heralded a gradual return to a Parliamentary régime.

## E The third constitutional cycle: 1870-1945

The third constitutional cycle to a certain extent constitutes an exception to the other stages in the development of France's constitutional history. It coincided with the Third Republic, which was a period of remarkable political stability, which is surprising since it included the troubled times of the First World War.

Following the defeat of the French in the Franco-Prussian war in 1871, political life in France settled down to a long period of Parliamentary supremacy. Initially there was a caretaker régime under the government of M. Thiers which restored the French legislature to full prominence with full approval of the population – no doubt the misery and defeat of the 1870-71 war were ascribed to the overbearing arrogance of an over-powerful executive. The Constitution which was adopted in February and July 1875 gave constitutional validity to this parliamentary system.

The Parliament consisted of a Chamber of Delegates and a Senate. The latter was very much the junior partner in the legislative process, since it was not directly elected and needed to be partially renewed every three years. The chamber, on the other hand, was elected by direct universal suffrage and entirely renewed every four years. The Parliament had full *residual* legislative powers, in the sense that it was able to legislate on any matter which was not specifically attributed to another authority under the Constitution. In addition, it had total control over the executive. The latter consisted of a President and a

Government, of which the former was a Head of State who 'reigned without governing', and the latter operated mainly through the Council of Ministers.

## F The fourth constitutional cycle: 1946 to the present

Once the period of stability of the third constitutional cycle came to an abrupt end through the events of World War II, France's constitutional development returned to the previously established pattern. The Third Republic came to an inglorious end when, in 1940, it gave full powers to Marshall Pétain's collaborationist executive to govern by means of *actes constitutionnels*. These were declared null and void by an order enacted by General de Gaulle in August 1945, which heralded the birth of a new Republic (the Fourth).

- **Preponderance of the legislature**: the constitution of the Fourth Republic re-established a full parliamentary régime by virtue of the prominence which it gave to the National Assembly. The latter was the senior partner in the legislature, and was assisted by a *Conseil de la République* whose powers were greatly reduced from those enjoyed by its predecessor, the Senate under the Third Republic. The full measure of the predominance of the Assembly manifested itself by the fact that, uniquely in French history, it had the power to topple the Government.

  The executive consisted of a President and a Council of Ministers. The President's powers were even less than those under the Third Republic, especially as regards his relations with the Parliament. The Council of Ministers was fully answerable to Parliament, and its President, who was appointed by the President of the Republic, but only after the National Assembly had given the candidate a vote of confidence.

- **Re-assertion of the executive**: the Fourth Republic was ended abruptly by the Algerian crisis of 1958, which brought France to the brink of civil war. Public opinion identified the weakness of the executive as one of the principal reasons for this crisis, and therefore gratefully accepted the new Constitution of the Fifth Republic which gave precedence to the President and the Government. The institutions and their powers are fully analysed below (p. 106 *et seq*).

- **Striking a balance: reassertion of the parliamentary system**. Few people now doubt that France is heading towards a new settlement between the executive and the legislature, which may even result from the establishment of a new Republic. The main factors which have caused this shift in public attitudes are the long period of relative political stability, which makes a strong executive less imperative, and the various scandals in which prominent members of the executive have been associated.

# III The institutions of the Fifth Republic

## A  General characteristics of the Constitution

### The democratic principle

The Constitution expressly asserts the democratic nature of its institutions, by stating that France is a democratic republic (Article 2) and that the authorities must at all times respect this democratic principle by ensuring that every method of voting shall take the form of universal suffrage (Article 3). Other expressions of the democratic principle are the opportunity given to the people to vote on certain issues by means of a referendum (Articles 11 and 89) and the civil liberties guaranteed by the Preamble to the Constitution.

### National sovereignty

As has been mentioned before, this abstract principle has come to replace the more concrete, but unworkable, notion of 'sovereignty of the people', and is enshrined in Article 3. This national sovereignty is mainly exercised indirectly through the representative institutions, although from time to time it may be exercised directly by referendum. It should be added, however, that the principle of national sovereignty is qualified in two ways: (a) by the provision in the Preamble which allows such limitations of sovereignty as are necessary to preserve the peace, and (b) by the Constitutional Amendment of 25/6/1992, which accepts that certain powers may be transferred to the European Union for the purpose of achieving economic and monetary union.

### The republican principle

Article 2 proclaims France to be a Republic which is (a) indivisible, which excludes the possibility of France becoming a federal state; (b) secular, in that the French state recognises no religion, and (c) social, in that the preamble expressly mentions social justice as one of the goals of the Fifth Republic. It also makes provision for some concrete expressions of this republicanism (in terms of its motto *Liberté, égalité, fraternité*, the national anthem *La Marseillaise* and the republican tricolour flag).

## B  The people

In the Constitution, the people are specifically mentioned as a constitutional organ. As such, they have three specific functions to perform: to appoint the holders of political authority, to participate directly in certain political decisions, and to take part in political life through parties and other groupings. Each function will be analysed in turn.

### Electing the political office-holders

The people are involved in this process as voters, and the Constitution regulates the manner in which they may act in this capacity.

As has been mentioned before, elections in France are governed by the principle of universal suffrage. The only restrictions on this principle relate to age, since only those aged 18 or over may vote; to nationality, since foreigners are normally excluded from participation in elections; and to civic behaviour, in that persons having incurred criminal convictions may be deprived of their electoral rights.

This right to vote is exercised by each citizen on an equal and individual basis, is secret, and is not subject to any compulsion, which means that the people are free to vote or to refrain from voting.

The electoral system itself has presented an unstable picture in the course of the Fifth Republic. In the first place, the President was initially not elected by direct suffrage, but by an extended electoral college: this system was abandoned in 1962. As to the elections to the National Assembly, a succession of changes occurred in the 1980s. From 1958 to 1986, the two-round list system was applied, under which the voters were required to vote for a list of candidates rather than for individuals. Where a list of candidates failed to obtain an absolute majority on the first ballot, a second round of voting occurred a week later between the lists which had obtained at least 12.5% of the votes; this time, the candidates on the list which obtained the highest number of votes were elected. This system was abandoned by the Socialist administration in 1986 to be replaced by proportional representation. Once the Centre-Right returned to power in 1988, the two-round list system was reintroduced.

The people may only vote in polling stations where they are entered in the electoral register. Those French nationals who reside abroad are also entitled to vote, which they may do in the constituency of their choice, subject to certain conditions.

### Direct participation: the referendum

The Constitution makes provision for direct participation by the people in the decision-making process, without, however, elevating the referendum to the status of a regular method of popular consultation as in Switzerland. Its use is restricted to the circumstances laid down in the following articles of the Constitution:

- **Article 11**: the President may subject to a referendum any draft law concerning the organisation of the public authorities, including the ratification of a treaty which, without infringing the Constitution, has an impact on the functioning of its institutions. Referenda under this provision have already been held on several occasions (eg that which took place on 20 September 1992 on ratification of the Maastricht Treaty).

- **Article 53:** the consent of the people involved is required for any transfer, exchange or supplementing of the French territory. Such consent would normally take the form of a referendum. This possibility has not as yet been taken up.

- **Article 89**: this provision lays down that no part of the Constitution may be amended unless it has been approved by a referendum. It has also been used on a number of occasions (eg the *Loi constitutionnelle* of 29/10/1974, which conferred on 60 senators and 60 National Assembly members the right to bring a challenge before the *Conseil constitutionnel*).

### Participation in political parties

Constitutional recognition is given to the existence of political parties. Article 4 states that the latter assist in the process of expressing the right to vote, and confers on them the right to be formed and act in total freedom, subject only to respecting national sovereignty and democracy. Official recognition of political parties was further enhanced by the *Loi organique* of 11/3/1988 relating to the financial transparency of political parties. This Law not only confers legal personality on political parties, with all the rights and obligations that this entails, but also gives Parliament the right to provide them with financial assistance.

## C The President

### General

The President and the Government constitute the bicephalous executive. The fact that the Constitution gives the Presidency pride of place in the order in which the Constitutional organs are mentioned testifies to the importance which it assumes in the 1958 constitutional settlement.

### Electing the President

The election of the President normally takes place between 20 and 35 days prior to the termination of the existing President's term of office, which is seven years. Where a vacancy arises before the normal term of seven years expires (eg by reason of the death or resignation of the incumbent, or his or her definitive inability to carry out his or her duties), the election must take place between 20 and 35 days following the date on which the vacancy arose. During the period of interregnum, the functions of the President are assumed by the President of the Senate. Voting takes place by elimination over two rounds, ie unless a candidate has secured an absolute majority on the first ballot, a second round of voting takes place a week later between the two candidates having secured the largest share of the vote.

To be able to stand for election, a candidate must be of French nationality and be older than 23. In addition, he or she must be sponsored by 500 national or local elected delegates (with the exception of municipal councillors) covering at least 30 *départements*, on the understanding that no single *département* may account for more than 50 signatures. The Constitutional Council has the task of verifying whether or not all these conditions have been met.

The election campaign itself is governed by the equality principle, in that (a) the candidates are given equal campaigning time on the public television networks, and (b) campaign spending is subject to an upper limit, and financed in part by the State.

### The presidential powers

These can be broken down into two categories: his shared powers, being those which require the signature of the Prime Minister and, where necessary, the relevant Minister, and his exclusive powers, which require no such formality. It is fair to state that, judging by the wording of Article 19 of the Constitution, the latter are seen as the exception to the rule.

The President's exclusive powers concern first of all the appointment of the Prime Minister. Under this heading, he may also decide that a referendum be held on draft laws regarding the organisation of the public authorities or seeking to ratify treaties which could affect the functioning of the public institutions (Article 11). He may also dissolve the National Assembly, but only after having consulted the Prime Minister and the presidents of both parliamentary assemblies, and subject to the restriction that the Assembly may not be dissolved again within a year of the date on which a new Assembly was elected (Article 12). He may in addition address special messages to the two Assemblies (Article 18), seize the Constitutional Council of the consistency of an international treaty with the Constitution (Article 54), appoint three members of the Constitutional Council (Article 56) and refer to the latter laws which have not yet been ratified (Article 61).

The President's exclusive powers are at their most radical under Article 16 of the Constitution, which deals with exceptional circumstances. Where the Republic, its institutions, its territory or its ability to perform its international obligations are in peril, the President may take such emergency measures as are necessary to enable the constitutional authorities to resume their normal duties. He may not, however, suspend the National Assembly during this emergency period. This measure has already been used in the course of the Fifth Republic, more particularly on the occasion of the Algerian crisis in 1961.

The shared powers of the President, on the other hand, are those which have formed part of the normal attributes of the Presidency under previous

Constitutions. These are the power to appoint and dismiss the members of the Government (Article 8); the ratification of laws adopted by the Parliament and, where necessary, to demand a new Parliamentary debate on a law or part thereof (Article 10); the signing of orders and decrees issued by the Council of Ministers (Article 13), the conduct of foreign relations (Articles 14 and 52), the leadership of the army (Article 15), etc.

# D The Government

## Organisation

The Government consists of two elements: the Prime Minister and the Ministers.

The Prime Minister is appointed by the President, who is in theory totally free in making this choice; in practice, however, he makes his appointment from among the ranks of the dominant party or coalition of parties within the National Assembly. The Prime Minister's functions are terminated by death, definitive inability to carry out his or her duties, and by compulsory or voluntary resignation. The Ministers are appointed by the President on a proposal by the Prime Minister. Their term of office ends in the following circumstances: (a) termination of the term of office of the Prime Minister; (b) death or definitive inability to carry out their duties; (c) voluntary resignation; (d) dismissal by the President on a proposal made by the Prime Minister; and (e) any decision made against them by the *Haute Cour de Justice* for a criminal offence committed in the pursuance of their duties.

Neither the Prime Minister nor the other members of the Government may exercise any other function in the course of their term of office, not even that of Member of Parliament. Any member of the National Assembly or of the Senate who is appointed Minister must therefore resign from Parliament (Article 23).

## Individual powers of the Prime Minister

In general terms, the Prime Minister directs Government action (Article 21). It is under this heading that he or she nominates the Ministers, takes part in the Council of Ministers which he or she sometimes chairs in the absence of the President, arbitrates in disputes between the Ministers, and exercises control over the Ministers, to the point of being able to propose their dismissal to the President.

More specifically, the Prime Minister exercises a number of duties which concern the relations between the Government and Parliament, as well as a number of administrative duties. As to the first, he or she has a number of tasks which concern (a) the functioning of Parliament, such as requesting the President to call extraordinary sessions of Parliament, (b) the legislative procedure, such as signing the decrees by which draft laws are put before Parliament, and (c) the responsibility of the Government to Parliament, such as pledging the responsibility of the Government before the National Assembly on the Government's programme or on a general statement of policy.

As regards his or her administrative functions, the Prime Minister has the power to (a) issue regulations of a general nature which take the form of *décrets* (Articles 21, 34 and 37), (b) make certain top civil and military appointments (Article 21); (c) co-ordinate the activity of the administrative departments, and (d) direct the military administration (Article 21).

### Powers of the Ministers

Acting collectively, the Government has two types of power: normal powers and exceptional powers. Its normal powers derive from Article 20 of the Constitution, which states that 'the Government shall decide and carry out national policy; it shall direct the administration and the armed forces'. This is a very general mandate, the limits of which have never been satisfactorily defined by law, although in practice they are restricted by virtue of the political responsibility of the Government before the Parliament. For the purpose of carrying out its collective functions, the Government has an executive organ called the Council of Ministers. In fact, many of the powers of the Prime Minister will in reality be exercised by the Council of Ministers.

The exceptional powers of the Government are exercised in two sets of circumstances: (a) where it is necessary to declare martial law (Article 36), and (b) where Parliament has given it authorisation to issue regulations (*ordonnances*) (Article 38). The Government may issue these Regulations on a wide range of subjects, and may even encroach on areas which in principle should be determined by Parliament by means of laws.

## E  Parliament

### General

The Constitution of the Fifth Republic retained the bicameral system, which is why Parliament consists of two chambers: the National Assembly and the Senate. However, the differences between the powers exercised by the two chambers is not as great as was the case under the Fourth Republic. Nevertheless, this equality of treatment serves to weaken the legislature, since it undermines the legitimacy of the chamber which obtains its mandate directly from the electorate, ie the National Assembly.

### Organisation

The National Assembly consists of 577 members, one per constituency but at least two for each *département*. They are elected for a fixed term of five years by the two-round voting system (cf. *supra p.* 107). Any challenge to an election result is brought before the *Conseil constitutionnel*, who may declare the elections void or revise the results.

The Senate, on the other hand, consists of 312 members (12 of whom represent expatriate French citizens). They are elected for nine years, but not simultaneously, since one-third are elected every three years. The Senate is not elected directly, but indirectly, ie by an electoral college for each *département* consisting of members of the National Assembly, regional councillors, *conseillers généraux* and representatives of the municipal councillors.

## Parliamentary sessions

There are three types of Parliamentary session: (a) the ordinary sessions, of which there are two: the first opens on 2 October and lasts 80 days, and the second opens on 2 April and may not last any longer than 90 days; (b) the extraordinary sessions, which may be convened in exceptional circumstances outside the ordinary sessions by the President on application by Prime Minister or by the majority of the National Assembly, and may only discuss a specific agenda; and (c) the exceptional automatic sessions which are held whenever the President decides to use his emergency powers under Article 16.

## The legislative process

Article 34 lists the general areas in which Parliament may legislate: these are (a) civil liberties, (b) the law relating to the status of persons and families; (c) criminal law (except for minor offences) and (d) taxation and currency.[2] Article 34 also determines areas, such as national defence, education and industrial law, in which Parliament shall only adopt general principles without going into detail, as well as special categories of legislation, ie the finance laws and the policy laws.

Both chambers take part in the process of adopting legislation on an equal basis, except where an *impasse* is reached after the second referral back, in which case the text adopted by the National Assembly may be ratified by the Government. There are three types of procedure, depending on whether the law in question is an ordinary law, a *loi organique*, a finance law or a law ratifying an international treaty.

The vast majority of laws adopted are *lois ordinaires*. They may be proposed by either the Government or by individual parliamentarians of either chamber. Once proposed, the draft law is examined by a committee of the chamber to which it has been proposed. The proposal is then put to the chamber in question after having received the opinion of the commission. In the course of the debate before the chamber, amendments may be suggested, both by individual parlia-

---

2   For a detailed list, cf. *supra*.

mentarians and by the Government. Once the draft has been adopted by the relevant chamber, it is transmitted to the other. Where the latter amends the draft as adopted by the first chamber, it is referred back to the latter; this *navette* process of referral back is continued until agreement is reached on the final version. However, where no agreement has yet been reached after two readings in each chamber, the Government will request the National Assembly to propose the definitive law.

**Other responsibilities of Parliament**

In addition to its legislative function, Parliament has a number of other responsibilities (a) judicial powers, in that it may bring charges against the President or a Minister before the *Haute Cour de Justice* and grant amnesties for certain categories of person having incurred a criminal sentence; (b) constitutional powers, in that only Parliament may adopt constitutional amendments; and (c) supervisory powers, by exercising political control over the Government.

# F Constitutional Council

The opportunities for obtaining constitutional review in France are extremely limited, in that the individual citizen has no access to the one body capable of assessing legislation in the light of constitutional provisions. The constitution is deemed to be adequately protected by giving a limited number of highly-placed individuals the right to challenge legislation before the *Conseil constitutionnel* before it actually reaches the statute book. The *Conseil* does, however, have responsibilities other than constitutional review.

For an overview of the organisation and functions of the *Conseil constitutionnel*, we refer to Chapter 2 (Organisation of the Courts, *supra*, p. 27).

# G Other constitutional organs

### The *Haute Cour de Justice* (Articles 67 and 68)

This is an organ which is responsible for hearing serious criminal charges brought against the President or the Ministers, or charges of crimes against the internal security of the state brought against ordinary citizens. It consists of 24 judges and 12 substitutes, elected by the National Assembly and the Senate on an equal basis. Thus far only one action has ever been brought before it (arising from the 'contaminated blood' scandal in 1993).

### The Economic and Social Council (Articles 69-71)

This organ had already seen the light of day under the Fourth Republic. It consists of representatives of the main social and economic interest groups (employers' and employees' organisations, agricultural associations, etc). They may advise the Government on social and economic policy, not only whenever the Government so requests, but even on its own initiative. The Government is in no way bound by its opinions.

### The *Conseil supérieur de la magistrature* (Articles 64 and 65)

This is the body which makes recommendations for appointments to the Bench and exercises disciplinary powers over judges for mistakes committed in the pursuance of their duties. It consists of 11 persons.

### The local authorities

These are dealt with in Chapter 7 (*infra*, p. 124).

# IV The civil liberties

## A Introduction

### General

Ever since it adopted the Universal Declaration of the Rights of Man in 1789, France has been proud of the fundamental freedoms which it confers on its citizens. These have invariably been considered to be as necessary an attribute of a democracy as the right to vote. Although France has a system of public authorities which has adequate checks and balances to prevent the State from acting in an oppressive way towards its citizens, its constitutional legislators have invariably sought to supplement these by a number of positive rights having constitutional status. The main characteristics of the French civil liberties are:

### Incorporation by reference

The Constitution of the Fifth Republic merely makes a brief reference to the 'rights of man' in its preamble, but pledges itself to uphold the Declaration of the Rights of Man, as well as the freedoms contained in the preamble to the 1946 Constitution.

### International dimension

This has manifested itself not only in the inspiration drawn by the French legislature from international declarations of human rights (such as that of the United Nations), but also in the fact that certain international instruments, such as the European Convention on Human Rights, have been fully incorporated into French law.

### No prior authorisation required

In principle, the citizen is entitled to avail himself of these liberties and guarantees without needing to seek prior authorisation. However, the public authorities may, in order to prevent any abuse of these freedoms, impose such restrictions as they may deem necessary in the public interest.

### Freedom to do or to refrain from doing something

The exercise of one's civil liberties expresses itself not only in the ability to perform certain actions – eg the right to join an association – but also in the right to refrain from engaging in certain activities, such as practising a certain religion.

### Fundamental, internal and external freedoms

The civic guarantees conferred on the French citizen are many and varied. It is, however, possible to make out four distinct categories: (a) the fundamental freedoms (ie those without which the others would be impossible to exercise); (b) the internal freedoms (which allow the free development of internal thought); (c) the external freedoms (which enable the citizen to give practical expression to the internal freedoms); and (d) the social and economic freedoms. They are analysed in turn below.

## B The fundamental freedoms

### General

The fundamental freedoms can be generally described as those which guarantee the integrity of the citizen's physical person, and which constitute the irreducible minimum which entitle the French state to call itself a free society. According to the drafters of the Constitution, there are three main categories of such freedoms: those which concern individual freedom, those guaranteeing the inviolability of the home, and those which protect the right to property ownership.

### Individual freedom

This is one of the most tangible legacies of the French Revolution, and is enshrined in Articles 2 and 7 of the 1789 Declaration of the Rights of Man, to which the Constitution expressly refers. We are dealing here with the right to come and go, and to remain, wherever one pleases, without fear of arrest or detention other than in the circumstances which are specified by law. It should be noted that this freedom is viewed here in terms of its individual, and not collective, exercise (the latter being guaranteed by other civil liberties, such as the right of assembly).

It is obvious that any unrestricted exercise of these rights could lead to abuses, and that the public authorities must have at their disposal means of protecting the public against such abuses, in particular where these take on a criminal dimension. Since, however, the criminal law constitutes an exception to these principles of individual freedom, it is for the legislation which imposes such restrictions to be very specific as to how, and in what conditions, individuals may be arrested, held or imprisoned. In addition, these restrictions must be imposed in a manner which is proportionate to the public interest which the legislation is attempting to protect.

This is why a number of safeguards have been built into the criminal law system in order to encroach as little as possible on the citizen's fundamental rights. Thus no person can be arrested without a warrant, except where he or she has been caught in the act. Once arrested, he or she cannot be held for inquiries beyond a certain time limit specified for each particular category of crime. If the proceedings reach the trial stage, there are a number of safeguards which protect the rights of the defence (eg the right to legal representation).

However, concern is growing in France at a number of developments which appear to be eroding these precious freedoms. The notion of 'being caught in the act' (*flagrant délit*) has been interpreted increasingly broadly by the authorities; measures ostensibly adopted to ensure State security are often disproportionate to the object pursued, and the exponential increase in electronic data processing also poses dangers to individual freedom, in spite of the recent enactment of data protection legislation.

**Inviolable nature of the home**

The home is regarded in France as the ultimate place of refuge for the individual, and therefore is inviolable. The public authorities only have the right to enter such private premises during certain hours of the day, and subject to the presentation of a search warrant.

**Right of property ownership**

This too is a right for which the Constitution refers to the 1789 Declaration (Articles 2 and 17). However, it would be misleading to think that private property continues today to hold the sacrosanct status which it enjoyed immediately after the French Revolution. This is borne out not only by the recent case law pursuant to the Civil Code provisions on property law (cf. *supra*, p. 62), but also because a number of other principles, such as the right to expropriation and nationalisation by the State, have also achieved constitutional recognition.

# C The internal freedoms

This category comprises the freedoms which enable the citizen to acquire and develop his or her knowledge and beliefs, as well as his or her fundamental philosophical and religious attitudes. As such, they can be broken down into two main categories: the freedom of thought and the freedom of education.

## Freedom of thought

The individual is free to entertain any thoughts on any topic whatsoever, be it religious, moral, political, social or philosophical, unless in doing so he or she would infringe the public order. The most important of these beliefs in terms of the ability to exercise them is religion.

France has been a secular state ever since the French Revolution. This has on more than one occasion caused severe friction with the Holy See, not least on the occasion of the adoption of the 1905 Law which currently governs the status of the various religious denominations in France.

Essentially, the 1905 Law guarantees freedom to celebrate the religion of one's choice. In fact, Article 32 lays down criminal penalties for anyone who interferes with this right. However, the exercise of this freedom must be consistent with the maintenance of public order, and therefore subject to certain restrictions, which are different according to whether they deal with the inside or the outside of the relevant places of worship.

Inside these places, worship is totally free. The public authorities may not interfere with any aspects of this building or form of worship, except where the public order is threatened (eg because of the parlous state of the building). Outside these places of worship, however, any manifestation of religious worship could inconvenience the public, for example by impeding the traffic. The most frequent form which these manifestations assume are religious processions: here, the Mayor of the municipality in question may adopt appropriate measures.

The principle of religious freedom also means that no-one may suffer any adverse consequences as a result of his or her religious beliefs – for example, when applying for posts in the public services. There have, however, been occasions when the conflicts between the religious allegiance of the citizen and the secular operation of the public services has been put to the test. This was the case a few years ago when a school decided to prevent two Muslim girls from attending classes on the grounds that they wore the Muslim veil (*l'affaire des foulards*).

## Freedom of education

This is one of the more difficult areas of civil liberties for the State to control. The latter could in principle restrict its role to providing a public education service free at the point of demand, and otherwise leave it to private initiative to provide a service for those who do not wish to avail themselves of this public service. However, this would mean that the element of *choice* would become the exclusive preserve of those having the means to meet the cost charged by private educational establishments – but to what extent can the State be seen to assist private education without infringing other fundamental constitutional principles, such as the secular nature of the State. Let us therefore examine these two essential aspects of the individual's educational rights, ie the right to receive education, and the right to have a choice when receiving this education.

The 'right' to receive education is perhaps a misnomer, since, in common with the vast majority of modern states, France considers that human dignity is inseparable from the acquisition of a minimum amount of knowledge, and that therefore education is compulsory up to a certain age. This carries with it the obligation of the State to provide public education to a satisfactory level. This means not only providing the necessary monies to fund it, but also to provide an integral service, ie as wide a range of educational outlets as possible. These extend beyond the traditional forms of teaching such as primary, secondary and further and higher education, and includes the notion of professional training and 'education for life'.

The right to exercise a choice in education is a more delicate matter to regulate. On the one hand, France rejects the notion of a State monopoly in education, and allows the general right to set up and operate private educational establishments, subject to certain administrative supervision procedures. However, this gave rise to the accusation that the freedom of choice in education was restricted to those who could afford private schooling fees. That is why a number of laws adopted over the course of the Fifth Republic have laid down a system whereby the State provides levels of financial support to private education which are commensurate with the extent to which the latter submits to official monitoring and quality control procedures.

# D The external freedoms

### General

These are the freedoms which enable the individual not only to exist and to think, but also to act, and to give practical expression to his or her fundamental freedoms and freedom of thought. The main manifestations of these external freedoms are the freedom of association and the freedom of the press.

### Freedom of association

In order to give practical expression to their freedoms, citizens must be allowed not only to meet on an occasional basis to this end, but also to associate on a more permanent basis. Such associations can either assume a commercial or a non-profitmaking form. Since the former are dealt with elsewhere (*supra*, p. 90), we will confine ourselves here to the non-profit-making associations.

Essentially, anyone is free to set up, and belong to, the association of his or her choice. However, French law does not restrict itself to laying down this principle: it has also laid down a number of measures which make it easier for the citizen to exercise this freedom. Thus it confers legal personality on certain categories of association, ie the ability for the association to exercise certain rights separately from the physical persons who constitute it. In addition, a law was adopted in 1901 which makes provision for several types of association: (a) the *association non déclarée*, which has no legal capacity, (b) the *association déclarée*, which must comply with certain requirements in exchange for the right to act at law, such as submitting its articles of association to the *Préfecture* and arranging for publication of its title and objects in the *Journal officiel*; and (c) the *association reconnue d'utilité publique*, which has extensive legal rights – including the right to have property bequeathed to it by will – in exchange for far-reaching monitoring procedures by the State, particularly as regards its finances.

### Freedom of the press

The term 'press' has, of course, been extended to include the various audio-visual media. This is generally recognised to be one of the more difficult freedoms to regulate by law, in view of its potentially subversive effect and the need to avoid the formation of media monopolies.

As regards the written press, the fundamental rule, as laid down in the relevant legislation (Law of 1881) is that no periodic publication may be subject to any prior authorisation or censure, but that the publisher must submit to two sets of rules: (a) those which lay down certain types of prohibited publication, such as obscene publications and reports on certain trials, and (b) the rule that certain formalities must be completed prior to commencing publication in order that, if necessary, the publisher's criminal liability may be brought into play by the authorities. However, any criminal proceedings brought against the press is subject to the safeguard that the trial will take place before the *Cour d'assisses*, ie in the presence of a jury.

As to the audio-visual media, these have been subjected recently to a number of convulsive changes by successive governments.[3] The present position is governed by a Law of 1986, substantially amended in 1989. The main effect of this legislation was to break the monopoly of the State in television and radio broadcasting. An independent administrative authority, called the *Conseil supérieur de l'audiovisuel*, has been established in order to monitor the observance of the principle of freedom of audio-visual communication.

---

3    For an account of these changes, see Dickson, B., *op cit*, pp. 95-97.

# E Social and economic freedoms

## General

The Constitution of the Fourth Republic recognised for the first time that there were a number of social and economic rights which should be given the same level of protection and constitutional status as the more traditional freedoms described above. The 1958 Constitution also recognises these new rights, if in a somewhat remote manner (by referring, in its preamble, to the relevant provisions of the 1946 preamble, which are thus deemed to have been incorporated into the 1958 Constitution).

## The status of the worker

It is on this subject that the 1946 preamble contains the most extensive set of provisions. Thus it guarantees the freedom of, and equality between, workers before their employers (para. 5(1)), the freedom to belong to the trade union of one's choice (para. 6), the right to strike (para. 7), the right to co-determination in the process of fixing working conditions (para. 8), the right to take part in the management of the firm (para. 8), and the right to professional training (para. 13).

## Economic rights

These concern not only the right to take part in the management of the firm for which one works (see above), but also the principle of nationalisation. Paragraph 9 of the 1946 Preamble states: 'Any property or business organisation whose operation has acquired, or acquires, the characteristics of a public national service or of a *de facto* monopoly, shall pass into public ownership' (translation by the authors). It must be stated that the enthusiasm with which this provision has been implemented has depended very much on the proclivities of the party in power.

## Social rights

These manifest themselves in the first place in the substantive rights which are conferred on the family (para. 10). In this and in other areas of social life, it is recognised for the first time that the State has an active part to play, rather than the *laissez faire* approach of the 1789 Declaration. Thus the State now has the obligation to organise social insurance (para. 11), to ensure that the people are equally responsible for the burdens resulting from national disasters (para. 12) and to guarantee equal access for children and adults to education, professional training and culture (para. 13).

# 7    Administrative Law

## I  Introduction

### A General

The term *'droit administratif'* can be interpreted in a number of ways. In the narrow sense of the term, it means the special rules and principles which have been developed by the administrative courts in France, which are distinct and separate from those to which the case law of the ordinary courts has given rise. In this interpretation, it is often used in the original French even in English works on administrative law, since it is particularly in this respect that the French system of justice differs from its English counterpart. In the very broad sense of the term, it encompasses everything which affects the organisation of public life other than the constitutional organs examined in the previous chapter. As such, it covers the local authorities, the other public bodies, the relationship between the public sector and the private sector, and the relations between the administration and the citizen – including various means of dispute settlement (mainly but not exclusively before the administrative courts). It is this broad interpretation of the term which will govern the approach adopted in this chapter.

Viewed in this light, the term 'administrative law' can be defined as the entire range of actions having legal implications which are engaged in by the government and the various decentralised authorities in order to serve the public interest and meet general needs. Its operation therefore involves a very wide range of actors, the main ones being the state, the local authorities, the autonomous public bodies (*établissements publics*), the private bodies having a more or less intense relationship with the public sector, as well as all the people who staff these bodies – both as elected representatives (*les élus*) and as appointed officials (*les fonctionnaires*).

It is useful to observe at this stage that the administration and its legal system have always occupied special status in French life which it has not quite achieved in other countries, particularly Anglo-Saxon. The main reasons for this is that administrative reform was one of the most lasting legacies of the state reforms introduced by the French Revolution.

# B Characteristics of French administrative law

### Autonomous nature

Ever since the major reforms introduced as a result of the Revolution, the French system of administrative law has been characterised by the adherence to the fundamental principle, developed by Montesquieu, of the separation of powers (*la séparation des pouvoirs*), under which the three constitutional authorities, ie the legislature, the judiciary and the executive (and therefore also the administration) must operate on a separate basis in order to prevent too much power from being concentrated into too few hands. It is perhaps the French administration which continues to bear the strongest evidence of the continued application of this principle.

This autonomy manifests itself not only in the separate system of administrative dispute settlement, but also by the different meaning and interpretation given to certain legal concepts according to whether it is being used in the context of administrative law or not. A good example of this is the notion of contractual and tort liability.

### Non-codified law

Unlike the civil or criminal law, there is in the area of administrative law no systematic body of rules which contains virtually all the legislation on the subject. There is in existence a '*Code administratif*', but this term is a very misleading one, since it merely refers to a collection of legislation issued by private publishers without any official sanction.

### Shaped by the case law

Although no French lawyer would ever admit to the term 'judge-made law', it is a fact that a good deal of the administrative law is what is known as *un droit prétorien*, ie a legal system which has been largely shaped by the court decisions. Many administrative law rules have no other origin than the decision which formulates them. This is particularly true of the case law developed by the *Conseil d'Etat*.

### From public authority to public service

Following the reforms introduced by the French Revolution, the ethic which dominated administrative law for much of the 19th century was that of public authority (*la puissance publique*), which was perceived to be the main justification for administrative action. However, under the influence of authors such as Duguit and Rolland, the notion that the main *raison d'être* of the administration was to provide a public service increasingly took hold, and now dominates the administrative law at all levels.

## C The legality principle

This is the rule that any action or instrument emanating from the administration must be in keeping with the applicable law. The administrative courts, headed by the *Conseil d'Etat*, will have the task of ensuring that this principle is adhered to. In most cases the legal standards which must be complied with concern the written law. However, there are some unwritten principles which the administration must also observe.

The *Conseil d'Etat*, which will be the body which ultimately will need to decide whether this principle has been observed or not, has always shrunk from assessing administrative action in the light of the Constitution, since this is the prerogative of the the *Conseil constitutionnel*.[1] However, the *Conseil* is fully entitled to assess administrative action and instruments in the light of legislation. This term must be interpreted in its broadest sense, as encompassing not only the *lois ordinaires, lois organiques* (cf. *supra*, p. 14) and the *lois référendaires* (being laws adopted by referendum), but also the *ordonnances* issued by the Government, which have the same legal effects as *lois*. In relation to legislation, the term *légalité* also means that the administrative authorities may not issue any regulations unless a legislative instrument expressly makes provision for this.

However, there are also a number of unwritten general principles which must be observed by the administrative authorities. These are the general principles of law which are based on the relevant case law. These range from principles of political philosophy (such as the principle of equality between the sexes, and equal treatment before the public services) to principles of a technical legal nature (such as the non-retrospective nature of administrative action, the respect of acquired rights, etc).

# II The law of administrative organisation

## A General

The administrative organisation of any modern society seeks to achieve a balance between the power of central government and local government autonomy. This amounts to making a choice between centralisation and decentralisation. Centralisation means that the administrative power is exercised by a central decision-making organ, whose decisions are carried out at the local level by agents appointed by the central authorities. Decentralisation is a system which confers decision-making powers on the local authorities, which are elected by those subject to their authority. (Decentralisation must not be con-

---

1   Cf. C.E. Decision of 6/11/1936, *Coudert et Arrighi*, S 1937, III, 33.

fused with the term *déconcentration*, which is merely a way of relieving the central authorities of certain administrative functions, which are exercised at the local level by field services of the central administration).

It is generally agreed that France has now achieved an in-between position called *la décentralisation contrôlée*. Having for a long time been the very model of a centralised state, France has recently made considerable moves towards decentralising the decision-making process (unlike the UK, which appears to be moving in the opposite direction). This has particularly been the case since the adoption of the *Loi Deferre* (Law of 2/3/1982), which has fundamentally changed the relationship between the local authorities and the State. Prior to this law, no decision of the local authorities was enforceable until such time as the *Préfet* (the representative of the State) had given his approval. This was known as *la tutelle administrative* (administrative supervision), or *le contrôle a priori*. Since the *Loi Deferre*, however, the role of the State representative (now renamed *le Commissaire de la République*) has become a more passive one. He or she continues to monitor the decisions made by the local authorities, but these now become enforceable as of right (*exécutoires de plein droit*) unless the *Commissaire* brings an action for annulment against them before the local *Tribunal administratif*. Thus any supervision by the State representative is now exercised *post factum* (*le contrôle a postériori*).

## B The system of local government in France

France is divided into six tiers of administrative subdivisions, ie municipalities (*communes*), *cantons*, *arrondissements*, *départements*, regions (*les régions*) and the State. Not all these administrative subdivisions of France are *collectivités territoriales* (local authorities). Only the municipalities, the *départements* and regions qualify for that description.

This territorial distribution does not imply the existence of strict demarcation lines between the powers of the State and the local authorities. Thus not all matters of regional concern fall within the powers of the *régions*, nor is the *commune* the sole organ to make decisions on municipal matters. The administrative organisation is, however, uniform for the entire territory of the country; thus the *département* of Var will have exactly the same organs as that of Bas-Rhin. In addition, all local authorities have a binary structure, in that they each have a decision-making body (*un organe délibérant*) and an executive body (*un organe exécutif*).

## C The State administration

The constitutional authorities which were examined earlier (cf. *supra*, p. 108) are also administrative authorities in their own right, since they are responsible for providing France with its central administrative authority.

Thus the President has extensive powers of appointment as well as certain regulatory powers, which he exercises by means of *décrets délibérés en conseil des ministres*. These enable him to adopt all such measures as are necessary for the purpose of ensuring the proper functioning of the public services. The Prime Minister also has powers of appointment and of regulation, but only in those areas which are not reserved for the President.

The Ministers, for their part, exercise administrative functions by means of *arrêtés* (generally applicable decisions) as well as *instructions* and *circulaires*, which are addressed to the various administrative units which operate under the authority of the ministerial departments. Parliament has, acting in its capacity of legislature, a number of administrative responsibilities, in that it may create and abolish public services.

In addition, the central state administration sometimes requires the intervention of specialist bodies or committees, such as the *Conseil d'Etat*, which has an administrative role to play in addition to its judicial functions (cf. *supra*, p. 40).

# D The regions

### General

The 22 regions constitute a relative newcomer on the French administrative scene. Although they existed as purely administrative units as a result of a decree adopted in 1959, it was only in 1972 that they became local authorities in their own right. The main reason for their establishment was the French system of economic planning. The five-year plans which have guided the French economy since the end of World War II require for their successful implementation a successful partnership between the central administration and decentralised bodies. The *département* had increasingly come to be considered as too small an administrative entity for this purpose. Its main actors are the Regional Council (the decision-making body), the President of the Council (the regional executive), the Economic and Social Committee, and the representative of the State. Corsica and the *Départements d'outre mer* form special status regions.

### The Regional Council

The Regional Council, which is the elected decision-making body of the regions, has a general responsibility for the administration of regional affairs. These relate mainly to economic development, but also include matters of social and cultural concern. For this purpose, it has its own budget.

The Regional Council is directly elected by the inhabitants of the region by a combination of the list system and proportional representation. The number of seats will depend on the strength of its population.

### The President of the Regional Council

As a result of the *Loi Deferre*, the President of the Council replaced the regional state representative as the regional executive. In this capacity, he or she prepares the meetings of the Regional Council, implements its decisions, directs the regional public services and represents the region at law.

### The Economic and Social Committee

Consistent with the notion of participation by the *partenaires sociaux* in the decision-making process, which has been part of French public life ever since the enactment of the constitution of the Fourth Republic (cf. *supra*, p. 105), the Economic and Social Committee is a body which consists of representatives of the main economic and social groupings within the region. It advises the Regional Council, which is obliged to consult it in certain well-defined areas; in all other cases its opinion is optional.

### The State Representative

The state is represented by the *Commissaire de la République*. He is appointed by the *Conseil des ministres* and is responsible for ensuring the application of national legislation within the region.

## E The *département*

### General

The *départements*, of which there are 96, constitute the archetypal French *collectivité territoriale*. It formed the cornerstone of the administrative reorganisation which took place after the French Revolution, and has developed from a mere subdivision of the State into a local authority in its own right. It operates through the *Conseil général*, its President and the State Representative.

### The *Conseil général*

Article 23 of the *Loi Deferre* tersely states: 'The *Conseil général* shall, by means of its decisions, regulate the affairs of the *Département*'. These general responsibilities include administrative powers, mainly in relation to the essential public services and public works programmes, as well as the maintenance of the infrastructure of the *département*. For this purpose, it has its own budget.

The *Conseil* consists of representatives, each representing a *canton*, elected on the basis of the two-round voting system. They are elected for a period of six years, although the *Conseil* is partially renewed every three years.

### The President of the *Conseil général*

The *Conseil* elects its President for a period of three years. Article 31 of the *Loi Deferre* confers on him the exclusive responsibility for the administration of the *Département*. He is therefore its sole executive organ. As such, he prepares and implements the decisions of the *Conseil général*, heads the public services of the *Département*, and acts as its paymaster.

### The State Representative

Although some authors of French public law continue to label him as *le Préfet*, the official title of the representative of the state in the *Département* is now the *Commissaire de la République*. His task is to ensure that national interests, national laws and the public order are respected in the *Département*. This includes monitoring the lawfulness of *Conseil général* decision making. As has been mentioned before, this now takes the form of *a posteriori* review. If the State representative considers such a decision to be unlawful, he will notify the *Conseil* of this fact. The latter may either amend its decision accordingly or maintain its original version. In that case, the *Commissaire de la République* will attempt to have the decision annulled before the local administrative court.

## F The *arrondissements* and *cantons*

These are administrative units without any legal personality or official organs, whether appointed or elected. The only reason for their existence is to serve as an electoral division (cantons) and as an administrative subdivision for which the *Commissaire de la République* may appoint a number of assistant state representatives.

## G The municipalities (*communes*)

There are 36,400 municipalities in France. Although the intention is to match municipal representation to the size of the population, there are frequent complaints about the rural bias in the whole system. More than 33,000 municipalities – ie 89% of all *communes* – are in rural areas, which only account for 14% of the French population. Although the boundaries of a number of municipalities have been altered from time to time, little appears to have been done to redress this fundamental imbalance. The municipalities operate through their elected Council and the Mayor and his assistants.

### The *Conseil communal*

This is the municipal decision-making body. Its members are elected for a period of six years by the voters of the *commune*, on the basis of a two-round voting system conducted between lists only (municipalities of more than 3,500 inhabitants) and between a mixture of lists and individual candidates (municipalities of fewer than 3,500 inhabitants). The size of the council can vary between 9 and 69.

The *Conseil* has the general responsibility of administering the affairs of the municipality. To this end, it votes on the municipal budget, appoints the Mayor and his assistants, and supervises the manner in which they discharge their duties, and manage the municipal property. A number of special responsibilities have recently been conferred on it, in the field of, *inter alia*, town planning.

The decisions of the *Conseil* are monitored by the State Representative of the *Département* in which the municipality is situated, in the same manner as the decisions of the *Conseil général*.

**The Mayor and his assistants (*le maire et ses adjoints*)**

The Mayor is an elected official whose powers and functions differ considerably from that of his English counterpart. Assisted by his *adjoints*, he has a triple role to fulfil:

- **to act as the municipal executive**, and as such to prepare the sessions of the municipal council and implement its decisions, to head the municipal staff, etc;

- **to act as the representative of the State**: in this capacity, he acts as an officer of the *police judiciaire* and fulfils certain administrative functions, such as publishing and implementing the national laws and regulations;

- **to exercise powers which are specific to the office of Mayor**: these concern chiefly the maintenance of law and order within his territorial jurisdiction.

# III The special public bodies

## A General

Although the local authorities account for many of the public services administered in France, they cannot be expected to shoulder the entire burden of the administration. Not only are there some special needs which can only be met by bodies which have no particular geographical associations (the *établissements publics*); there are also a number of concerns for which it has been found both efficient and appropriate for the local authorities, and even other administrative units, to organise themselves on a collective basis, ie the joint boards (*les groupements de personnes publiques*).

# B The *établissements publics* (public corporations)

## General

The *établissements publics* can probably be best defined as public bodies having legal personality, other than the State or the local authorities, which enjoy administrative and financial independence and are responsible for administering a public service. The notion is very difficult to translate into English for want of comparable institutions this side of the channel. Probably the term 'public corporations' comes closest to the objects and purpose of the *établissements publics*.

The principal characteristic of the *établissements publics* are their specificity. This is why their scope for action is a good deal more limited than that of the local authorities, whose brief tends to be more general. They are therefore subject to strict *ultra vires* rules, and the administrative courts normally apply these very strictly. On the other hand, they do enjoy a good deal of autonomy, in that they have their own decision-making organs and their own financial means and property.

The *établissements publics* should not be confused with *établissements reconnus d'utilité publique*, which are legal persons governed by private law, although in certain circumstances they may be subject to public law and therefore to the jurisdiction of the administrative courts. There are essentially two types of *établissements publics:* those of an administrative nature and those which operate on a commercial and/or industrial basis.

## The administrative public corporations

These are the most unambiguously public of the *établissements publics*. They are entirely governed by public law, and, under Article 34 of the Constitution, may only be created by Parliament (although once a *loi* has established a category of *établissements publics administratifs*, individual ones may be set up by decree). They are staffed mainly by public officials and any action on their part will have the rank of *acte administratif*. They even have the power to order expropriations and impose levies. Their action is capable of being challenged before the administrative courts.

At the same time, they are decentralised institutions, in the sense that, subject to the supervision exercised by the administrative courts, they have a considerable amount of autonomy, have their own financial resources and budget, and have the rights and obligations normally associated with other legal persons. They are also specialised institutions, in that their organs may not engage in any activities other than those conferred on them by the law (or decree) which established them. Being defined primarily on the basis of this specialist activity, they represent a wide variety of individual areas: economic (Chambers of Commerce and Agricultural Chambers), educational (*ecoles normales supérieures*, universities, *lycées*, the *Ecole nationale d'administration*), financial (*Caisse des dépôts et consignations*), social assistance (the public hospitals, the National Employment Agency) scientific and artistic (the *Académies*, the National Council for Scientific Research, even the *Centre Pompidou*!) and public works (National Association of Authorised Landowners).

### The industrial and commercial public corporations

Political and social trends in the course of this century have increasingly prompted the public authorities to undertake a number of industrial and commercial activities which had hitherto been considered to be the preserve of the private sector. The *établissement public* was considered to be the best institutional form in which this initiative could be developed, albeit in an adjusted form.

This is why the industrial and commercial public corporations have a less pronounced public character than their administrative counterparts. In fact the rules which govern them are a mixture of public law and private law, giving the *établissements publics* concerned the appearance of public sector companies (although they should not be confused with the *sociétés nationales* and the *sociétés d'état*, cf. *infra*, p. 134). Rules of private law apply in their relations with the corporation staff, in that they are expected to act as a private employer; in their relations with its users, as regards their contractual relations with the latter; and in their relations with other third parties, for whom the corporation will be expected to observe the same rules as any other trader. The *établissement public* in question will, however, be subject to rules of public law as regards its structure, in that (a) it can only be created by the public authorities and its management structures are controlled by the latter, and (b) it enjoys a number of privileges which are associated with its responsibility for providing a public service (eg it may order expropriations and its creditors may not impound its assets to meet its debts).

Industrial and commercial *établissements publics* cover a wide range of activity. In broad terms, the areas covered are agriculture (the various *offices nationaux interprofessionnels* dealing with broad agricultural products such as cereals, meat and table wines), chemical industry (the potash mines corporation in Alsace), financial credit (the *Caisse centrale de réassurance*), information (the *Institut national de l'audiovisuel*), research (the *Bureau de recherche du pétrole*), transport (the Paris airports, the autonomous ports, the French national railway company) and various other specialist areas, such as tourism (the *Office du tourisme*).

## C The Joint Boards (*Groupements de Personnes Publiques*)

### General

Already towards the end of the last century, it became obvious that there were various matters which affect more than one local authority, particularly as the various conurbations began to assume vast proportions, involved several local authorities and required co-operation in such matters as public transport and traffic control. The first local authorities to set up joint boards aimed at institutionalising this form of co-operation were, inevitably, the *départements* (who did so as early as 1871), and now every form of local authority is associated with this type of grouping.

### Interregional co-operation

Although the sheer size of the regions makes it less imperative for them to associate, two forms of co-operation are laid down by law: (a) the interregional agreements (*les conventions interrégionales*) on matters of regional concern (eg the 1977 agreement concluded between three regions on the modernisation of the Midi canal) and the interregional boards (*les ententes interrégionales*) which take the form of *établissements publics* and are established to perform such tasks as are agreed by the regions involved.

### Co-operation between the *départements*

The Law of 1871 on this subject makes provision for three types of co-operation: (a) the *conventions interdépartementales* (which are similar to the regional agreements), (b) the *conférences interdépartementales* which are meetings organised between the regions to discuss topics of mutual interest, and (c) the *ententes interdépartementales*, which are *établissements publics* organised along the same lines as their regional counterparts.

### Municipal co-operation

It is at the municipal level that co-operation between local authorities is its most widespread – perhaps inevitably in view of the modest size of most *communes*. Various forms of co-operation are laid down in the existing legislation (mostly, but not exclusively, the *Code des communes*):

* The *Groupements intercommunaux sans personnalité juridique*: these are loose forms of association, and can be either organised on an *ad hoc* basis (the municipal conferences and conventions) or have a more permanent character (the *commissions syndicales*).

* The *Syndicats de communes*: these have by now assumed sizeable numbers (nearly 20,000) and can be constituted for specific objectives or in order to form a permanent multi-purpose forum for co-operation. Their establishment does not require the unanimous assent of the participating municipalities. They are administered by a permanent Committee consisting of representatives from each municipal council, and their decisions are capable of judicial review by the administrative courts.

- The *Districts*: these were set up in 1959, and take the form of *établissements publics* grouping together the municipalities or conurbations, for which they replaced the *syndicats des communes*. They are responsible for administering intermunicipal services such as housing and firefighting, those services which previously were the responsibility of the *syndicats*, and any new functions which the municipal councils or the *Conseil de district* may confer on them.

- The *Communautés urbaines*: these are *établissements publics* which administer public services in the larger conurbations. They have a wide range of responsibilities, including town and country planning, various forms of land use, transport and education.

- The *communautés de communes* and *communautés de villes*: these are two new forms of intermunicipal co-operation which were introduced in 1992, and are aimed at improving co-operation in land use and economic development.

## D The Joint Committees of different administrative bodies

Provision has also been made for co-operation between administrative bodies of various types. They were inspired by the British 'joint committees', and can assume two forms:

### The *syndicats mixtes*

These are *établissements publics* grouping together the widest possible range of public bodies, including the various intermunicipal associations described above, the chambers of commerce and industry, *the ententes interdépartementales* and various *établissements publics*. There are now approximately 550 such *syndicats* in existence.

### The *agences départementales*

These were introduced by the *Loi Deferre*, and enable both local authorities and *établissements publics* to set up *agences départementales* responsible for providing the members of these agencies with various forms of technical, legal and financial assistance.

# IV Administrative law and the private sector

However broad a range of activities is deployed by the administration, it cannot be entirely self-sufficient in a society such as that of France which operates on the basis of a mixed economy. It will need to conclude contracts with the private sector for some of its most essential needs, and some matters of mainly public concern are sometimes entrusted entirely to the private sector (subject to the necessary supervision by the public authorities). In addition, the public sector involves itself in the world of commerce and industry not only through the *établissements publics*, but also through public sector companies, which operate exactly like any private company, except for the extent to which they are supervised by the public authorities.

# A Administrative contracts

## General

In order to meet their needs, the public authorities may conclude either ordinary contracts which will be governed by the *Code civil* (cf. *supra*, p. 63), or administrative contracts, which are governed by rules of administrative law, and for which any disputes will be settled by the administrative courts. They come in a wide variety of forms: (a) the public works contracts (*marchés de travaux publics*) by which a public authority entrusts a private or public person with the performance of public works, such as the construction of a bridge; (b) the *concessions*, by which a public service is sub-contracted to a private or public person; (c) the *concession de travail public*, by which a public authority not only invites a private or public body to carry out a public work, but also allows the latter to operate it for a certain period; (d) the *offres de concours*, whereby private or public persons invite a public authority to provide the former with a certain service; (e) the *marchés de fournitures ou de services*, which are straightforward contracts purchasing furniture or certain services; and (f) the public loans (*emprunt d'Etat*), whereby public authorities borrow money from the private sector.

## Criteria for identifying administrative contracts

The fact that administrative contracts are governed by administrative law will cause some disputes as to whether specific agreements are administrative or not. It will then be the task of the relevant court – in most cases the *Tribunal des conflits* – to assess whether or not the contract is administrative on the basis of a number of criteria.

One very straightforward identifying criterion is a legislative one: where Parliament or the Government have determined the administrative nature of contracts by expressly attributing jurisdiction over any disputes arising from them to the administrative courts. This is the case, for example, with the public works contracts, contracts of employment for professional soldiers, and contracts involving the occupancy of public land.

However, there are also two fundamental criteria which have been laid down by the case law, which determine that a contract is administrative where (a) the object of the contract is to entrust the very performance of a public service to a third party[2] and (b) the contract contains a clause which takes it beyond the scope of private law. This is for example the case where a contract stipulates that only one party, the administrative authority, has the right to rescind the contract.

### The performance of administrative contracts

It is particularly on this aspect of the contract that the administrative contracts differ from those governed by the *Code civil*. The administration enjoys certain privileges which mark a departure from the equality between contracting parties which is laid down in the private law rules. The other party is protected against any disadvantage he may suffer as a result of this by a system of damages which may be awarded to him.

This privileged position manifests itself in several ways. First, the administration has the right to issue instructions to the other party as to the manner of performance of his contractual obligations. In addition, the administration may change unilaterally certain terms of the contract, it has the power to impose certain penalties (not in order to penalise the other party, but to enable the contract to be performed), and it has the right to rescind the contract if the public interest so requires (compensation being payable to the other party).

# B Public sector companies

### General

These *sociétés* are companies whose legal structure is governed by private law, but remain associated with the public sector because of their links – with varying degrees of intensity – with the administration and because of the supervision by the public authorities to which they are subject. They consist not only of companies which are wholly owned and controlled by the public sector, but also of companies in which the public sector is a shareholder (not necessarily a majority shareholder). With very rare exceptions, all these companies take the form of a *société anonyme*, ie the equivalent of an English public limited company.

### *Sociétés anonymes* which are wholly owned by the State

These companies break down into two categories: the *sociétés nationales* and the *sociétés d'Etat*. The former are companies which were taken into public ownership on the occasion of two major exercises in post-war nationalisation, ie that which took place immediately after the liberation, and that which was the result

---

2    Cf., for example, the *Conseil d'Etat* decision of 20/4/1956, *Epoux Bertin, Grands arrêts de la jurisprudence administrative*, No. 91.

of the election of a left-wing Executive and Parliament in 1982. A curious aspect of these companies is that they continue to be governed by (slightly adapted) rules of private company law before the major reforms of 1966. The *sociétés d'Etat* on the other hand are companies which were created in France's overseas dependencies by the State, and whose capital is supplied entirely by the latter.

**The mixed status companies (*sociétés d'économie mixte*)**

These are joint-stock companies in which a public person (which can be the State, local authorities or *établissements publics*), is a shareholder. The courts have consistently held that all such mixed-status companies, regardless of the size of the shareholding held by the public body, must be considered as a legal person governed by private law.[3] However, special legislation, or the Articles of Association, may lay down certain rules departing from the applicable private law. In addition, the status of the *sociétés d'économie mixte* is governed by a special Law (dated 7/7/1983).

## C Private persons associated in the provision of public services

This association can take two forms: private persons can either participate in, or actually provide the public service. As to the first, there are many private organisations – many of them with charitable status – which assist with the provision of public services, sometimes to the point of constituting disguised public bodies (this is sometimes a deliberate ploy in order to elude certain public accounting rules).

There are also private persons who actually operate a public service. This they can do either on the basis of a special *loi* or by virtue of a contract. Those created by a *loi* include the *sociétés mutualistes* which manage and dispense social security funds, and the *fédérations sportives*, ie the sports administration bodies.

# V The administration and the citizen

Apart from the opportunity for obtaining judicial review, which constitutes the subject-matter of the final section, and the commercial relationships described in the previous section, the main causes of legal relationships between the administration are administrative actions and the liability of public agents.

---

3    Cf., for example, the *Conseil d'Etat* decision of 21/7/1972, *Société Entreprise Ossude, Rec. Cons. d'Et.* p. 562.

# A Administrative action (*actes administratifs*)

## General

The concept of *actes administratifs* is a notion which is virtually impossible to translate into English – which is all the more regrettable in view of the fact that this is a concept which is fundamental to the functioning of the entire administrative system in France. To translate it by 'administrative instrument' would be inadequate, since not only does the *acte administratif* not require the form of a written document, but does not even need to consist in a positive action, since an abstention may also constitute an acte administratif. Probably the term 'administrative action' is the nearest approximation to this concept in English law.

The most distinctive feature of the *actes administratifs* is their unilateral nature. They can be defined as legal actions which emanate from the administrative authorities and which are capable of being challenged by those whose legal position they affect. They need not necessarily take the form of a written document, as they may also be issued by word of mouth. They should not be confused with enforceable decisions (*la décision exécutoire*) which is merely a particular expression of administrative action. A decision rejecting a planning application is not enforceable, but nevertheless remains an *acte administratif*.

## Types of administrative action

Unilateral administrative actions in France are remarkable by their diversity. *Express administrative actions* mostly take the form of a written document – eg a *décret* – but may also be issued orally, or even visually (eg a signal given by a policeman). *Implicit decisions* result from the silence of the administration, ie their failure to respond, which must last at least four months to qualify as an *acte administratif*. *Implicit acceptances or authorisations* are periods of silence observed by the administration in response to an application, which amounts to its acceptance. These actions are governed by individual legislative provisions.

Sometimes doubt arises as to whether a particular action will qualify as an *acte administratif*. Here, we will need to turn to the available case law for guidance. Thus it has been held that measures leading up to an *acte administratif* only have the status of information; preparatory measures such as a notice inviting applications cannot qualify as administrative action.[4] However, formal notices demanding payment (*mises en demeure*)[5] and standard documents such as model contracts or Articles of Association[6] do qualify as unilateral administrative actions.

---

4   *Conseil d'Etat* decision of 12/10/1988, Rec. 367.

5   *Conseil d'Etat* decision of 27/5/1988, Rec. 212.

6   *Conseil d'Etat* decision of 2/7/1982.

A distinction must also be drawn between actions which are internal to the administration and those which have general application. Of the former, there are, broadly speaking, three types: (a) *circulars*, which are instructions issued by Heads of Department to their staff (here, a distinction is drawn by the case law between *circulaires réglementaires* and *circulaires interprétatives*); (b) *directives*, which are more general in their application, which lay down policy guidelines for the administration, and (c) *minor internal measures* (*mesures d'ordre intérieur*) which apply merely within individual departments.

Those which have general application, on the other hand, fall within the scope of regulatory powers (meaning the power to issue *règlements*). These are the generally applicable instruments issued by the Executive on the basis of various articles of the Constitution, and which have already been dealt with, ie the *ordonnances* (orders), the *décrets* (decrees) and the *arrêtés* (decisions). There are also certain special regulatory powers which enable the Executive from time to time to encroach on certain matters normally reserved to Parliament – eg Article 47, which allows a proposed finance law to be enacted by means of *ordonnance* should Parliament fail to adopt or reject it within a time limit of 70 days of the proposal being submitted to it.

### Implementation of *actes administratifs*

Administrative actions enter into effect as soon as they have been brought to the attention of those involved (*la publicité*). This can be done either on a personal basis (*la notification*) in relation to non-regulatory actions, and by publication (*la publication*) for regulatory actions. Administrative actions are subject to the non-retroactivity principle, which means that they may not produce any effects which pre-date the date of their entry into effect.

In principle, the *actes administratifs* have indefinite application, and will only disappear by an express repeal (*abrogation*) or withdrawal (*retrait*). If repealed, the administrative action will only cease to apply for the future (*ex nunc*), whereas if a withdrawal takes place, the *acte* will be removed retrospectively.

# B The liability of the public authorities

## General

Even in the best run of administrations, mistakes will occur, and at least some of these will cause damage to other persons. The legal question will then arise as to who will be liable for any losses thus incurred. Three issues need to be examined in this context: the liability of the individual administrative official, the liability of the administration as a whole, and the nature and size of the compensation to be paid.

## The liability of the individual official

The individual official may incur liability both towards the citizen and towards the administration. (It should be made clear from the outset that we are dealing here only with the mistakes committed in the course of the official's employment; for any mistakes committed 'off duty' the official will be subject to the ordinary rules of private law tort liability.) As regards the former, a distinction needs to be made between the *faute de service* and the *faute personnelle*.

The former are mistakes which, however inexcusable, can nevertheless be occasionally committed by any administrator – thus, for example, the granting of a planning of application which should, on the basis of the information available to the administrator, have been refused. They result, in the delicious phrase of one leading author on public law, from *la mauvaise habitude de l'administration*.[7] These will be tried before the administrative courts, applying the rules of public sector liability which are different from those of the ordinary tort liability found in Articles 1382 *et seq* of the *Code civil*.

*Fautes personnelles*, on the other hand, are those which, although committed by the official in the pursuance of his duties, show a degree of seriousness which somehow takes the mistake beyond the scope of the official's duties – for example, a policeman who commits an assault on a colleague whilst on duty. These will be subject to the ordinary rules of the private law of torts, and will be judged by the ordinary courts. Obviously, the case law has played an important part in developing the criteria aimed at drawing the distinction between these two types of liability.

As regards the individual official's liability towards the administration, the rule is that this can only be incurred through the official's *faute personnelle*; since the *faute de service* is an error committed on behalf of the administration, the latter cannot claim reparation from itself. However, the situation may occur whereby a singly tortious event involves both a *faute de service* and a *faute personnelle*. In such cases, two possibilities arise. The injured party may institute an action against the official responsible, in which case the latter will be able to recover from the administration that part of the damages awarded for *faute de service*; or the injured party may claim against the administration, in which case the latter may recover from the official that part of the compensation awarded which was attributable to the *faute personnelle*.

## The liability of the administration

The term 'administration' here must be understood as meaning any administrative unit, be it the State itself or even the smallest local authority. The adminis-

---

7    Trotabas, L. and Isoart, P., *Droit public et administratif* (1982, LGDJ) p. 297.

tration can be held liable, not only for damage caused to third parties as a result of a fault, but also on grounds of no-fault liability.

As far as the liability based on fault is concerned, the only fault that concerns us here is the *faute de service*, since the personality of the individual official or officials is of no relevance. This *faute de service* may result either from an infringement of the lawfulness requirement (*violation de la légalité*) – such as a failure to respect a substantial formality – or from a material fact (*fait matériel*), such as negligence, error, delay, or failure to act.

No-fault liability may also be incurred by the administration. Here, liability is based on the risk which is inherent in certain activities (somewhat akin to the basis for liability identified by the House of Lords in *Rylands v Fletcher* (1868)[8]). The administrative courts first started to apply this doctrine in relation to public works, but subsequently extended it to the manipulation of dangerous objects (eg, where a third party is injured on the occasion of a police operation involving the use of firearms[9]), the existence of dangerous activities (such as the damage resulting from the provisional discharge of a mental patient[10]) or the existence of a dangerous situation (eg the case of a pregnant teacher exposed to the risk of infection by German measles[11]).

### The nature and extent of the compensation

In principle, the judgment awarding compensation must endeavour to restore the loss incurred (*la remise en état*). However, this will invariably take the form of a cash payment, specific performance being impossible to enforce against the administration since no administrative court may issue injunctions against the administration.

As regards the amount at which the compensation payable is assessed, a distinction must be drawn between the material damage and the moral damage caused. As regards the former, the sum awarded will essentially consist of two elements: (a) the principal and related damage (eg the damage caused to a car and the fact of being deprived of its use respectively), and (b) the additional charges and expenses (such as court costs, expert assessments, etc). As regards the moral damage caused (eg the long-term shock effect caused by a particularly traumatic accident): here, the *Conseil d'Etat* used to be extremely reluctant to take this into account, unlike the *Cour de cassation;* however, in recent years the administrative courts have been increasingly inclined to award compensation for *le préjudice moral*.

---

8   (1868) LR3 HL 330.
9   Decision of the *Conseil d'Etat* of 24/6/1949, Rec. 347.
10  Decision of the *Conseil d'Etat* of 13/7/1967, Rec. 341.
11  Decision of the *Conseil d'Etat* of 6/11/1968, AJDA 1969, p. 117.

# VI Judicial review of administrative action

## A General

It has already been explained (cf. *supra*, p. 39) that the administration is subject to a separate system of judicial treatment from that which deals with disputes between private parties. Both the structure and the jurisdiction of the administrative courts have been dealt with at length in Chapter 2 (*supra*, p. 39), whereas the procedure before them is explained in Chapter 9 (*infra*, p. 184). What we are concerned with here are the grounds on which judicial action may be taken against the public authorities before the administrative courts. These are known collectively in French law under the term *le contentieux administratif*.

## B Annulment proceedings for *ultra vires* action (*contentieux de l'annulation pour excès de pouvoir*)

What is particularly original about this procedure is that it is brought, not against a person, but against an administrative action. The citizen may apply for its annulment, and if his or her action succeeds, the *acte administratif* will be deemed never to have existed, and its legal effects will be cancelled *erga omnes* (as far as every citizen is concerned).

In order to succeed, the action will need to overcome two hurdles. The first concerns the *admissibility* of the action: here, all the conditions stipulated must be met by the action. The second concerns the *substance* of the claim, for which only one of the substantive grounds (*les ouvertures*) must be satisfied.

### The admissibility criteria (*conditions de recevabilité*)

Four criteria must all be met for the action to be admissible:

- **The *acte administratif* must be unilateral and emanate from a French administrative authority**. Since the action must be unilateral, it is not possible to bring annulment proceedings against administrative contracts. Any type of unilateral action may be challenged, be it express or implicit, individual or general. The action must also emanate from a French administrative authority – which means that neither *lois* nor court decisions will be capable of administrative review; this authority must also be a French authority.

- **The applicant must be capable of bringing court proceedings, and have an interest in challenging the administrative action**. This means not only that the applicant must have the civil status to bring court actions (eg that he or she must have attained the age of majority). It also requires that the challenged action not only has legal implications for the applicant, but also that his or her interests have thereby been affected.

- **The action for annulment must be the only possible remedy.** The action for annulment has traditionally been viewed as an exceptional procedure, which is why it may only be brought if no alternative remedy exists in order to obtain satisfaction. Thus a taxpayer cannot bring annulment proceedings against a decision made against him or her, since there is another remedy open to him, which is the *action en décharge de l'impôt*. The administrative courts have, however, recently displayed signs of greater flexibility in relation to this requirement.

- **The applicant must comply with all the relevant time limits and formal requirements.** The time-limit for bringing the action is two months as from the date on which they were brought to the attention of those concerned (*la publication* or *la notification*, cf. *supra* p. 137). For some administrative actions, such as election proceedings, the time limit is even shorter. As to the application itself, this must contain a number of particulars, such as the facts, the reasons why the action has been brought, as well as the names and addresses of the parties involved. It must be written in French and accompanied by the appropriate substantiating documents (*les pièces justificatives*).

### The substantive grounds (*les ouvertures*)

Once the first hurdle, that of admissibility, has been cleared, the administrative court will be able to assess the substance of the action. To this end, the court will need to establish whether any of the five substantive grounds (*ouvertures*) set out below have been met. However, in so doing the court may only assess the lawfulness of the action. It may make no judgment on whether the decision was the right one in policy terms (*l'opportunité*).

- **Lack of powers (*incompétence*).** Any administrative action must have an author; if the author exceeded his or her powers in issuing an *acte administratif*, this will be a ground for judicial review. Sometimes, however, the administrative court will consider that it is in the public interest for such actions to be validated. For example, if a marriage has been celebrated before a local councillor to whom the power to do so had been improperly delegated, the court will validate the marriage nonetheless because there was an *apparence de compétence* (appearance that the correct authority was in charge).

- **Statutory infringement (*violation de la loi*).** This is a condition which seeks to establish whether the subject matter of the *acte administratif* has not infringed any legislative provision. The term 'legislation' has always been interpreted very broadly by the administrative courts, as embracing any general and binding rule. Therefore mot only the Constitution and the laws adopted by Parliament must be observed by the administrative action, but also generally applicable regulations and even general principles of law.

- **Failure to observe the formal requirements** (*vice de forme*). The grounds for annulment here consist in an omission of all or some formalities imposed by law or regulation. Here, only essential formalities will count as invalidating factors.

- **Misuse of power** (*détournement de pouvoir*). This is a ground which concerns what the French call *la morale administrative*, ie the ethical standards which must be observed by the administration. This issue arises where the administration has observed the letter of the law when adopting an *acte administratif*, but has used its powers to do so for a different purpose from that for which these powers had been conferred on it. Thus where a mayor uses his powers to regulate the organisation of dances in such way that these could only take place in a dance hall owned by him, he would be guilty of misuse of power.

- **Lack of adequate grounds for adopting the administrative action** (*inexistence de motifs*). The grounds in question must be understood as meaning the concrete situation which gave rise to the action. For example, where a person has his or her application for planning permission refused on the grounds that his or her building would spoil an area of scenic beauty; if no such area existed, the refusal to issue the planning application would be capable of annulment on grounds of *inexistence de motifs*.

## C The unrestricted action (*contentieux de pleine juridiction*)

This is an action for which the court will have more extensive powers, and which may be brought on wider grounds, than is the case with annulment proceedings. The following actions are possible under this procedure:

- Actions for the cancellation of administrative contracts (*contentieux des contrats administratifs*);

- Actions in tort liability against the administration (*contentieux de la responsabilité*) cf. *supra*, p. 138;

- Actions for the recovery of fiscal debts by the State, local authorities and other public authorities (*contentieux des dettes de l'Etat et des collectivités publiques*);

- Actions challenging electoral proceedings (*contentieux des élections*);

- Actions to change a decision (*contentieux de réformation d'une décision*).

Unlike the *ultra vires* proceedings, the unrestricted procedure has no limit on the grounds on which an action is brought, and the admissibility criteria are much less strict. In addition, the effect of the decision made under the *contentieux de pleine juridiction* is limited to the parties involved in the dispute, whereas the effects of an *ultra vires* action apply *erga omnes*.

## D Actions in interpretation (*le contentieux de l'interprétation*)

Under this procedure, the administrative courts can be requested to clarify the scope and meaning of an administrative action. The role of the court in this case is therefore to act as a legal adviser. The most frequent circumstances in which this procedure is used is where for some reason a civil court needs to interpret an *acte administratif*. Proceedings before this civil court will then be stayed whilst the administrative court deals with the matter. This is known as a *question préjudicielle* (preliminary ruling).

## E Other proceedings before the administrative courts

The administrative courts may also hear emergency actions (*la procédure d'urgence* – for example where a public building is being unlawfully occupied); be required to assess the lawfulness of administrative actions (where a plea of illegality relating to an *acte administratif* has been raised before an ordinary court); and even act as an administrative criminal court, for minor offences committed against the public highway (*la grande voirie*) or the public domain, such as the removal of materials, and in certain financial and disciplinary matters.

# 8    Criminal law

## I General introduction

Like its English law counterpart, the criminal law in France seeks to penalise those actions and omissions which are deemed to be so unacceptable even in a free society as to threaten the very foundations of the social order if no corrective action is undertaken. Although in recent years there has been a trend away from confining such corrective action to the mere imposition of punitive sentences and towards a combination of preventative action and rehabilitating the perpetrators of crime, the notion of penalising criminal offences remains central to the French *droit pénal*.

Widespread ignorance and popular misconceptions – eg the notion that in France anyone accused of a crime is deemed to be guilty until proved innocent – have tended to exaggerate the differences between the British system of criminal justice and its French equivalent. Yet it must be admitted that, even though the practical effects of the two systems do not reveal any spectacular differences, there can be considerable disparities between some of the underlying principles, as well as a large number of individual substantive and procedural rules, applied in the criminal courts on either side of the Channel. Bearing this fact in mind, it is possible to identify below a number of general characteristics of the French system of criminal law and procedure.

### Law based on codes

Like the other major areas of the French legal system, the criminal law has been the subject matter of large-scale codification. The first such codes, ie the 1810 *Code pénal*, which governs the substantive criminal law, and the 1808 Code de *procédure pénale*, which lays down the criminal procedure (and which had already been replaced once before, in 1975) have recently been comprehensively overhauled and replaced by codes which were introduced by four Laws of 22/7/1992 (entering into effect on 1/3/1994). Although the two new codes have retained the text of many of the old provisions, these have been placed in a new, more systematic order, and follow a numbering system which is infinitely more flexible than their predecessors. Instead of simply numbering the articles in a successive sequence, the modern system of 'recognition numbering' is used – thus enabling a provision immediately to be placed in the context of a certain area of the law. (Thus, Article 225, dealing with various forms of assault on the persons, can be immediately located under Book II, Chapter 2, Section 5). This reform also provided a welcome opportunity for consolidating the piecemeal changes which had been made in the original codes since their adoption.

## Close correlation between the substantive and the procedural law

The English system bears all the hallmarks of a system which has gradually evolved over the years, and therefore lacks a systematic correlation between the substantive and procedural rules. The fact that the two original French Codes were introduced virtually simultaneously enabled them to constitute a rational and a closely integrated system. Thus there are three types of offence which correspond to three types of court and court procedures. As a result, the French criminal law is much more accessible than its English counterpart.

## Correlation between the criminal law and other legal areas

The French criminal law to a certain extent reinforces the other areas of the law by penalising the failure to comply with the latter. Thus the civil law is reinforced by providing that, in certain conditions, failure to comply with the rules on personal property may constitute theft. In addition, there is close relationship between the criminal law and the civil law aspects of offences committed, in the shape of the ability of the victim to add civil proceedings to the criminal action (the so-called *partie civile*, cf. *infra* p. 172).

## *Nullum crimen sine lege*

Here, the underlying philosophy is the same as in English law. No crime can exist, and no punishment inflicted, unless it has a direct basis in the statute law. It protects the French general public against any unwarranted extension of the scope of the criminal law by the judiciary, and against any retrospective application of the law. This rule has, however, given rise to the occasional difficulty in view of the many constitutional changes which have taken place in France since the original codes were enacted. Article 34 of the present Constitution of the Fifth Republic lays down that Parliament may legislate only for the two more serious types of offence, *crimes* and *délits*. As regards the *contraventions*, which constitute the least serious of infringements, it is the Government which, under Article 37 of the Constitution, legislates by means of *règlements* (regulations).

## Changing trends in interpretation

As has been the case in the French civil law, the provisions of the Criminal Codes have been sufficiently flexible to be able to accommodate far-reaching changes in the approach by the French courts towards criminal behaviour, which has manifested itself in changing trends in legislative interpretation. This approach has evolved from a classical theory, which was based almost entirely on the notion of punishment, to the current notion of *la défence sociale*, for which the author Marc Ancel must take a great deal of credit. This new approach considers the criminal action in the light of the concrete and individual circumstances in which it was committed, rather than on the basis of abstract notions of law and order.

### Distinction between the 'general' and the 'special' criminal law

The *Code pénal* is divided into two parts: a general part, contained in Book I of the new Code, whose rules apply to all offences regardless of their nature or implications, and a specific part, forming the subject-matter of Books II to V of the new Code, in which the individual offences are regulated in great detail.

# II The classification of criminal offences

## A The basic distinction

### General

The basic distinction which underpins the entire system of criminal law is stated in Article 111-1 of the new Code, which disposes that, in terms of their seriousness, offences are divided into *crimes* (serious crimes), *délits* (intermediate offences) and *contraventions* (minor infringements). This classification has a great deal of merit from the point of view of the interests which it seeks to serve, but has been subjected to a large measure of criticism.

### The interests served

There are both substantive and procedural interests which are served by this classification. In substantive terms, the distinction is important from the point of view of attempted offences and the complicity in criminal activity, since these forms of criminal liability are excluded from *contraventions*. In addition, the penalty imposed will be different for each of these categories – not only the actual severity of the punishment, but also the penalty imposed on re-offenders, the conditions in which suspended sentences can be imposed, the criteria for serving one's sentence under the system of 'semi-freedom' (*semi-indépendance*), etc.

As to the procedural interests, the distinction is relevant not only from the point of view of establishing which court shall have jurisdiction, but also the manner in which the offence will be investigated, the extent to which an accused can be remanded in custody, the appeals which can be instituted against sentences, the time limit for bringing criminal proceedings, etc.

## The criticism

The classification referred to has been subjected to fierce criticism for a number of years now, both in terms of the principle of the distinction and from the practical point of view of their application. As to the former, it is argued that the classification is hopelessly outdated, based as it is on an old distinction which goes back to a time well before the French Revolution, when the author of major crimes was considered to be irredeemable. Present-day notions of criminology take a less forbidding view, which means that the distinction between *crimes* and *délits* has lost a great deal of its purpose. The practical difficulties arise mainly where the effect of mitigating or aggravating circumstances convert an offence from one category to another. Many commentators consider it a mistake not to have taken advantage of the introduction of a new Code in order to apply a new classification.

# B Political offences

Another major distinction made is between 'ordinary' and 'political' offences. Generally speaking, political offences tend to be dealt with less severely on the grounds that their authors display fewer antisocial tendencies than the 'ordinary' offender.

## Types of political offence

The new Code makes provision for three categories: (a) offences against the nation, the state and the public peace (Articles 410-1 *et seq*); (b) the 'mixed' offences, which have been committed with a political objective but infringe private interests (eg the murder of a Head of State); (c) 'related' political offences, ie those which are committed on the occasion of a political event (eg riots during a political demonstration).

## Implications of political offences

Political offences have particular implications both in terms of the penalty imposed and at the procedural level. The penalties imposed are different from those inflicted on the 'ordinary' offenders, but only at the level of the *crimes*. In other words, there are no specific penalties at the level of the *délits*. In addition, the penalties imposed do not have the same consequences as ordinary offences (eg they do not cancel a previously incurred suspended sentence or cannot give rise to the extradition of its author).

At the procedural level, the differences are less stark than they used to be. Since the abolition of the *Cour de sûreté de l'Etat*, political offences fall within the jurisdiction of the ordinary courts. However, certain differences remain in the procedure followed before these courts, in particular where the offence concerned is classified as a 'terrorist' infringement.

# III  The essential elements of a criminal offence

## A  General

It has already been mentioned that there are three types of criminal offence under French law, *crimes*, *délits* and *contraventions*. The general term which covers all three categories is *infraction* (which in this chapter will be invariably translated as 'offence'). An *infraction* could be defined as any positive or negative action whose perpetrator will be subjected to corrective measures – in the form of either a penalty or a safety measure. For any action to qualify as an offence under this definition, it must meet two sets of criteria: (a) the four *general* conditions which must be met by any offence, ie a statutory basis, a substantive element, a moral factor and the injustice criterion, and (b) the specific conditions which every particular type of offence must satisfy. We will deal here with the general conditions only; the specific elements will emerge from the discussion of the 'special' criminal law (*infra*, p. 160).

## B  Statutory basis

As has been noted earlier, the French criminal law is based on the principle of *nullum crimen sine lege*. Two issues arise from this element: how is the applicable legislation interpreted, and what happens where conflicts arise between statutes in time.

### Interpreting criminal legislation

The French criminal courts are faced with a problem not encountered by their civil law counterparts. On the one hand, they may not refuse to give a judgment in a case brought before them on the grounds that there is a gap in the applicable law. On the other hand, they are bound by the principle that criminal legislation is to be interpreted strictly.[1] Therefore the criminal courts may not be as inventive or 'creative' as the civil courts, and under no circumstances may they decide cases by analogy (at least if this is to the detriment of the accused).

However, the fact that interpretation is strict does not necessarily imply a *literal* interpretation. Obviously, where the text of the provision is clear, the court may not depart from it. The criminal courts are, however, given a certain degree of discretion where the law is less than clear. Imperfections of legislative drafting sometimes make for unclear and even contradictory statutes. In such cases, the French courts may allow the spirit of the law to prevail over the letter. Other circumstances may also serve to detract from the clarity of the law. This is the case, for example, where situations have arisen which are not covered by the

---

1    Article 114-4 of the *Code pénal*.

relevant statute because of scientific and technical progress made since its enactment (eg interference with a computer database belonging to someone else). In such cases, the courts may apply legislation by analogy if this works to the benefit of the accused.

### Conflicts of legislation in time

On the one hand, criminal law statutes apply to all actions committed after its entry into effect; on the other hand, they may not apply to actions which were committed, and on which a final judgment has been made, before their entry into force.[2] However, this leaves a grey area in the shape of actions committed under a certain statute, but which had not yet received a final judgment at the time when that statute was replaced or repealed. Here, a distinction is made between substantive statutes and procedural statutes.

- **Substantive statutes**. As regards substantive law, the non-retroactivity rule will mean that, in principle, the new statute cannot apply to actions on which no final decision has yet been made. However, this rule will not apply if the new legislation is less restrictive than the old. This has given rise to the rule of *l'application de la loi la plus douce* (the least severe law shall apply). This principle in turn admits certain exceptions.

- **Procedural statutes**. As regards procedural criminal law statutes, on the other hand, the rule is invariably that the new statute shall apply as from the moment of its entry into force. This rule is justified by the general assumption that new rules of procedure have the inevitable effect of improving the administration of justice, and that they can have no influence on the conduct of the accused.

## C The substantive element

No-one can be penalised for merely entertaining the thought of committing an offence. This thought must acquire the concrete expression of an action, words or even attitudes if it is to be punishable. Here, a distinction must be made between *completed* and *attempted* offences.

### Completed offences

In the case of offences of commission, three elements must be present: the physical action which constitutes the action of commission described by the law; the result of this action, and a causal link between the two. However, the criteria are a good deal less clear-cut in the case of offences of omission, which has resulted in a number of unsatisfactory court decisions on this issue.

---

2    Article 112-1 of the *Code pénal*.

### Attempted offences

These occur where, for whatever reason, an offence has already gone beyond the stage of merely being a thought in the perpetrator's mind, but is interrupted before it can be completed. Although the object of the exercise was not achieved, considerations of public policy require action to be taken in such cases. Two issues arise here: what stage needs to be reached before an attempted offence becomes punishable, and what are the penalties which are applied to them?

The answer to the first question is supplied by Article 121-5 of the new Code, which states that 'an attempt shall have been made where its execution has already commenced but was only suspended or failed to achieve the desired effect through circumstances beyond the control of the perpetrator'. The notion of 'commencement of execution' has been interpreted very broadly by the courts. Thus, for example, attempted theft was inferred by the *Cour de cassation* from the fact of following a cashier on his usual rounds.[3] As to the other element, that of the actual commission of the crime being frustrated through circumstances alien to the would-be perpetrator, this has generally been interpreted as a requirement that there be a failure on the part of the would-be perpetrator to refrain voluntarily from committing the crime. This means that if this failure has its origin in an internal cause from the point of view of the perpetrator, the latter cannot be charged with an attempted offence, regardless of the motive – be it fear, remorse, pity, etc – which inspired it. However, any external element, such as resistance on the part of the victim, the arrival of witnesses or the police, etc, which caused this failure will remove the voluntary element from the would-be perpetrator, and therefore render him criminally liable.

On the second issue, that of the penalty applicable to attempted criminality, the new Code maintains the system of the original *Code pénal* in insisting that the perpetrator of an attempted offence must undergo the punishment as if the offence had actually been completed. However, this only applies where attempted offences are actually held to be punishable. In this regard the following rule is laid down in Article 121-4 of the new Code: (a) if the attempted offence is a *crime*, it will be punishable in all circumstances; (b) if it is a *délit*, it will only be punishable where a specific provision so disposes, and (c) *contraventions* can never be the subject matter of a punishable attempted offence.

## D The moral element

Unlike the substantive criterion, which is objective, the moral element represents a subjective criterion which must be met by the action if it is to qualify as an offence. In committing the punishable action, the perpetrator must also have

---

3    Decision of 29/12/1970, *JCP* 1971, 16770.

committed a fault (*une faute*). He must therefore have had a *mens rea* (criminal intent), which must be interpreted in a very broad sense, since criminal action can be the result not only of intended criminality, but also be negligent behaviour. a certain intellectual ability to appreciate that one's behaviour is unlawful. However, before judging whether a person has committed a fault, it must also be examined whether he or she had sufficient intellectual powers of appreciating that the action he or she was committing was unlawful, ie whether he or she is *blameworthy* (*imputable*).

### The element of blameworthiness (*l'imputabilité*)

For this element to be present, French law requires two factors: the perpetrator must be fully aware of his or her actions and he or she must have acted voluntarily.

Two categories of persons are in principle not deemed to be fully aware of their actions, ie minors and the mentally disturbed. As to the former, a distinction must be made between those under 13 years of age (who cannot in any way be held criminally liable) and those between 13 and 18 (for whom there is only a rebuttable assumption of blamelessness). The second category, that of the mentally disturbed, is fraught with more onerous legal difficulties. Cases of complete loss of mental control can be established by expert medical opinion, and will discharge the perpetrator of the criminal action from any liability. Less straightforward, however, are the cases of 'partial mental disturbance' (*aliénation mentale partielle*). Article 122-1 of the new Code provides that perpetrators thus afflicted are in principle punishable, but that the courts must take account of their mental condition when fixing their sentence.

As to the requirement that the person in question must have acted voluntarily, Article 122-2 states that those who were compelled to act by an irresistible force cannot be punished. This force can be either physical or moral. Physical force is that which deprives a person of his or her will by influencing his or her body in a particular way (eg a car which is pushed onto the kerb by another car and thereby kills or injures a person). Moral force, on the other hand, is moral influence, exercised by a third party in the form of threats, provocation or suggestion, which deprives the perpetrator of his or her free will.

### The fault

Under Article 121-3 of the new Code there are two types of fault: faults of intention and faults of omission. A fault of intention requires a combination of three factors, ie (a) the will to perform an action which achieves the criminal result: thus in the case of murder, the perpetrator must have willed the action which resulted in the death of the victim, such as the pulling of the trigger of a gun; (b) the will to achieve the criminal result: in the case of murder, this criterion would require the perpetrator to have anticipated and desired the death of his victim;

and (c) the will to accomplish (a) and (b) in the full knowledge that in so doing, the perpetrator is breaking the law; however, here the burden of proof on the part of the prosecuting authorities is lightened considerably by the general principle that ignorance of the law is no defence (*nul n'est censé ignorer la loi*). Only very exceptionally will the courts accept a departure from this principle (eg Article 122-3 of the new Code).

Faults of omission, ie criminal negligence, used to be regarded as a less important form of criminal activity, but has gained in significance because of the growth of industrialisation and mechanisation as can be seen from the thousands of deaths recorded each year through motor accidents. There are three types of criminal negligence: (a) conscious negligence: here, the perpetrator willed an action and anticipated its result, but did not desire the latter, eg where a person consciously fails to stop at traffic lights and in so doing injures someone; (b) unconscious negligence: this is the case where the perpetrator sets out to perform a certain action, but acts in a manner different from the one intended and thus causes damage to someone else (eg a doctor who prescribes the wrong kind of medicine); and (c) failure to observe a *règlement de police* where the latter results in manslaughter or injury.

# E The element of injustice

### General

This is essentially a negative factor, which consists in the absence of any circumstances justifying the action which, without this justification, would constitute an offence. There are three such justifying circumstances: instruction by law or by legitimate authority; legitimate self-defence and necessity. The consent of the victim is not a justifying circumstance *per se*, but may be admitted in exceptional circumstances.

### Instruction by law or by a legitimate authority

No-one can be prosecuted for the commission of any action which was prescribed or authorised by legislation, or which was ordered by a legitimate authority, unless, in the latter case, the action in question is obviously unlawful.[4]

There are circumstances in which legislation prescribes or authorises actions which otherwise would constitute an offence. Thus an infringement of the principle of professional confidentiality will not be punishable where the law requires or authorises the disclosure of the secret in question. As regards actions ordered by a legitimate authority, it is necessary not only for the authority in

---

4   Article 122-4 of the new Code.

question to have the power to order enforcement of the law; the authority in question must also have acted within its powers, and there must exist a link of subordination with the person to whom the order was issued. This rule can give rise to considerable difficulties where the offence was committed on the instructions of a legitimate authority, but in violation of the law.

## Legitimate self-defence

No person can be penalised for having committed an action necessitated by the requirements of legitimate self-defence, unless the means of self-defence are grossly disproportionate to the threat to which the person was exposed.[5] Both the aggression and the defensive action must meet a number of criteria in order to be acceptable as a justifying factor.

The act of aggression normally emanates from a person (but could also emanate from an animal) and must be directed against the person who defended himself. The danger presented by the aggression will mostly be physical in character, but may also in certain conditions be of a moral nature or – more controversially – involve the property of the person in question. It must also be unjust, in the sense that any aggression ordered by law or by a legitimate authority cannot give rise to a plea of self-defence; and it must be present and immediate, since any threat of future aggression will enable the victim thereof to seek the assistance of the public authorities.

The defensive action must be (a) necessary, in the sense that there was an absence of means of escape enabling the victim to alert the authorities; (b) measured, which is generally held to mean that it must be proportionate to the seriousness of the assault or of the threat; and (c) intentional, since the notion of self-defence is inconsistent with negligence.

- **Necessity**. Circumstances can arise whereby a person considers it necessary to commit an offence in order to avoid a danger threatening him or a third party – eg the stealing of water in order to extinguish a fire. Whereas the 1810 Code was extremely ambiguous on this subject, Article 122-7 of the new Code now specifically admits this circumstance as a defence against criminal prosecution. The requirements which the state of necessity must satisfy in order to excuse crime are similar to those relating to self-defence, in that the danger threatening the perpetrator must threaten him or her or a third party (or even, in some circumstances, a thing) and the act committed must be necessary and proportionate to the danger threatening its author. However, the civil liability to which the action in question may give rise will be more onerous for the author of an act of necessity than it is for a person acting in self-defence.

---

5    Article 122-5 of the new Code.

- **The consent of the victim.** In spite of the old Roman law rule *volenti non fit injuria*, the consent of the victim is not in principle allowed as a defence against crime in French law. However, the harshness of this rule is sometimes mitigated in certain circumstances, ie where the victims' consent removes one of the elements which are necessary for an action to constitute an offence, where the victim failed to complain about an offence for which a complaint is necessary in order to be able to prosecute (eg criminal libel), and, in certain circumstances, where the victim is a medical patient who consented to the treatment given.

# IV Offences involving more than one person

## A Complicity

Where offences are committed by several persons, a distinction is made between those directly involved, ie the author or the co-authors – and those involved indirectly, ie accomplices.

### Who is an accomplice?

Three conditions must be fulfilled for a person to be prosecuted as an accomplice: a legal requirement, a substantive element and a moral factor. The legal requirement is that the participation of the accomplice can be linked to a principal action which is not only punishable – regardless of whether the principal author has actually been penalised for it or not – but also constitutes a *crime* or a *délit*. Therefore no-one can ever be accused of complicity in a *contravention*. The material criteria are stated in Article 121-7 of the new Code, under which the punishable material acts of complicity are aid or assistance, provocation, or the issuing of instructions. The moral requirement is that, by his actions in which he participated in the offence, the accomplice actually intended to take part in the offence committed.

### How is complicity penalised?

Unlike the old Code, which laid down that the accomplice was to undergo the same penalty as the perpetrator of the offence, Article 121-6 of the new Code provides that the accomplice shall be punished as if he or she had been the author of the offence committed. This means that, even if in principle the offence attracts the same penalties for the author and for the accomplice, the court is not obliged to impose the same penalty, since the accomplice could have certain attributes which the author does not have (and *vice versa*).

## B Liability incurred for third parties

Fundamentally, French criminal law operates on the principle of *individual liability*, which means that the author of the offence, and only him or her, may be prosecuted and penalised. However, circumstances may arise whereby a person, without having physically taken part in the offence, facilitated its commission by perpetrating an error (fault). This is why in certain conditions, the person operating a business may be held liable for the financial implications of an offence committed by one of his employees. For example, Article L 21(2) of the Road Traffic Regulation Code provides that, where the driver of a vehicle which has caused an accident was acting as an agent, his or her principle may be required to pay both the fine and the court costs.

## C  Liability of legal persons

In principle, the criminal law only concerns physical persons, and until 1992 the criminal liability of legal persons (businesses and associations) was not recognised by law. However, with the recent proliferation of organisations to which legal personality has been attributed, the new Code has to a limited extent acknowledged that the latter may sometimes be punishable. Article 121 provides that they may be liable for offences for which their liability has been expressly laid down by law and which were committed on behalf of the legal person by its organs or representatives. This applies to all legal persons except for the State.

# V  Criminal sanctions

## A  General

The most traditional of criminal sanctions is the penalty or punishment, which has the objective of atonement, rehabilitation, compensation and deterrence, and normally takes the form of a loss of freedom, pecuniary loss or the loss of certain rights (the death penalty having been abolished in 1981). However, towards the end of the 19th century, another sanction began to see the light of day, ie the safety measure, which merely has the object of preventing (further) crime, and can take the form of internment of the mentally disturbed, disintoxication of alcoholics, or a prohibition on residence in a particular area. However, the punishment remains the principal form which criminal sanctions take. The French system provides for a flexible system of penalties. The general principle is laid down in Article 132-24 of the new Code, which requires the courts to take account not only of the circumstances of the offence and the personality of its author, but also, when imposing fines, to consider the offender's resources and expenses.

## B  Penalties applied to single offences

The flexibility referred to above gives the court scope for both reducing and increasing the penalty officially laid down for an offence.

### Reducing the penalty

The penalty may be reduced by the courts on their own initiative, or by legislation. As to the first, the *Code pénal* lays down two types of penalty: those which have a maximum but no minimum, and those which have both. Obviously where there is no minimum provided, the court can reduce the penalty right down to the lowest conceivable level (although the Code also provides that in the case of offences punishable by life imprisonment, the court may not impose any sentence which is less than two years). The penalty may also be automatically reduced by virtue of certain legislative provisions. Thus, for example, Article 224-1 of the new Code provides that the author of a kidnapping offence will have his or her sentence reduced if he or she voluntarily releases the victim before the fifth day of the kidnapping has expired. Indeed, the relevant legislation may exempt the author or accomplice of a crime from any penalty whatsoever if he reports the author or co-author of the offence.

### Increasing the penalty

The courts have no power to increase the penalty beyond the maximum laid down on their own initiative; they may only do so on the basis of specific legislation. There are both *general* reasons why the penalty may be increased, such as re-offending behaviour, and *special* aggravating circumstances which are related to a specific offence, such as the various reasons why Article 311-4 of the new Code provides that the penalty for theft may be increased.

## C Penalties for multiple offences

In principle, each offence committed will attract its own penalty, and the punishment administered in the case of multiple offences will simply amount to an accumulation of the penalties incurred for each separate offence. However, there are two circumstances in which this rule will not be applied: where there is a real concurrence between the multiple offences, and where the author reoffends.

### Real concurrence between offences

Here, we are dealing with various offences which are not separated from each other by a definitive sentence. Because the offender did not have the warning as to his or her future conduct which is deemed to be one of the results of a sentence, he or she cannot be subjected to the aggravating circumstances of the reoffender. The court can opt for one of the following: it may (a) apply a cumulative penalty, (b) apply the highest punishment, or (c) apply the punishment for the most serious offence.

## The author re-offends

As has been mentioned before, the fact of committing one or more subsequent offences of the same nature as that for which a sentence has been imposed constitutes an aggravating circumstance. The effect of this circumstance is to increase the maximum sentence which may be imposed on the author. However, since the courts are generally loath to apply maximum sentences for a first offence, reoffenders in most cases receive a sentence which is still within the maximum of the penalty laid down for the first offence. This circumstance gives rise to special requirements of evidence, since the case file must contain details of the previous conviction or convictions incurred.

# D Deferral of sentences

Present-day criminal policy holds that at times, society is better served by deferring a penalty than actually carrying it out. This can be done in two ways: by imposing a suspended sentence and by granting a conditional release.

## Suspended sentence

This confers a conditional dispensation from carrying out the sentence either wholly or in part, and is granted by the court which imposed the sentence. They may be either unconditional or have certain conditions attached to them.

Unconditional suspensions have the object of deterring the author of the offence from reoffending and assume that the fact of being sentenced will constitute an adequate warning for the latter, whilst subjecting this favourable treatment to his or her good conduct in the future. However, it is not granted to every person: only those having had no prison sentence imposed on them during the previous five years will be eligible. In addition, it may only be applied to financial penalties and to prison sentences not exceeding five years. It is a conditional favour, and may be withdrawn within a period of five years as from the date on which the sentence became a definitive one.

Conditional suspensions defer the sentence subject to the fulfilment of certain obligations by the offender. This type of deferral is both more liberal than the unconditional suspensions – since no sentence, however recently imposed, will stand in its way – and more stringent, since it is only applicable to prison sentences not exceeding five years. The obligations on which this suspension is dependent can be either positive – eg the obligation to reside in a certain area or undergo a certain course of period of training – or negative, such as refraining from driving or from visiting certain areas.

## Conditional release

This is a mechanism which enables the offender to be released prior to the expiry of his sentence, subject to good behaviour. It can only be applied to a sentence which has already been served to a certain proportion, ie half the penalty for a first offender, two-thirds for a reoffender, and 15 years for life sentences. In addition, the offender in question must give certain pledges as to his or her readjustment to society, and meet a number of obligations.

# E Extinction of sentences

Sentences are naturally extinguished by the sentence having been served by the death of the offender. However, there are other ways in which the sentence can be extinguished, ie as a result of an intervention by the authorities.

### Pardon

This is quite a controversial method of extinguishing sentences, and is the privilege of the Head of State. It may only be granted for sentences which are actually being carried out. The initiative may emanate not only from the offender, but also from his or her Counsel or any other person who can prove an interest. It is issued in the form of an order signed by the Prime Minister and the Minister of Justice. Normally, pardons are conferred on individuals, but collective pardons are also possible.

### Reduction or postponement of the sentence

This is a relatively recent mechanism and is pronounced by the court which imposed the sentence. The sentence may thus be reduced for a maximum of three months per year of imprisonment or of seven days per month for sentences of less than a year.

### Time-barred sentences

The social usefulness of penalising an offender disappears after a certain period has elapsed after the commission of an offence. Article 133 of the new Code provides that this period is 20 years for a sentence imposed for a *crime*, five years for those which result from a *délit*, two years for those resulting from *contraventions*. The date from which this period starts to run is that on which the sentence became definitive. If the sentence has been imposed *in absentia*, it will be definitive within ten days of its official notification. This period can, however, be interrupted by acts of enforcement such as arrest, or suspended by certain obstacles.

### Discharge

This too is a relatively recent mechanism. It enables the court which imposes a sentence to discharge the offender from the various 'secondary' effects of a sentence, such as the loss of various rights which result from certain sentences.

### Amnesties

This is a power exercised by the legislature to issue a general pardon for certain offences. If it is issued before a sentence is imposed for that particular offence, the prosecutor's action will fall; if it is issued after the sentence has been passed, it will extinguish both the sentence and the penalty being served.

### Rehabilitation

This is a mechanism which enables an individual who has had a sentence imposed on him or her to recover those rights which he or she had lost as a result of the sentence. It is therefore aimed at making it easier to reintegrate the offender, subject to good behaviour. Rehabilitation may be ordered either by the courts or by legislation.

# VI Specific offences

# A General

The rules stated above constitute the general criminal law, ie those which apply to every type of offence. However, a sophisticated system of criminal law such as that of France also provides for a number of special rules which apply to specific offences. They are contained in Books II to V of the new Code. Book II concerns offences against the person, and involves not only the traditional crimes of murder and injury, but also the relatively new ones of genocide and even the invasion of privacy. Book III applies to offences against property, such as theft and fraud. Book IV relates to offences against the public order, ranging from treason and terrorism to counterfeiting money and setting up or taking part in unlawful associations. Book V covers a number of offences which cannot be classified under any of the above categories. At present, it contains only one article, ie on cruelty to animals, but it is intended that it will cover a wide range of 'unclassifiable' offences such as misappropriating public funds, environmental pollution, economic and industrial crimes, etc.

# B Offences against the person

The new Code has not only created new types of offences which simply did not exist at the time of the 1810 Code, but is also given priority treatment, since the protection of the person against violence was one of the specific reasons for revising the Codes. The main categories of offences are dealt with below.

### Genocide and other crimes against humanity

Before 1992, it was impossible to deal with this crime other than by merely adding up the number of murders or assaults committed. However, the fact that a number of international organisations and conventions had increasingly concerned themselves with this type of crime prompted wholehearted recognition by the French legislature; indeed, the definition of genocide stated in Article 211-1 is taken over literally from the United Nations convention on this subject. The punishment inflicted for this type of offence is invariably life imprisonment. It penalises any action which contributed towards the intentional destruction of a group of persons defined by race, religion or on any other such arbitrary basis. However, crimes of a similar nature are also penalised, such as the devising of plans to deport, enslave, systematically execute, kidnap, or torture the members of any arbitrarily defined group. The defence that the perpetrator was only following orders will at no time be accepted.

## Intentional homicide

There are two cases of homicide: murder (*meurtre*) or assassination (*assassinat*). Murder is defined by Article 221-1 as wilfully causing the death of another person. It carries a maximum prison sentence of 30 years. Murder committed with premeditation, on the other hand, is classified as assassination, the term 'premeditation' being defined as a planned decision to make a homicidal attack on a certain person or on anyone who may be encountered, regardless of any circumstances on which the act may be dependent.

Book II then proceeds to list a number of specific types of murder or assassination, such as (a) killing a child under 16, (b) killing one's own parent or grandparent, (c) the homicide of vulnerable parties such as the disabled, elderly or the pregnant; (d) the killing of a person who was acting in the pursuance of the administration of justice, and (e) poisoning, which is punishable as soon as any attempt is made against the life of a person by administering substances which are capable of causing death more or less quickly, regardless of the manner in which the substances were administered and regardless of whether the death of the person poisoned was actually caused by that substance or by some other effect.

Finally, Article 221-6 deals with unintentional killing – ie negligent – which is punishable with a maximum of three years' imprisonment and a maximum fine of FF 300,000.

## Intentional and unintentional assaults

This covers the general offences of assaults on a person's health and well-being, as well as such crimes as sexual assaults and drug trafficking. The severity of the penalties provided is commensurate with (a) the harm caused, and (b) the relationship between the author of the crime and the victim. Thus the penalty will be considerably higher for the striking of one's parents or of one's children. Here too, the new Code has added to the offences which existed under the 1810 Code, such as torture and barbarity.

## Abortion

As is the case in most countries, this is a highly controversial part of the criminal law and has undergone a number of changes in recent years. Under Article 317 of the 1810 Code, anyone who caused an abortion by any means on a pregnant woman, regardless of her consent, could face up to five years' imprisonment. This rule has now been mitigated to a considerable extent, although abortion has not been completely decriminalised. The following remain indictable offences: (a) the performing of an abortion without the consent of the mother (maximum sentence five years' imprisonment and a fine of FF 500,000), (b) the carrying out of an abortion elsewhere than in hospital or by a person other than a medical practitioner, or beyond the tenth week of pregnancy, except for health reasons (maximum sentence two years' imprisonment and a fine of FF 200,000, or five years' imprisonment and a fine of FF 500,000 for habitual offenders), and (c) giving a woman the means of carrying out an abortion on herself (a maximum sentence of three months' imprisonment and FF 300,000, or five years' imprisonment and FF 500,000 for habitual offenders).

## Sexual offences

The offence of rape is punishable by 15 years' imprisonment (increased to 20 years where certain aggravating circumstances, such as the relationship between the rapist and the victim, apply). Unlike the 1810 Code, however, the new Code includes in Article 222-23 a definition of rape (*le viol*), as being any sexual penetration committed on any person, regardless of its nature, by means of force, duress, threat or surprise. Another new feature is that the husband can now be punished for raping his wife.

As to prostitution, under the new Code it remains the case that prostitution by itself is not punishable. However, various related activities are indictable offences, such as the wilful aiding and abetting of prostitution or pimping or partaking in the profits of prostitution.

Two other innovating features of the new Code are worth noting. On the one hand, adultery is no longer a criminal offence, reflecting the more permissive sexual climate of the second half of the 20th century. On the other hand, the new offence of sexual harassment has been created, and is defined in Article 222-33: the fact of harassing others through the medium of orders, threats or forms of compulsion, with a view to obtaining sexual favours, by a person who abuses his or her authority attracts a maximum penalty of one year of imprisonment and a fine of FF 100,000. In addition, the old crime of 'outrage to public morality' has now been replaced by sexual exhibitionism imposed on others in a place which is accessible to the public (maximum sentence: one year of imprisonment and FF 100,000).

## Discrimination

This too is an innovation introduced by the new Code. It is defined in Article 225 as any distinction made between physical persons because of their origin, gender, family status, state of health, handicap, customs, political convictions, trade union activity, or the fact of belonging, or being suspected of belonging, to a certain ethnic group, nation, race or religion). The maximum sentence for discrimination thus defined is two years' imprisonment and a fine of FF 200,000.

### Other offences against the person

Article 225-17 makes it an indictable offence to commit any assault on a dead body or any violation of a place of burial. The maximum sentence is one year of imprisonment and a fine of FF 100,000. It is an aggravating factor if considerations relating to the race, nationality or religion of the dead person motivated this desecration, which increases the maximum penalty to five years' imprisonment and a fine of FF 500,000.

The following are also new offences: (a) the invasion of another person's privacy.[6] This offence is defined as the recording or communication of words spoken privately, or the features of a person where the latter is not in a public place; (b) the misrepresentation of another person's features (*atteinte à la représentation de la personne*), which is an offence where a person's features or statements are incorporated into an assembly of pictures or words without that person's consent and without a clear explanation that this is in fact an assembly of words or pictures or *montage*; and (c) criminal slander or libel (*la dénonciation calomnieuse*).

# B Offences against property

Here again, the new Code has extended the range of indictable offences to take account of modern developments in criminal behaviour.

### Theft

Like its predecessor, the new Code starts with a very terse definition, which is followed by a series of special circumstances in which theft may be committed, some of which are mitigating factors and others constitute aggravating circumstances.

Article 311-2 states that anyone who fraudulently removes anything of which he or she is not the owner is guilty of theft. There is every reason to believe that the broad interpretation which the courts have given to this notion under the 1810 Code will continue to apply under the new rules.

---

6    Article 226-1 of the new Code.

The mitigating circumstances are mostly concerned with family relationships. It is not deemed to be expedient from the point of view of criminal policy to deal with thefts committed between close relatives with the full rigour which applies to other types of theft. They merely give rise to a civil action. This will be the case for thefts committed between spouses, by descendants from ascendants and *vice versa*, and a restricted number of relatives by marriage.[7]

The Penal Code makes provision for a large number of aggravating circumstances. Theft committed (a) by breaking and entering, (b) by using force, (c) by choosing as victims particularly vulnerable persons, (d) by virtue of a planned action by two or more perpetrators, (e) by using lethal violence, torture or barbarity, (f) whilst trespassing (ie burglary), all constitute such aggravating circumstances.

As to the penalties which these offences attract, ordinary theft (*vol simple*) gives rise to a maximum penalty of three years' imprisonment and a fine of FF 200,000, whereas in the aggravating circumstances specified above the maximum sentence is five years' imprisonment and a fine of FF 500,000.

**Fraud**

This is a closely-defined offence requiring the fulfilment of a number of precise criteria. Article 313-1 lays down the essential elements of fraud (*escroquerie*) as being the assuming of a false name or attribute, the misuse of an existing attribute, or the deploying of deceptive activity, as well as the obtention, or the attempt to obtain, money or other valuables and in so doing swindle another person out of his or her property. Here again, the new Code does not content itself with the general offence, but refines the concept into a number of related or similar offences (*infractions voisines à l'escroquerie*): breach of trust, exploiting the ignorance or weakness of others in such a way as to induce then to engage in actions which cause them serious harm, the fixing of auctions, etc.

# D  Offences against the public order

This is covered by Book IV of the new Code. Here too, various offences of the 1810 Code have been abolished and new crimes, such as terrorism and infringing the fundamental interests of the State, have been introduced.

The provisions relating to terrorism have been introduced as a result of an increasing incidence of this type of behaviour since the 1970s. There are two types of terrorist offence. On the one hand, there are those actions which are criminal offences in their own right, but which are linked to an individual or collective design to cause serious disruption to the public order by means of ter-

---

7    Article 311-12 of the new Code.

ror or intimidation.[8] These will be punished more severely than if they had been committed without any terrorist intention. Secondly, Article 421-2 identifies a new kind of action which, if linked to an individual or collective plan to disrupt the public order, ie the discharging into the air, soil or water substances capable of endangering the health of humans, animals or the environment. This type of crime attracts a maximum penalty of 15 years imprisonment and a fine of FF 1.5 million where no human life has been lost, and a maximum penalty or life imprisonment and a fine of FF 5 million where such actions have caused death.

This type of crime is subject to various mitigating circumstances: by warning the authorities and preventing it from occurring, as well as identifying the other responsible parties, the author of terrorist actions will evade punishment altogether,[9] whereas the provision of information which prevents the action from taking place or prevents death or injury, accompanied by the identification of any other persons responsible, will halve the sentence.[10] Foreign nationals convicted of terrorist offences may be banned from France for life.[11]

---

8   Article 421-1 of the new Code.

9   Article 422-1 of the new Code.

10  Article 422-2 of the new Code.

11  Article 422-4 of the new Code.

# 9     Court Procedure

## I Introduction

The fact that we decided to devote an entire chapter of this work to court procedure is explained by more than a desire for the systematic marshalling of subject matter. It also reflects the attachment of French legal circles to this aspect of the law, which is greater than on this side of the channel. In France – and in continental Europe generally – there are not a few academic lawyers who call themselves 'proceduralists', whereas in Britain, very few teachers and commentators of the law would lay claim to such a qualification. To this must be added the fact that the formal distinction between the procedural law and the substantive law is much greater in France than in England – if only because there are several codes which are entirely devoted to this branch of the law (*Code de procédure civile, Code de procédure pénale*, etc).

The sharpness with which French procedural law distinguishes itself from its English law counterpart is less acute than it is sometimes made out to be, and differs according to the type of procedure in question. Whereas the conduct of a criminal case is substantially different from the manner of adjudication in England, the same cannot be said of civil procedure, as Brice Dickson points out in his work on French law.[1] (As regards administrative procedure, of course, no comparison is possible in the absence of any specific administrative courts of procedures in England). This is why the following characteristics of French procedural law are set out mainly to highlight the differences between the two systems.

### Inquisitorial approach

For the purpose of settling the disputes brought before them, French court proceedings rely much more on the investigation of the case by a specific section of the court than on cross examination of, and the confrontation between, witnesses, which is the accusatorial approach adopted in the English courts. This is not only the case in relation to criminal proceedings, since it is evident in civil law and administrative law also. See, for example, the role of the *juge de la mise en état* in civil proceedings.

---

1    Dickson, B., *op cit*, p. 124.

### Greater emphasis placed on documentary evidence

Partly as a result of the inquisitorial approach, French court procedure relies much more heavily on documentary evidence than is the case in England. This is particularly the case in respect of the reporting stage, where the *juge rapporteur* presents a summary of the investigation stage to the full court.

### Greater involvement of the public authorities

Court procedure in France is much less of a private matter than in England. Quite apart from the role played by the investigating authorities referred to earlier, the prosecution of crime is – at least as far as public prosecutions are concerned – a purely state-run affair (*le Ministère public*, or *parquet*); no private lawyer is ever entrusted with bringing the case against the accused, as happens in England. In civil proceedings too, the role of the authorities is much more pronounced. The *Ministère public* is more in evidence in civil proceedings where matters of public policy are at stake (for example in family law disputes) than is the case with the Attorney General in England. See also the role of the *Commissaire du Gouvernement* in administrative proceedings.

### Greater degree of formalism

Court procedure in France is much more subject to standard forms and proceedings than is the case in England. Whereas in England it is sometimes difficult to tell in a court decision where the grounds of judgment end and the actual decision begins, French judgments are strictly divided into the grounds of judgment (*les motifs*) and the enacting terms (*le dispositif*). Even the submissions exchanged by the barristers are highly formal although there is no rule which requires them to be so. (It has to be said, however, that most lawyers have now discontinued the practice of introducing every ground of their submissions with the words *'considérant que'* or *'attendu que ...'*.)

### Standards of proof required

In England, there is a sharp distinction between the standard of proof required in criminal procedure, where the prosecution must prove its case beyond all reasonable doubt, and that which will apply in private disputes, which operates more on the balance of probabilities. In France, this distinction is less pronounced, if only because, as we will see later, the instructions contained in the rules on this subject tend to be on the vague side, in both cases.

### Duty to give reasons

Although recent trends in English law show that increasingly, the courts see themselves as being under an obligation to answer all the arguments raised during a dispute and give reasons for their decision, it has not yet become the gen-

168

eral principle of law which it has undoubtedly achieved in France. Although stopping short of constitutional status, *la motivation* nevertheless is one of the fundamental rules of French court procedure.[2]

### The *audi alteram partem* principle

Although this rule of natural justice has always been accepted by the English courts, it has never quite reached the same status as in France, where the *principe du contradictoire* is expressly laid down by law.[3] This rule ensures that, in principle, no court will give a decision before both parties have had an opportunity to be heard. This does not, of course, prevent judgments from being made *in absentia* where one of the parties fails to avail himself or herself of this opportunity.

# II Criminal procedure

## A General

As has been the case with the substantive criminal law, criminal procedure in France has been the subject matter of intense revision over the past few years. The main object in so doing was to strengthen the rights of the defence whilst not in any way detracting from the need to punish the guilty. In fact this is the third major revision to occur since the original 1808 *Code d'instruction criminelle* was introduced.[4] However, the change in government which immediately followed the 1992 revision has already resulted in some of the changes made being reversed.[5]

It has already been stated that French criminal procedure is essentially inquisitorial and written. This means that a great deal more will have been settled in a French criminal case before the actual trial than is the case in English proceedings, ie during the investigation stage conducted by the *juge d'instruction*. Therefore the defence has fewer opportunities for springing surprises on the prosecution than is the case in England.

Essentially there are six distinct stages in proceedings before the French criminal courts, regardless of whether this is the *tribunal de police*, the *tribunal correctionnel* or the *Cour d'assises*. First, the offence needs to be *reported*, which

---

2   Here, it is interesting to note that countries such as Belgium, whose system is based very much on the French model, have actually given constitutional status to this principle.

3   Articles 14-17 of the new Code of Civil Procedure.

4   The Code now in force is called the *Code de procédure pénale*.

5   For a detailed study of this recent chain of events, cf Trouille, H., 'A Look at French Criminal Procedure' (1994) *Criminal Law Review* p. 735.

will be followed by a *preliminary investigation*. A decision must then be made whether or not to *initiate proceedings*. If it is decided to proceed with criminal prosecution, there will in most cases first occur a *judicial investigation*, which then paves the way for the *main trial*; finally, the judgment needs to be *enforced*. We will examine each of these stages in turn. This will be followed by an examination of the various possibilities or appeal and review which may be brought against the decision.

## B  Reporting the offence

In the vast majority of cases, offences will be notified to the police force. However, it is also possible to bring an alleged offence directly to the attention of the organ which is responsible for bringing charges in respect of all serious offences, *crimes* and *délits*. This is the public prosecutor's office (*le Ministère public* or *le parquet*), which acts on the basis of information supplied by either the police or the individual citizen. Where the offence is reported by the aggrieved citizen, he or she will *porter plainte*, whereas if the report is made by a third party, the relevant term to use is *dénoncer*.

However, the role of the victim in actively prosecuting the office does not necessarily end there. If as a result of the preliminary investigation, the public prosecutor decides not to bring charges, the aggrieved party may bring a private prosecution. In addition, the civil action for damages brought before the criminal courts (*la partie civile*) is also something for which the initiative lies entirely in the hands of the victim (cf. *infra*, p. 172).

## C  The preliminary investigation

At this stage, the police play a very important part in the proceedings, in particular the *officiers de la police judiciaire*, who operate directly under the direction and supervision of the public prosecutor's office. (They will also have a role to play in the course of the judicial investigation by the *juge d'instruction*.) Once the offence has been reported to them, the police will start the process of collecting evidence and looking for the presumed offender or offenders. A distinction must be made here between the *enquête en cas d'infraction flagrante*, or *enquête de flagrance* (where someone has been caught in the act) and the *enquête préliminaire*, which is the ordinary investigation.

An *enquête en cas d'infraction flagrante* is allowed only in the case of *délits* and *crimes*. The concept of *flagrant délit* (that of being caught in the act) is a very broad one. Article 53 of the *Code de procédure pénale* (henceforth CPP) defines it as not only an offence which is being, or has just been, committed, but also where there are circumstances incriminating the suspect within a short time after the commission of the offence (general agitation shown by witnesses, being found with various items of property on him or her, etc). In such cases, the main task of the police will be to preserve such evidence as is capable of disappearing or changing its nature. To this end, they may carry out such operations as searches (*perquisitions*) and seizures (*saisies*).[6] The police may also prevent the suspect or key witnesses from leaving the premises, and interview anyone who is thought to be likely to provide information on the offence.[7] In addition, the police may arrest the suspect or place him in police custody.[8]

Where no *flagrant délit* exists, the ordinary preliminary investigation (*enquête préliminaire*) will be conducted by the police, either on their own initiative or on instructions issued by the *Ministère public*. The powers available to the police under this type of investigation are more restricted. Thus they have no powers to arrest persons for questioning; they may only be invited for questioning by means of a *convocation*. However, since 1981 the police now have the power to carry out identity checks (*contrôle d'identité*), which hitherto had been restricted to the *enquête de flagrance*. Searches and seizures may not take place without the consent of those involved.[9]

# D Initiating court proceedings

## General

Once the police investigation is completed, the relevant documents are conveyed to the public prosecutor's office. The prosecutor will have complete discretion as to whether to bring charges or not: here, he or she must use his or her judgment known as *l'opportunité des poursuites*. There are safeguards against the arbitrary use of this discretion, the most important one being the victim's right to bring charges independently of the *Ministère public*, by summoning the accused directly to appear before the court (*citation directe*) or by applying to the *juge d'instruction*. In addition, there are certain state authorities, such as the customs administration, which may compel the public prosecutor to bring charges.

Having considered all the relevant reports and statements, the public prosecutor may do one of two things. he or she may either decide that there is insufficient *prima facie* evidence, or consider that it would not be wise to proceed (eg in the case of a minor offence where the publicity given to the perpetrator would outweigh any penalty which could be inflicted on him or her). In such cases, he or she will discontinue the action by means of a *classement sans suite* (subject to the safeguards referred to in the previous paragraph).

---

6   Article 60 of the CPP.
7   Article 61 of the CPP.
8   Article 63 of the CPP.
9   Article 76 of the CPP.

## The *action publique*

If he or she decides to proceed with the action (*l'action publique*), he or she is yet again faced with a choice. If he or she considers that the facts are so clear as to dispense with the need for any investigation, he or she may by-pass the *juge d'instruction* and seize the court direct. To this end he or she may invite the accused to attend for hearing by means of an *avertissement*, but as this procedure relies upon the co-operation of the suspect, it is very rarely used. In most cases, the direct summons method (*la citation directe*) will be resorted to. Here, the suspect is ordered to appear by means of a writ issued by a *huissier*. This writ must contain a precise specification of that of which the suspect stands accused.

Where an investigation is required, the action will be initiated by means of a *réquisitoire introductif* or *réquisitoire afin d'informer*. By issuing this document, the *Procureur de la République* instructs the *juge d'instruction* to open the judicial investigation. Once again, this *réquisitoire* must contain an exact specification of the facts which are to be investigated. If the name of the suspect is known it must appear on the document which will then be called a *réquisitoire nominatif*.

Once an *action publique* has been initiated, it may only be terminated by the death of the suspect, an amnesty (cf. *supra*, p. 160) or the repeal of the law which makes the action complained of an offence.[10]

## The *action civile*

In England, any damage caused to the victim can only be pursued before the civil courts (even though recent amendments in criminal law have given the courts limited powers to exact some compensation from the author of the crime). In France, however, the victim is given the opportunity to spare himself or herself the cost and time consumed by a civil action, and may simply add the tortious implications of the offence to the criminal action before the criminal courts. This is, however, without prejudice to the victim's right to seize the civil courts. However, once the victim has opted for the civil courts, he or she will have forfeited the right to initiate the *action civile* before the criminal courts. In addition, where the victim has brought the action before the civil court, the latter must suspend judgment until after the verdict of the criminal courts. This is the rule known as *le criminel tient le civil en état*.

# E  The judicial investigation

For an introduction to the main actor at this stage of the proceedings, the *juge d'instruction* (and his counterpart with the Court of Appeal, the *Chambre d'accusation*) we refer to Chapter Two (*supra*, p. 33).

---

10  Article 6 of the CPP.

As soon as he or she receives instructions from the public prosecutor, or sometimes the victim, to investigate a case, the *juge d'instruction* will open the inquiry. However, this does not mean that he or she will need to investigate the case in full. The investigating judge may decide that the case falls outside his or her geographical jurisdiction, that the facts stated in the public prosecutor's instructions are not conclusive of any offence, or that the action has become time-barred. In this case, he or she will issue an *ordonnance de refus d'informer*.

The *juge d'instruction* has a wide range of powers at his or her disposal in order to collect the necessary evidence. He or she may visit the scene of the crime and conduct such searches as he or she considers necessary[11] and even seize any objects and documents which he or she considers relevant to the crime.[12] In addition, he or she may question all those who are thought to be able to provide useful information. It is, however, in his or her relations with the suspect that his or her powers are at their strongest, even though the latter's rights have been considerably strengthened by the recent review of criminal procedure.

Before the 1992 reforms to the CPP, the accused was formally brought into play by means of the *inculpation*. This mechanism has now been replaced by the *mise en examen*,[13] which notifies the accused of the fact that there are serious indications against him or her (*indices graves et concordants*). From that point onwards, the suspect may no longer be heard as a witness, but as an accused person, with all that this implies in terms of rights of the defence and having the right at all times to be assisted by a lawyer. Where a suspect has not been interviewed for three months, he or she may request an interview within the next 15 days. In addition, the new procedure has abolished the *détention préventive*, which formerly could last for a long time. (In fact, the manner in which some investigating judges abused this power was one of the more powerful reasons behind the 1992 reforms.) Under the new procedure, it is only the president of the *Tribunal correctionnel* who may order the detention of the suspect after full hearing held in accordance with the *principe du contradictoire*. The *juge d'instruction* retains the right to ordain the *détention provisoire* by way of pre-trial detention, but only for the most serious offences, and for a maximum period of one year.

Nevertheless, the *juge d'instruction* retains some very far-reaching powers for use during his investigation. He or she still has the right to issue a wide variety of *mandats* by which he or she may require the accused, witnesses or other potential providers of information to attend for interview.[14] If the person con-

---

11  Article 92 of the CPP.

12  Article 97 of the CPP.

13  Article 80-1 of the CPP.

14  Article 122 of the CPP.

cerned fails to appear as a result of the first summons (*mandat de comparution*), his or her presence may be compelled by the issuing of a *mandat d'amener*, which is an instruction issued to the police to take the person in question to the place of interview.

Once the examination is completed, the *juge d'instruction* must inform the suspect of that of which he or she is formally being accused, and draw up an official report (*procès-verbal*) of the entire proceedings to date. The accused and his or her lawyer are then given a further 20 days in which to apply for further investigations; once this period has elapsed, the entire case file is communicated to the *Ministère public* with an *ordonnance de présomption de charges*, which is a document stating which charges should be brought. If the public prosecutor decides nevertheless not to bring charges, the *mise en examen* may be re-opened if new facts come to light.

Another safeguard against the extensive powers of the *juge d'instruction* – which predates the 1992 reforms – is the role of the *Chambre d'accusation*. This is a section of the *Cour d'appel* which has two functions. One is to hear appeals against any of the orders issued by the *juge d'instruction* in the course of his or her investigation. Secondly, the *Chambre* must also provide a second opinion on the investigation of the *juge d'instruction* in crimes which in principle should go to the *Cour d'assises*, regardless of whether an appeal has been made or not. In the latter case, the *Chambre* will conclude its re-investigation with (a) an *arrêt de non-lieu* (which is a discharge order[15]), or (b) an *arrêt de renvoi* if the chamber considers the offence in question to be a less serious offence to be dealt with by the *Tribunal de police* or the *Tribunal correctionnel*,[16] or (c) an *arrêt de mise en accusation* which is a committal for trial of the accused before the *Cour d'assises*.[17]

## F The main trial

At the trial stage, the procedure, whilst not becoming entirely accusatorial, loses some of its inquisitorial characteristics, in that the oral element will be more pronounced, and the parties will in principle be present in person, and the witnesses may be examined by the parties (although there is no cross-examination in the English sense). The trial will be different in the three types of criminal court.

### The *Cour d'assises*

This is the most solemn and formal of all the French courts. Essentially, there are two stages: first, the *instruction définitive* (concluding investigation) and the

---

15   Article 212 of the CPP.

16   Article 215 of the CPP.

17   Article 215 of the CPP.

closing speeches (*plaidoirie* – often mistranslated into English as 'pleadings' – for the accused, *réquisitoire* for the public prosecutor).

The main trial proper commences with the *interrogatoire*, at which a number of questions are put to the accused by the public prosecutor, counsel for the defence, and the *partie civile*, which regard his or her identity and the accusation made against him/her. Although the President's role has been considerably diminished by the post-1992 rules, it is still he or she who will control the whole process and, towards the end of the *interrogatoire*, may question the accused himself or herself.[18]

At this stage one of the most time-consuming stages in the trial commences, ie the hearing of the witnesses: first the *témoins à charge* (witnesses for the prosecution) and then the *témoins à décharge* (witnesses for the defendant). The order in which each individual *témoin* is questioned is determined by the President. However, Article 332 CPP determines a strict order in who may conduct the questioning. The *témoins à charge* are heard first by the prosecutor, then by counsel for the *partie civile*, then by the defence counsel (except for those witnesses who are called by the *partie civile*, in which the order of questioning is first the partie civile, then the public prosecutor, then the defence). The *témoins à décharge* are heard first by the counsel for the defence, then by the prosecutor, then by counsel acting for the *partie civile*. The witnesses must give their testimony separately and take the oath.[19] Expert witnesses may also be heard.

This stage of the proceedings having been completed, the second main phase begins, ie the closing speeches. The order of appearance is as follows: first the counsel for the *partie civile*, then the public prosecutor, and finally the counsel for the defence. All three are allowed to make rejoinders, on the understanding that it is the defence which will always have the last word.

The jury, as well as the three judges, will then retire to consider their verdict (unlike the position in England, where only the jurors make the final pronouncement). Voting must be in writing and in secret.[20] For the accused to be found guilty, at least eight members must cast their vote to that effect; anything less – eg seven votes in favour, five against – will lead to the accused being found not guilty. Another difference with the English jury system is that in France, the jury will also take part in determining the sentence; this time, the decision will be made by a simple majority.[21] Finally, the three judges alone will deal with the claim by the *partie civile*.[22]

---

18  Article 328 of the CPP.
19  Article 331 of the CPP.
20  Articles 356-358 of the CPP.
21  Article 362 of the CPP.
22  Article 371 of the CPP.

### The *Tribunal de police* and the *Tribunal correctionnel*

Before these courts, proceedings are both speedier and less formal than before the *Cour d'assises*. However, the sequence of events is similar to that before the *Cour*. First, the President will confirm the identity of the accused and establish that all the parties involved as well as the witnesses are present. The public prosecutor will then outline the facts of the case, which is followed by a hearing of the accused, first by the *Ministère public*, then by the *partie civile*, and finally by the defence counsel. The evidence will then be produced in the form of witnesses, official reports and experts' reports, as well as the various exhibits (*pièces à conviction*).

Subsequently the closing speeches will be heard: first that of the lawyer for the *partie civile*, then the *Ministère public*, and finally by counsel for the defence. The court then retires to consider its verdict and give sentence. Before the *Tribunal correctionnel*, there are invariably three judges in attendance; therefore if unanimity cannot be reached, a majority 2:1 verdict must be found. The verdict will then be read out in open court.

Before the *Tribunal de police*, a simplified procedure may be applied in the case of minor offences which only involve payment of a fine (Article 524 CPP). Here, the public prosecutor merely requests the court to issue an *ordonnance pénale*, without any hearing or even appearance of the accused. The subsequent judgment does not even need to be reasoned.

## G Enforcement

Two parties will be involved in enforcing sentences of the criminal courts: the public prosecutor and the *partie civile*.[23] As regards the order for civil compensation, these must be enforced by the *partie civile* using all the remedies at the disposal of any other person to whom money is owed under a civil claim. The judgment will be the *titre exécutoire* (enforcement deed) of the *partie civile*.

As regards the penal implications of the sentence, enforcement is the exclusive preserve of the public prosecutor's office, and this regardless of whether the sentence was that which the public prosecutor had originally applied for. In case of *relaxe* (acquittal by the *Tribunal de police* or *Tribunal correctionnel*) or *acquittement* (acquittal by the *Cour d'assises*), it is for the *Ministère public* to secure the release of the accused.

Where penalty has been imposed, the means of enforcement differ according to the nature of the punishment. Where a fine is imposed, the public prosecutor will need to use all such remedies as are available to the creditor of a civil claim (with the added power of *contrainte par corps*, by which defaulters can be impris-

---

23   Article 707 of the CPP.

oned). If the penalty imposed involves imprisonment, the administration of the punishment will become the responsibility of the *juge de l'application des peines*, who is a special judge with the *Tribunal de grande instance* who has a three-year mandate for fulfilling this particular function.[24] In this task, he or she will be assisted by a wide range of officials such as probation officers and social workers.

## H Appeals and review

On this subject, we would refer to the relevant section in Chapter 2 (*supra*, p. 36 *et seq*).

# III Civil procedure

## A General

For the purposes of this section, the term 'civil procedure' must be interpreted very broadly, as encompassing not only the proceedings which govern purely civil claims, but also those which arise before such other judicial bodies as the commercial courts, the land lease courts (*Tribunaux paritaires des baux ruraux*) and the industrial courts (*Conseils de prud'hommes*). Any dispute between private parties will fall within the scope of the term 'civil procedure'.

Civil procedure has also been the subject matter of intense revision in the past few decades. The main reason for these reforms has been the exponential increase in litigation in recent times, which has led to attempts – with varying degrees of success – at streamlining and accelerating procedures. This was the main focus of the new *Code de procédure civile*, which was introduced in 1975.

As regards the nature of the proceedings, there is a considerable difference between the procedure before the *juridictions de droit commun* (*Tribunal de grande instance* and *Cour d'appel*) on the one hand, and the *juridictions d'exception* (*Tribunal d'instance*, *Tribunal de commerce*, etc) on the other hand. Before the former, proceedings are more formal and written, the oral part of the procedure being confined to the hearing stage. With the specialist courts, on the other hand, the oral part of the proceedings predominates.

## B Issues which are common to all proceedings in private disputes

### Standards of proof

As to the standards of proof required at the civil level, the general rule is that it is for the parties involved to prove the facts which underlie their arguments. For

---

24   Article 709-1 of the CPP.

this purpose, they may use any legal means – whether by document, witness or legal presumption. The latter is used much more frequently in French law than in English law, and many articles of the various codes are based on them (eg the presumption that the possessor of an object – particularly a moveable item – is deemed to be its owner unless a better title to ownership is found). Other means of proof are the *aveu judiciaire*, by which one of the parties has made a formal admission to the court, either orally or in writing[25] or the *serment décisoire*, comparable to the English affidavit, by which one party is required by the other to confirm the truth of a particular fact substantiating his claim by means of an oath.[26]

## Role of the *Ministère public*

It has already been observed (*supra*, p. 168) that civil proceedings are a much less private matter in France than in England, and that the public authorities are more likely to intervene in civil disputes than is the case in England. This is made manifest by the role played by the *Ministère public*. The latter's judicial responsibility is not confined to acting as public prosecutor in criminal cases. It is also expected to represent the public good whenever matters arise before any court which affect the interests of society.

In civil cases, the *Ministère public* may take part either as a plaintiff, or as an intervening party. In the former capacity, it may commence an action whenever it is in the public interest to do so. Thus the *Ministère public* may apply to have a company wound up, or to take certain actions involving the protection of children. As an intervening party, the *Ministère public* is frequently called upon to deliver an opinion in the public interest to the court. Thus no guardianship for minors may be decided without the opinion of the *Ministère public* having been heard.

## *Locus standi*

As is the case in England, not just anyone can bring a case to court. To be able to do so, a person – natural or legal – must have a legitimate interest. Under Article 31 of the new Code of Civil Procedure (henceforth NCPC), actions may be brought by anyone who has a legitimate interest, except where legislation confers the right of action exclusively to those whom it deems fit to bring or challenge a claim. The courts have tended to interpret this condition fairly strictly, and have tended to rule inadmissible actions brought in respect of some hypothetical future event. The interest claimed by the plaintiff must also be legitimate: thus actions for the recovery of money which has been unlawfully acquired are in principle inadmissible.

---

25   Article 1356 of the Civil Code.
26   Article 1357 of the Civil Code.

# C The procedure before the *juridictions de droit commun*

The procedure before both the *Tribunal de grande instance* and the *Cour d'appel* is virtually identical. Some differences are due to the personnel involved – thus, for example, before the courts of appeal the submissions will be drafted, by *avoués d'appel* instead of *avocats*.

### Initiating the action

In the vast majority of cases, the action is initiated by means of an *assignation*. This is the equivalent of an English writ of summons. It is served (*signifié*) on behalf of the plaintiff on the defendant by a *huissier de justice*, who for this purpose uses a special document called the *exploit d'huissier*. The summons must contain all the relevant information, such as the court before which the action will be brought, and the identity of the *avocat* representing the plaintiff. However, the action will only be recognised by the Court if, within four months of the *signification* the *assignation* has been presented to the court registrar (*secrétariat-greffe*). In addition, the defendant will have 15 days from the *signification* in which to submit the name of his or her lawyer, who must then inform the plaintiff's *avocat*, as well as the court registrar, that he or she has been appointed.[27] Where the defendant fails to respond to the writ, the case will normally heard *in absentia* (*jugement rendu par défaut*), against which the defendant may object if he or she can prove that the *assignation* never reached him or her.

It must be observed at this point that an action must be brought within certain time limits in relation to the facts which gave rise to it, failing which it will become time-barred. This matter is governed, not by the NCPC, but by the *Code civil*. The principle is that the action must be brought within a period of 30 years following the facts constituting its cause.[28] However, for some actions this period can be reduced to 20 (actions against those who acquired personal property in good faith) and even to 10 years (tort liability).

### The preliminary examination

As is the case with criminal proceedings, there are straightforward actions which can be dealt with immediately, and those which require a preparatory stage. Most cases require the preliminary examination or *la mise en état*. This stage will be controlled by a special judge called the *juge de mise en état*. his or her role is different from that of the *juge d'instruction* in that in civil proceedings, it will be the parties involved, or in some cases third parties, who perform the various actions of the *instruction*; the role of the judge will be to control the entire process.

---

27   Articles 755 and 756 of the NCPC.
28   Article 2262 of the Civil Code.

In the first instance, the *juge de mise en état* will set a variety of time limits in which the parties are to perform certain procedural actions, such as the exchange of pleadings (*l'échange de conclusions*). This exchange can be a somewhat lengthy process, since the defendant can make a counterclaim (*demande reconventionnelle*) in his or her pleadings – to which the plaintiff will then need to reply – and the plaintiff is also allowed to file additional claims even after the original exchange of pleadings. Then the examining judge proceeds to the examination proper, for which he or she has a number of powers (*mesures d'instruction*). Thus he or she may (a) conduct *vérifications*,[29] which are visits to the scene of the dispute; (b) order *comparutions personnelles*,[30] by which he or she may order any party to appear personally before him or her, usually in the presence of their *avocats*; (c) obtain *attestations*, which are written pieces of evidence provided by witnesses[31]; (d) order *enquêtes*, which are oral testimonies provided by witnesses,[32] which if not obeyed may lead to the imposition of a fine; (e) require *constatations* and *consultations*,[33] which are straightforward investigations carried out by expert witnesses, and (f) order *expertises*, more complex findings by experts.[34]

Once the *juge de la mise en état* considers that he or she has adequately investigated the case, he or she will issue an *ordonnance de clôture de l'instruction* to close the preliminary stage, and transmit the case for trial to the main court.

## The main trial

The date for the main trial will either have been fixed by the *juge de la mise en état*, or will be set by the President of the court.[35] The trial proceedings will normally take place in public[36] or in chambers (*en chambre du conseil*[37]) where there are reasons of public policy for doing so. Many cases involving family law are heard *en chambre du conseil*. The main trial will take place over the following three stages:

- **the oral discussion (*les débats*).** There is no stage comparable to the hearing of witnesses which takes place during the criminal proceedings, since this will already have been done at the stage of the *mise en état*. (However, where

---

29  Article 179-183 of the NCPC.

30  Article 184-198 of the NCPC.

31  Article 199 of the NCPC.

32  Article 199 and 204 of the NCPC.

33  Articles 249-262 of the NCPC.

34  Articles 263-284 of the NCPC.

35  Article 779 of the NCPC.

36  Article 433 of the NCPC.

37  Article 435 of the NCPC.

it considers it necessary to do so, the trial court may order an *enquête* to take place.) Therefore the hearing will proceed direct to the *plaidoiries* (closing speeches). The first to speak will be counsel for the plaintiff, who will not only set out the arguments in support of his or her client, but also refute those which were advanced by counsel for the defendant in his or her *conclusions*. Then counsel for the defendant will present his or her speech, along much the same lines. Finally, the *Ministère public* will address the court in cases where it is involved as an intervening party (cf. *supra*, p. 145). Once all the speeches have been made, the President will close the hearing (*clôture des débats*).

- **consideration of the verdict (*le délibéré*)**. The court then retires to reach a verdict. This stage of the proceedings is governed by absolute secrecy.[38] Since normally there are three or more judges in attendance, a majority verdict will need to be reached. Once reached, the verdict will be read out in open court (*le prononcé de la décision*).[39] This does not mean that the entire document is read out: only the dispositif, ie the enacting terms of the judgment, will be read.

- **the judgment (*le jugement*)**. Unlike its English counterparts, this is a very formal document. Normally, it contains the following elements:

  (a) identification particulars: these are details such as the court issuing it, the date of issue, the names of the judges, names of the parties and, in most cases, their *avocats*, and the name of the court registrar.

  (b) the grounds of judgment (*la motivation*). Each ground of judgment will commence with the words '*attendu que*' or '*considérant que*'.

  (c) the enacting terms (*le dispositif*). This is invariably introduced by the words '*par ces motifs*' (on these grounds). Standards terms used here are '*dit et juge que*', '*déboute que*', '*condamne*', etc.

  (d) the enforcement terms (*la formule exécutoire*). Here too, the same expression is invariably used: '*La République française, mande et ordonne*).

The judgment must be notified to all the parties.[40]

Once issued, the judgment will have three effects: (a) *le déssaisissement*, which means that the dispute is now removed from the court's jurisdiction; (b) it will be enforceable (*force exécutoire*) and (c) it will have *autorité de la chose jugée* (best translated as *res judicata*). It is particularly the latter element which distinguishes

---

38  Article 448 of the NCPC.

39  Article 451 of the NCPC.

40  Articles 675-682 of the NCPC.

French court decisions from their English law counterparts. Under Article 1351 of the Civil Code, the effects of the decision are restricted to the parties and the dispute between them, and under Article 5 of the Civil Code, no court may make a judgment with a view to issuing a binding rule. This is a result of the principle that in France the courts must be the servants, not the masters, of the law; their role is restricted to interpreting and applying legislation. This does not mean that the court decision will have no implications for third parties: like contracts, court decisions are legal actions, and must be respected as such.

### Enforcement of the decision

It has been mentioned before that one of the compulsory parts of a court decision is its enforcement terms (*formule exécutoire*).[41] Any judgment bearing this formula is a *titre exécutoire* or enforcement document. It will enable the winning party to compel enforcement of the enacting terms of the decision should the losing party fail to do so. Therefore the former may apply to a *huissier de justice* in order to perform the usual enforcement actions (*les saisies*). It has been known to happen, however, that the public authorities have refused to enforce decisions where to do so would involve unacceptable disturbances of the public order.

## D Proceedings before the *juridictions d'exception*

### General

Although in recent years attempts have been made at expediting proceedings before the *Tribunal de grande instance*, these are still considered to be inappropriate for the specialised courts. One of the main reasons for this is that the cost of legal representation by means of an *avocat*, which is obligatory before the *Tribunal de grande instance*, often acts as a major deterrent to potential litigants. This is why the specialised courts accept that (a) the parties may represent themselves; (b) they may be represented by people other than *avocats* (for example, trade union representatives before the *Conseil des prud'hommes*), and (c) they do not need to submit pleadings in substantiation of their case. In addition, there is no intervention by any *juge de la mise en état*.

### The *Tribunal d'instance*

One of the characteristics of the procedure before this court is the attempts made at conciliation. This is the purpose of the introductory writ, which can

---

41   Translated by the authors from: '*La République française mande et ordonne à tous huissiers de justice, sur ce requis, de mettre ledit jugement (arrêt) à exécution, aux procureurs généraux et aux Procureurs de la République près des tribunaux de grande instance d'y tenir la main, à tous commandants et officiers de la force publique de prêter main-forte lorsqu'ils en seront légalement requis*'.

either be the *assignation à toutes fins*, which seeks a solution of the dispute by either judgment or conciliation, or by a *citation à seules fins de conciliation*. If the conciliation fails, the case will either be heard immediately or postponed to a later date.[42] Although the procedure is mainly oral, and, as has been mentioned before, no *conclusions* are required, the parties in fact often present written pleadings to the court.

### The *Tribunal de commerce*

Here again, there is a choice of writs by which to initiate the action: (a) the *assignation*, (b) the *requête conjointe* or (c) *présentation volontaire*.[43] Unlike the cases before the *Tribunal d'instance*, however, disputes before the commercial courts may, where the subject matter appears to be complex, require a preparatory stage which will be controlled by a *juge rapporteur*. The latter has a wide range of powers during this preliminary stage, including the right to summon the parties to appear before him/her and produce the necessary documentary evidence. However, his or her powers are more limited than those of the *juge de la mise en état*.

### The Conseil de prud'hommes

It should be recalled that this court deals exclusively with disputes arising from contracts of employment, and the rules governing its procedure are contained both in the NCPC and in the *Code du travail*. Here again, every attempt is made at conciliation before adjudication. In fact, the procedure commences with a *compulsory* conciliation stage before the *bureau de conciliation* (conciliation committee). Only if a settlement before this committee fails will the matter go forward for adjudication.

As is the case before the commercial courts, the subject matter of the dispute placed before the adjudication body may be too complex to be settled without a thorough examination. For this purpose, one or more examining officers (*conseillers rapporteurs*) may be appointed to conduct the *instruction*; however, their findings are not binding on the adjudication body. The parties are then called before the adjudication body, after which the procedure is entirely oral. At the end of the hearing, the adjudication body will take its decision by a simple majority.

## E  Special procedures

### The *procédure des référés* and *ordonnances sur requête*

It has already been noted (cf. *supra*, p. 30) that the President of a court occupies a special position in French judicial procedure. Not only has he or she a number

---

42  Article 840 of the NCPC.

43  Article 854 of the NCPC.

of important administrative duties, such as the allocation of cases between the chambers of a court; he or she also has judicial powers in his or her own right. In the first place, he or she may make *ordonnances sur requête*, which are straightforward authorisations issued on a simple application by the interested party, such as the rectification of a civil status deed (*rectification d'un acte de l'état-civil*[44]).

However, his or her most important judicial power is exercised when acting as *juge des référés*. However streamlined the procedure before a court may be, there are certain situations which require an immediate and provisional measure. Thus for example it would be of no avail to the plaintiff in an action for damages if the defendant had moved all his or her assets to a country where they could not be seized. This does not mean, however, that the *principe du con-tradictoire* will be sacrificed to expediency: not only does the defendant have the opportunity to defend his position; he must also be given ample time to prepare his defence.[45] However, although the *ordonnances de référé* are enforceable, they do not have the authority of *res judicata*. The *référés* procedure is available not only before the *Tribunal de grande instance* and the *Cours d'appel*, but also before the commercial courts, the *Conseil des prud'hommes*, and the *Tribunaux paritaires des baux ruraux*.

### The *compétence grâcieuse*

Not every case which comes before the French courts involves a dispute between two or more parties. Sometimes a court decision is required in order to confer official status on certain actions or events. It is especially in the area of family law that the courts are required to act under their *compétence grâcieuse*, which is why it is mainly the *Tribunal d'instance* which is called upon to act in this way. Where a divorce takes place by mutual consent, or a minor needs to be adopted, or it is necessary to appoint a trustee who will administer the property of minors or of persons deemed to be incapable of attending to their own legal affairs, a decision, albeit without any dispute, must be made. This is why this procedure is characterised by a complete absence of formalism.

# IV Administrative procedure

## A General

The fact that disputes involving the administration have been divorced from the ordinary courts for over 200 years would suggest the procedure before the administrative courts to be radically different from that before the *juridictions*

---

44  Article 99 of the Civil Code.
45  Article 486 of the NCPC.

*judiciaires*. However, this is far from being the case. The main reason for this is the fact that the administrative courts were developed much later than the ordinary courts, bearing in mind that it was not before 1872 that judicial status was conferred on the *Conseil d'Etat*, and that the *Tribunaux administratifs* were only created as recently as 1953. Those responsible for designing these new courts could not help being influenced by existing models, in particular those of the ordinary courts, since some of the disputes between the administration and the citizen are similar to those settled before the *juridictions judiciaires* (eg the actions in tort).

There are, however, a number of differences. First of all, the procedure before the administrative courts is much more inquisitorial and written than is the case before the ordinary courts (in particular since the changes introduced in the latter since 1975). In addition, the equality between the parties, which is so fundamental to civil disputes, is lacking before the administrative courts. Since the administration must continue to function regardless of any disputes with the citizen, the former must enjoy certain privileges. This explains why, for example, an action brought before the administrative courts cannot have the effect of suspending the enforcement or implementation of the administrative action complained of.

Subject to a few minor differences, the procedure is the same at the three levels of administrative justice – the *Tribunaux administratifs*, the *Cours administratives d'appel* and the *Conseil d'Etat*.

# B Admissibility criteria

It is important to point out at this stage that we are dealing here with admissibility criteria for any administrative court action, whether it be under the *contentieux de l'annulation* or the *contentieux de pleine juridiction*. Both types of action have their individual admissibility criteria which are discussed elsewhere (cf. *supra*, p. 140). Viewed in this light, there are four elements which determine the admissibility of an action: the person of the applicant,[46] the *décision préalable* rule, the deadlines to be respected, and the formal conditions which must be met by the application (*la requête*).

### The applicant

Two criteria must be met by the applicant if his or her/its action is to be admissible. In the first instance, he or she/it must be capable of engaging in court proceedings (*ester en justice*). This issue will be of particular importance in relation to the administrative organs; as we have seen (cf. *supra*, p. 123 *et seq*), some have

---

46 The term 'applicant' is preferred here to the word 'plaintiff', which is more appropriate for the ordinary courts.

legal personality – and are thus capable of acting at law – whereas others have not. Among those which are legal persons, the question of who is capable of representing them at law will need to be addressed (the local authorities, for example, will be represented by their executive organ duly authorised by the decision-making organ).

The second criterion is that of *locus standi*. Here, there is a distinction between that which is required of natural persons and the conditions which must be met by legal persons. Natural persons must be able to show a *direct* and *personal interest (un intérêt direct et personnel)*. The *Conseil d'Etat* has tended to interpret this condition broadly – thus in one case, the fact that a natural person was a user of a particular public service qualified him for *locus standi* to challenge an action of that service.[47] Legal persons, on the other hand, must demonstrate a professional and collective interest (*un intérêt professionnel et collectif*). Here again, the relevant case law tends to be generous in its interpretation of this condition.[48]

### The *décision préalable* rule

Except in the case of disputes involving public works, no action may be brought before an administrative court unless a previous decision has been made by the administration. In the absence of a decision, the applicant will first need to provoke it from the administration before being able to bring court proceedings. This will obviously produce few enough problems as regards the *contentieux de l'annulation*. In relation to the *contentieux de pleine juridiction*, the question may become more involved. For example, where a citizen has suffered damage as a result of administrative action, he or she cannot for that reason alone take the administration to court: first, he or she must apply to the administration for a sum by way of compensation; if the administration refuses, that will be the decision which will form the basis of the application to the administrative court.

### The time limits to be observed

In principle, the deadline for bringing an administrative action is two months. There are a number of exceptions to this: for disputes involving public works, there is no time limit, as is the case in respect of *questions préjudicielles* (applications for interpretation of administrative law made by the ordinary courts – cf. *supra*, p. 143). For challenges brought to election results, a series of deadlines well short of two months applies. The deadline can be extended for a variety of reasons, such as the fact that the action was brought to the wrong court (*juridiction incompétente*), applications for legal aid, and for actions where distance is a factor (eg actions emanating from the *DOM-TOM* regions).

47  *Conseil d'Etat* Decision of 21/6/1906, *Syndicat des propriétaires et contribuables du quartier Croix-de-Seguey v Tivoli*, GAJA No. 17.

48  *Conseil d'Etat* Decision of 28/12/1906, *Syndicat des patrons coiffeurs de Limoges*, GAJA No. 18.

Any action brought after these time limits will be inadmissible. This requirement is a strict one, and extends even to the pleadings: any extension of modification of the *conclusions* which are deemed to constitute new arguments and which are advanced beyond this deadline will be inadmissible.[49] It will, however, be possible to raise a plea of illegality (*exception d'illégalité*) beyond this deadline (where the defendant argues that the administrative regulation which he is alleged to have infringed is itself unlawful).

## The *requête*

The application must contain a statement of the facts and arguments raised, as well as the names and addresses of the parties. It must be worded in French, signed and accompanied by the relevant documentary evidence, not least the decision complained of.

# C The trial

There are three main elements to the trial: *the instruction*, the hearing and the decision itself.

## The *instruction*

The manner in which the proceedings commence is the reverse of that in civil proceedings: the application (*mémoire introductif d'instance*) is first entered with the court registry (*greffe*), then notified to the parties. Another difference with the civil proceedings is the inquisitorial nature of the instruction, with the pace being set entirely by the *juge rapporteur* (who is a member of the court appointed for this purpose on an *ad hoc* basis). The parties will be given a series of deadlines in which to communicate the *mémoires* (pleadings) and the productions (documentary evidence) to the other parties by registered letter.

The *rapporteur* may order all such measures of investigation as he or she deems necessary, such as requests for clarification, the verification of administrative documents, or even a visit to any premises involved in the dispute. he or she may also order an *enquête*, or the performance of *expertises*. Once he or she is satisfied that the case is ready for trial, he or she issues an *ordonnance de clôture d'instruction*.

## The hearing

The hearing is normally held in open court. First, the *rapporteur* will present his report, which gives a brief outline of the issues involved. The parties, or their counsels, may make oral observations provided that they do not exceed the terms of their written pleadings.

---

49 *Conseil d'Etat* Decision of 20/2/1953, *Société Intercopie*, S. series 3, 79.

It is at this stage that the *Commissaire du gouvernement* enters into play. The *Commissaire* is cast in the role of *Ministère public* before the administrative courts. In spite of his or her title, however, he or she does not put forward the viewpoint of the Government, but that of the public interest. The legal opinion which the *Commissaire du Gouvernement* is required to present to the court during the hearing is highly authoritative. (The Advocate-General before the European Court of Justice was closely modelled on the *Commissaire du Gouvernement*.)

Once the hearing is concluded, the court retires to consider its verdict in secret (*en chambre du conseil*). The decision itself, however, is read out in open court.

# D The judgment

The judgment must remain within the limits of the pleadings submitted by the parties. This means that the judgment may be neither *infra petita* (rule on fewer issues than those applied for – eg failure by the court to give a ruling on a claim for compensation added to an action for annulment) nor *ultra petita* (grant more than that which was applied for – eg award larger damages than those which were claimed by the applicant).

The rulings (*décisions* in the case of *Conseil d'Etat*, *arrêts* in the case of the *Cours administratives d'appel* and *jugements* in the case of the *Tribunaux administratifs*) formally consist of four components:

- **the *visas*,** which analyse the arguments and the pleadings of the parties, as well as the applicable rules;

- **the *considérants*,** which are the grounds of judgment;

- **the *dispositif*,** which is the enacting terms of the decision. These take the form of numbered articles;

- **the *formule exécutoire*,** which orders the enforcement of the decision.

# E Enforcement

The administrative courts are limited in the measures which they may enact in their decision. They may (a) reject the application, (b) annul the contentious administrative action or (c) order the payment of damages. The court cannot, however, issue any injunction to the administration – it may not, for example, order it to demolish a building which had been unlawfully erected.

The implications of the decision differ according to the nature of the action. The annulment of administrative action has an effect *erga omnes*, whereas any other decision – eg order to pay compensation – is restricted in its effects to the parties involved in the dispute.

Until relatively recently, the enforcement of administrative court decisions could give rise to a great deal of difficulty. Taking advantage of the fact that the courts could make no injunction against them some administrative authorities either ignored the decision or only carried it out slowly and incompletely. This situation was remedied by a Law of 16/7/1980, which made it possible for the *Conseil d'Etat* to impose financial penalties (*astreintes*) on recalcitrant administrative authorities, as well as fines (*amendes*) on any public official who obstructed the enforcement of administrative court decisions.

# 10 Legal Translation

## I General introduction

Legal translation is in many respects the ultimate linguistic challenge, in that it combines the inventiveness normally associated with literary translation and the attention to terminological correctness which is usually the hallmark of technical translation. The difficulties involved in this field are aggravated in no small measure by the limited nature of the traditional tools of the translator's trade, ie dictionaries and glossaries, and require an in-depth knowledge of the subject matter – to the point where some have even suggested that linguists without any legal qualification are unequal to this particular challenge.

The authors hope to be able to convey the full range of the challenges facing the legal translation in this chapter, more particularly that which involves the two languages with which we are dealing in the context of this book, ie French and English. Essentially we intend to do this by first of all attempting to explain the background to these difficulties and challenges, which reside not only in the differences between the two legal systems, but also in the disparities in philosophical attitudes and in practical approaches towards the resolution of social issues. We will then point out some of the main pitfalls inherent in legal translation involving French and English, some of which are not unfamiliar to translators in any discipline, whilst other are more subject-specific. Thirdly, we will provide a brief overview of the main tools which should be available to the legal translator. Finally, we will provide a word of explanation on the methodology of legal translation.

## II Background to the main difficulties of legal translation between French and English

One of the first tasks of the legal translator will be to acquaint himself or herself with the major differences in approach between the two systems. Although we have already drawn attention to this factor in previous chapters, it is useful to repeat them here briefly in order to provide as comprehensive a context as possible for this specific skill. However, there are other difficulties with which the legal translator must contend, and which relate to the conceptual difference between the two languages, even beyond any legal context.

# A Differences in philosophical approach

As we have already had occasion to point out earlier (*supra*, p. 4), the law is not a self-contained social science. It bears the clear imprint of underlying thought patterns, philosophical attitudes and approaches towards solving human problems. In this respect there is already a considerable gap between English and French thinking.

The French intellectual approach is conditioned by the philosophical thought processes introduced by René Descartes, to wit, deductive rational thinking. Under this approach, rules and dogmas are derived from broad principles in an ordered and methodical manner. English intellectual thinking, on the other hand, was dominated from approximately the same period as that of Descartes by the inductive, pragmatic approach, according to which rules and principles are based on empirical observation of individual cases.

As we have explained more fully in Chapter One (cf. *supra*, p. 4), this is fully reflected in the legal systems of the two countries. It is obvious, then, that this has also had an effect on the terminological differences between the two systems.

# B Differences in the role of the courts

This too has been fully explained in the first chapter. The fact that the courts in the Anglo-Saxon systems have a creative role to play, whereas in the French codified tradition, the courts are expected – at least in principle – to be solely the servants, rather than the masters, of the law has had important repercussions for the legal terminology used under both systems.

# C Differences in legislative drafting

It has also already been explained (*supra*, p. 5) that there is a major difference in the drafting techniques employed in both countries. The British tradition has always been for Parliament to formulate legislation with as many detailed provisions as possible. This is explained by the traditional rivalry between the statute law and the common law, which leads the Parliament which adopts the statute law to endeavour to leave as little as possible to the discretion of the courts.

In France, on the other hand, there is a tendency for legislation to be drawn up in very broad terms by the Parliament, leaving the details to be filled in by Government action (hence the aforementioned 'lois-cadre'). This difference in approach also has its effect on the legal language used in both systems. (It must be said, however, that in Britain, under the pressures of the Parliamentary timetable, there is also a tendency to opt for this type of legislation as well).

# D The role of codification

It has been noted earlier that in France the major bodies of law are grouped together in codes. They have a language of their own, which has perhaps survived longer than it would have done had the laws in question been structured less cohesively. There is also the fact that these codes, and therefore also their language, were incorporated into several countries other than France – this again is a factor which has contributed to the specific nature of the legal language used in these codes being maintained for longer than would otherwise have been the case.

# E Conceptual differences between the English and French languages in general

In his highly informative work *An English Reader's Guide to the French Legal System*,[1] Martin Weston points out that the principal difficulty in translation, regardless of the subject matter, is the question of overcoming conceptual differences between the two languages. This is a particularly thorny problem when it comes to translating into the target language (being the language into which the text is being translated) concepts which differ from those which are familiar to its speakers, not only in minor denotational respects, but also for cultural and institutional reasons.

Thus to translate the term *'porte'* by 'door' or 'gate' presents no conceptual problems. Even though the reader will need to be aware of the fact that the word *porte*, along with so many others, is capable of being translated by two equivalents in English, there are no conceptual difficulties for the simple reason that a door or a gate is an object and a notion which is familiar to English speakers. However, the term *petanque* presents conceptual problems because it denotes a game which is simply not played in England; nor is there any game commonly known to the English-speaking public which is even remotely comparable to it. (Similarly, the term 'cricket' would present the French speaker with similar conceptual differences.) Therefore, any such term will need to be explained rather than translated. This problem is exacerbated, as Weston points out,[2] where the terms are used by way of, or in the course of, metaphorical expressions – how, for example, does one translate into French 'to be on a sticky wicket'?

---

1   (1993, Berg) p. 9.

2   *Ibid* p 10.

## F 'Legal register'

In linguistic science, the term 'register' denoted the specific manner in which language is used in a particular field of human knowledge. This involves more than mere differences in vocabulary, and embraces differences in grammatical use, the permissible use of idiomatic expression, greater formality or informality of language, etc. Thus, for example, the subject of criminal behaviour will have a totally different 'register' according to whether it is reported in a newspaper, in a law journal, or in Parliamentary proceedings. Within the legal register, there are other variants which enter into operation; the language in which a particular problem of landlord-and-tenant law is discussed in consultations between a lawyer and his or her client will of necessity be different from that used by a court called upon to settle the issue.

# III The main pitfalls lying in wait for the legal translator

## A The *faux amis*

In the jargon of the translator, *faux amis* are words which look or sound the same in both the target language and the source language. These are legion as between French and English, if only because many English words have French, rather than Anglo-Saxon, origins. The classic example is *éventuellement*. In French, this word means 'possibly' or even sometimes 'hypothetically'. It should never, however, be translated as 'eventually', which in English means 'finally' or 'definitively'. It is obvious that, because of the conceptual nature of the law, these '*faux amis*' can, if misconstrued, lead the reader to misunderstand completely the subject matter under discussion, and not just the odd paragraph or sentence.

Take the case of the word '*société*'. If used in the context of commercial law, this term is the equivalent of 'company' in English. However, the person who thought that he or she was dealing here with societies – as in friendly societies – would in many cases misunderstand the whole context and meaning of the text in question.

Similarly, the French term '*conclusions*'. In English, these are the equivalent of 'submissions' or 'pleadings'. To misconstrue the word as 'conclusions' – as in the conclusions drawn by a judge or court – could again lead to the entire text being totally misunderstood.

The '*faux amis partiels*' can also play a treacherous part here. Some words are only partly misleading because of the similarity with the other language. Here, the term '*titre*' is a good example to consider. This can in some contexts – such as the law of property – indeed mean 'title' in English, where it is intended to convey the rightful claim to ownership ('to have title to the property'). However, in the field of banking law, the term '*titre*' should be translated as meaning 'security', since in this field of the law, the term *'titre'* refers to commercial documents such as stocks, shares and bonds.

## B Terms having more than one meaning

This is obviously a problem that occurs extremely frequently in ordinary translation,[3] but worth reiterating for all that, particularly as some of the meanings can be extremely divergent. Take the case of the term *'voie de fait'*. In a criminal law context, this term means assault and battery. In administrative law, however, this term denotes circumstances which take the dispute in question beyond the jurisdiction of the administrative courts.

## C The role of indirect speech in French court decisions

This is an aspect to which the legal translator must pay particular attention. Whenever a fact, right or circumstance is alleged to have happened – eg by one of the parties, or by the public prosecutor, French courts tend not to preface these statements with a warning that these are mere claims (as would be the case in an English court). They will tend to use indirect speech – eg *'Il s'agirait ici d'un vice de forme plutôt que d'un vice de fond'* will often not be prefaced by a 'warning' statement such as *'selon le défendeur'*. The reader often has to divine this from the context. Ignorance of this use of the conditional can lead the translator into severe difficulties.

## D Legal concepts existing in one system but not in the other

This is a concrete application of the general conceptual difficulties explained earlier (cf. *supra*, p. 5), and truly represents one of the trickier aspects of legal translation. Let us take as an example in this context the term *'dispositif'*, meaning that part of the court decision which contains the actual judgment (as opposed to the *motifs*, which are the grounds of judgment). There is simply no equivalent in English to this term, so one has to resort to either the nearest equivalent – the best equivalent which we have been able to find so far is the expression 'enacting terms of a judgment' – or circumlocution (which can, moreover, differ according to the particular syntactic context in which the word needs to be translated). The other technique which could be appropriate is the use of translator's notes. In the other direction, from English into French, let us take the term 'consideration' in the English law of contracts. This is the promise to do or give something in return for that which one stands to obtain under a contract. Again, there is no precise French equivalent, and the temptation to use

---

3   The student who translated the phrase *'le chômage est un des facteurs principaux dans la criminalité croissante'* as 'unemployment is one of the main postmen in growing crime' will haunt the authors indefinitely.

a one-to-one equivalent which only partially covers the original term – or only has the remotest connection with it – should be strongly resisted.

## E Concepts used in the source language which are covered only in part in the target language

This too can present considerable difficulties. There are certain legal concepts which have an equivalent in the other only in certain circumstances. Let us take, for example, the term *'huissier de justice'*. This term can only be translated by the English equivalent 'bailiff' if the concept is being used in the context of an activity which the *huissier* and the bailiff have in common, ie the seizure of goods. If, on the other hand, the activity in question is the serving of court documents on another party involved in a lawsuit, the corresponding English term to be used would be 'process server'. And if the term is used in the context of the drawing up of official reports establishing certain facts (*'procès-verbaux'*) there is simply no equivalent in English law; once again, circumlocution or translator's notes will need to be resorted to. The same problem occurs from English into French – eg the term 'mortgage', which can only mean *'hypothèque'* in certain circumstances.

## F Failure to understand the concept to be translated

Even if the text is being translated by someone who is either a lawyer or has a very sound knowledge of the legal system whose terms are to be translated, there is still the strong possibility that he or she will be faced with concepts which he or she simply does not understand. Let us take the term *'évocation'* in French. This denotes the power of the *Conseil d'Etat* to remove from any lower administrative court any case which it considers so important as to warrant its personal attention. We have yet to come across a dictionary which translates or explains this term in the legal sense. How then can a translator be expected to understand this term unless he or she is an expert in French administrative law? Similarly, when translating from English into French, how is the translator expected to be acquainted with terms such as 'fee simple' unless he or she has a thorough knowledge of the English law of property? It is true that the same problem of terminological difficulty may arise in the field of technical translation, yet in most cases, there are technical glossaries which will provide a one-to-one equivalent. This is much less frequently the case in legal translation.

## G Differences in use of certain terms as between several French-speaking countries

Since virtually all the French-speaking countries have legal systems based on that of France, this is not a frequent occurrence. Nevertheless the danger does exist. Thus the term *auditeur*, which in France means a junior member of the *Conseil d'Etat*, means a public prosecutor before a military court in Belgium.

# IV The main tools of the legal translator

## A General

We have already indicated earlier (cf. *supra*, p. 7) that legal translation is an area in which dictionaries are of limited value – in fact, sometimes they can be downright misleading. The reason for this is that dictionaries look for the convenient 'one-to-one equivalent' solution, and very seldom if ever provide an explained translation. Thus in one dictionary, the *Ledocte* four-language legal glossary (French-English-Dutch-German), we found the term 'consideration' translated as '*rémunération*', which is again an example of convenience taking precedence over accuracy. There are exceptions, of course. The *Quemner* dictionary of legal terms (English-French), for example, goes to some pains to provide explanatory translation, but it is hopelessly incomplete.

Of much more consequence for the translation professional are the instruments stated below.

## B Explanatory legal dictionaries

In so many cases, it is only once a term has actually been explained that the translator is equal to the task of translating it. In both languages there a number of very good explanatory dictionaries available. The *Lexique de termes juridiques* published by Dalloz, and the *Oxford Law Dictionary* are justly praised for their completeness and accuracy.

## C Textbooks, handbooks and manuals

In many cases, one may have little option but to try to glean the relevant terminology from manuals and handbooks in the particular field of the law to which the text to be translated relates. This is fully borne out by our own experience as professional translators. When faced with a very complex and technical text on fiscal law, for example, it may be advisable to read very thoroughly, in the target language, several chapters of an introduction to the law of taxation. Here again, it is fair to state that this is a problem which arises more in the context of legal translation than in any other field. Indeed, the authors express the sincere hope that legal translators will find this work useful for the purpose of understanding and translating a considerable number of legal terms.

## D Existing translations of codes and law reports

In recent years, there has been a significant increase in the number of codes from various legal systems which have been published in translated form. We use the term 'code' in a very broad sense here, as including not only bodies of law such as the French Civil Code, but also constitutions of nations, treaties and large pieces of legislation such as the English Land Property Act. Here again, of course, a certain familiarity with the legal system in question will be a useful asset.

As a slight variant on this theme, legal translators may also from time to time usefully consult the Civil Code of the US state of Illinois. Although there is no (official) French version, it is largely inspired by French codified law (Louisiana having been a French colony until the early 19th century), and therefore the legal translator may sometimes find it to contain a number of useful civil law terms, stated in English, but being French in origin.

## E EU legislation and court reports

Since EU legislation and court reports are all equally authentic in all Community languages, this too can provide a useful source of reference material for the legal translator. This is particularly the case since EU legislation is covering an increasing number of legal fields. Take for example the area of company law. As the number of EU directives on this subject increases, so too does the amount of terminology which is available in all the official languages of the EU.[4]

For translation between English and French, there is an additional, related source, ie the instruments issued by the Council of Europe (including the court reports of the European Court of Human Rights), French and English being the sole official languages of the Council of Europe.

# V Translation methodology

To have the tools at one's disposal is not enough. The legal translator must also use the right methodology if he or she is to be successful. The methods described below are not provided in any order of preference. They are those which the legal translator must constantly keep in mind and apply where appropriate.

---

4   It should be added here that the EU has published glossaries in various fields, and has organised a sizeable database of terms in the official languages of the EU.

# A Equivalent concepts

In many circumstances, it will be appropriate to use the nearest equivalent concept in the target language. Thus the term *Conseil d'administration* can be safely translated as 'Board of Directors': even though the powers and function of these two organs are not exactly the same under the two systems, they are sufficiently similar to avoid any danger of misleading the reader. The same applies to the term *exécution du contrat*, which can safely be translated as 'performance of the contract'.

A number of dangers must, however, be borne in mind and avoided by the legal translator. First, the danger that the equivalent concept in the target language only partially covers the term of the source language. Thus the term *'notaire'* should never be translated as 'solicitor', since, although the function which the *notaire* and the solicitor have in common is the conveyancing of land, that is where the resemblance ends. Secondly, the danger posed by the *faux amis* is particularly acute here. For example, it is fatally tempting, but mistaken, to translate the term *'magistrat'* by 'magistrate', since the former denotes a professional judge, whereas the latter *only* refers to lay judges (except where accompanied by the term 'stipendiary magistrate', which would be a highly inappropriate translation anyway, for reasons set out below). Similarly, the term *Gardien des sceaux* (*Minister of Justice*) should not be translated as 'Lord Privy Seal', in view of the totally different function fulfilled by these two figures.

Closely related is the danger of *faux amis partiels*: a good example is the term *'administration'*. This may only be translated as 'administration' where the source-language term denotes the body of people responsible for carrying out the duties of the State towards the citizen. However, in a commercial context it will mostly mean the management of property or businesses, in which case the term 'management' should be used. Then again, when used in the context of a trustee to whose care property has been entrusted, the term 'administration' in English is very often the correct translation.

Thirdly, care must be taken not to use a term which, although it does represent the nearest equivalent in the target language, nevertheless is too specific to the legal system in question to be able to serve as an appropriate translation. The term 'Act' is a good example. It is inappropriate to use this term as a translation for the word *'loi'*, since a British or American Act is adopted as a result of procedures which are very specific to the British and American parliamentary systems. Similarly, it would be inappropriate to use the term 'Home Secretary' as a translation for *'Ministre de l'intérieur'*, or 'Cabinet' as a translation for *'Conseil des Ministres'*, for the same reasons.

Fourthly, there is the obvious danger that, in his or her quest for the nearest equivalent, the wrong one is used. Some mistranslations of this kind are more obvious than others. It will be clear to even the most inexperienced legal translator that it is totally inapt to translate *'Assemblée nationale'* as 'House of Commons', or the term *'Haute Cour de justice'* as 'High Court'. However, there are other examples which are perhaps less immediately obvious.

It is tempting, for example, to translate the term *'département'* by the term 'county'. This is totally inappropriate, since the equivalence is purely superficial; the place of the county in the English system of local government is totally different from that occupied by the *département* in France. There is a similar temptation to translate the term *'Code de la route'* as 'Highway Code', even though the two are totally different: the former is a set of binding road traffic rules having legislative status, whereas the latter is more in the nature of a 'Code of Practice', which is provided merely for guidance.

Another dimension which could be taken into account in endeavouring to find the correct equivalent is the difference between the various Anglo-Saxon systems. Thus when translating a legal text intended for a Scottish readership, it is probably acceptable to translate the term *usufruit* as 'usufruct' without any further explanation, since this is a known concept of Scottish law which fulfils the same role as *usufruit* does in French law. Here again, however, we have to be very careful and selective. Thus it would in our view be incorrect to translate the term *Ministère public* as 'District Attorney' even if the translation was intended for an American readership, since the two concepts are too far apart to be regarded as true equivalents.

## B Word-for-word translation

It is clear that there will be many circumstances in which the nearest equivalent concept of a term will merely amount to a word-for-word translation. The term *'Cour d'appel'* can obviously be safely translated as 'Court of Appeal', and the appropriate translation for *'contrat de vente'* is clearly 'contract of sale'. However, there are other circumstances in which a word-for-word translation will be appropriate.

In the previous section, it has been observed that there are several cases in which the equivalent concept is inappropriate and likely to cause confusion. In these circumstances, it is preferable to adopt the unimaginative, but safer, method or word-for-word translation. In Section A above, we saw how the use of the term 'Home Secretary' as a translation for the notion of *'Ministre de l'intérieur'*, is inappropriate; here, it is better to use the straightforward 'Minister of the Interior'. Similarly, for *'Conseil des Ministres'*, it is safer to use the bland 'Council of Ministers' (even allowing for the slight danger of confusion with the 'Council of Ministers' of the European Union), rather than the misleading 'Cabinet'.

Two observations must be made at this point. First, there is a danger that, in trying to avoid misleading the reader by using what appears to be the nearest

equivalent, the translator uses a word-for-word equivalent which is equally misleading, or is totally meaningless to the reader. This is why it would be unacceptable to use the term 'Council of State' as a translation for *Conseil d'Etat*, since the former term could very well mislead the reader into believing that the author is referring to body consisting of leading statesmen, or even a general advisory body assisting the state bodies, whereas the *Conseil d'Etat* has a very special function: to act as the supreme administrative court as well as acting as a legislative adviser to the Government and to Parliament. This is also why we disagree with Weston[5] where he considers the term 'court of cassation' to be an acceptable translation for '*Cour de cassation*', since this is a term which will be totally meaningless to the reader.

Secondly, the danger must be avoided of using word-for-word translation as an admission of defeat and therefore look for an equivalent concept at all costs, at the risk of misleading and misinforming. The golden rule for the translator, and particularly for the legal translator, must be: 'when in doubt, err on the side of safety'.

Naturally, there are the inevitable borderline cases. For example, is it appropriate to translate the term '*crime*' in French by 'crime' in English? Strictly speaking this should not be the case, since the word *crime* in French law is a specific term denoting one particular type of punishable offence, whereas the term 'crime' is used much more loosely in English. Yet it might be argued that to use the explanatory method described in the following section would be unnecessarily long-winded and artificial, and therefore the use of the term 'crime' in English would be acceptable. Obviously a great deal will depend on the context. When translating a French textbook on *droit pénal* in which the difference is being explained between a *contravention*, a *délit* and a *crime*, it is obvious that an explanatory approach will need to be adopted.

## C Use of the original source language term (accompanied by a translator's note where appropriate)

From the above, it will be clear that there are circumstances in which neither the nearest equivalent method nor a word-for-word translation will be equal to the task. Many terms simply have no equivalent in the target language, and must therefore be explained rather than translated. It must immediately be added, however, that for some terms this is an easier proposition than for others.

First, there are terms which have become sufficiently familiar to an English-speaking audience as to require no explanation, either in brackets or in footnote. The term *département* is a case in point. At the next level of difficulty, there are some terms for which an explanation consisting of a few words will be perfectly

---

5    *Op cit*, p. 25.

adequate. Thus the term *'Commissaire de la République'* can be translated by simply stating the original French term in full, followed, in brackets, by the words: 'Government representative in the municipality' (or *département*, or region, depending on the local authority in question). However, there are some terms which require a more elaborate explanation.

Let us take the term *'partie civile'* in French. This refers to the mechanism enabling the victim of a crime to add an action for civil damages to the criminal proceedings. However succinctly one endeavours to explain this, the gloss in question will be rather lengthy; in which case a footnote will probably be more appropriate.

Another problem concerns the question whether an explanation, once given, should be repeated. We take the view that if the term in question is repeated on several occasions throughout the text, an initial explanation will be sufficient. If, however, the term is used some 30 pages apart, it is probably appropriate to repeat the explanation (or to add a footnote referring the reader to the earlier explanation provided). Here, the legal translator will need to use his discretion and rely on his intuition and experience.

Weston[6] proposes an alternative method for solving the problem presented by terms having no equivalent in the target language: on the first occasion, the term is stated in the original language together with an explanation (eg the term *'auditeur'* is translated by the French original term, followed by the explanation 'junior members of the *Conseil d'Etat'*). Subsequently, however, the explanation may be incorporated in the text, with the original term added in brackets, eg 'the junior members of the *Conseil d'Etat* (the *auditeurs*)'.

Here again, there will be borderline cases. Let us take the term *'Conseil constitutionnel'*. To translate this term as 'constitutional court', using the word-for-word method, is probably acceptable; yet at the same time it may produce a misleading impression. As is explained more fully in Chapter Six (cf. *supra*, p. 113), the *Conseil constitutionnel* is a body to which only certain leading statesmen have access, and which can only invalidate proposed legislation (ie legislation before it reaches the stage of promulgation by the President of the Republic). There are therefore some grounds for arguing that it is preferable to keep the original term and add an explanation to that effect in a footnote.

A similar problem arises in relation to the term *'conseil de prud'hommes'*. It could be argued that the translation 'industrial tribunal' is perfectly acceptable by using the 'nearest equivalent term' method. However, it could be argued equally plausibly that the *Conseil de prud'hommes* has certain characteristics which make it a totally different animal from an industrial tribunal; therefore the original term should be retained, followed by an explanation concerning the bipartite nature of this particular type of court.

---

6   *Op cit*, p. 26.

# D The creation of new terms and concepts

There are occasions where, if none of the above methods appear to be suitable, it may be appropriate to use a new term or concept by way of translation. However, extreme caution is counselled when using this method, which is why it should be an exceptional procedure, to be used either when all else fails, or where the translator is absolutely sure that neither a misunderstanding nor an outrage on the target language will be perpetrated.

Let us take the case of the term *'Tribunal de grande instance'*. It is probably acceptable to translate this as 'court of first instance' even though there is no such thing in England, since the *Tribunal de grande instance* is the court which, in principle, has jurisdiction to deal for the first time with all civil disputes. The term *'Tribunal d'instance'* could be translated as 'district court' as conveying the notion that this court is the lowest civil court in the judicial system.

It is by applying this method that, in Chapter 9 (cf.*supra*, p. 188), we suggested the translation of *'le dispositif'* as 'the enacting terms of a judgment', even though there is no such term in English law. Rather than use a long-winded explanation and rely on the reader's memory to remember it, the use of this term is perfectly acceptable: it creates no confusion with any other term, and conveys reasonably accurately that which is the function and purpose of the formulation in question. However, we repeat that this method should only be used as a last resort.

# VI Conclusion

It is, in our view, appropriate to draw two conclusions from the difficulties and particularities of legal translation.

One is that it lays to rest once and for all the notion that machine translation will be a suitable substitute for the experienced legal translator. This concept is already a highly dubious one even in the field which allegedly best lends itself to it, ie technical translation. In view of the limited relevance of one-to-one equivalent dictionaries and glossaries to legal translation, the use of computers is also of very doubtful assistance. Those who claim otherwise are either mischievous or charlatans.

The other conclusion is that some expertise in the underlying subject matter of legal translation, ie the law, is an absolute must for any successful legal translator. It would be exaggerated to claim, as some do, that only lawyers should be allowed or licensed to engage in this particular activity. However, this is an area of translation in which background knowledge is an absolute must for all but the most general texts on the subject.

# Appendix 1

In this appendix three judgments of the French courts have been reproduced along with a suggested translation of each one in order to demonstrate the style adopted.

The first two are taken from the *Cour de cassation* and concern the Law of 5/7/1985 which (controversially) allowed victims of traffic accidents an automatic right to compensation unless it could be proved that the accident was due to the 'inexcusable fault' of the victim.

The third case is taken from the *Conseil d'Etat* and concerns the Law of 17/7/1978 which gives citizens the right to inspect files concerning them held by administrative bodies – the French equivalent of a 'Freedom of Information' Act.

In distinct contrast to what one would expect from a judgment of the House of Lords (a court of similar nature within the English hierarchy), the three judgments involved are extremely short and do not include any discussion or extended reasoning. It is to be remembered that French courts operate on a collegiate basis and therefore no individual judge's opinion is ever cited. It is a judgment of the court, not of the individuals on the bench.

No previous decisions are cited within the judgments and no judgment can set a binding precedent for cases which follow – indeed, as has been seen earlier, French law does not allow a court to base its decision on any previously decided case. The only guidance available is the wording of the relevant law.

## *Cour de cassation*

### Consorts Monnois et autre -c- Anfry

**La Cour. - Sur le moyen unique, pris dans ses deux branches:**
Attendu, selon l'arrêt confirmatif attaqué (Rouen, 29 mai 1986), que, de nuit, dans une agglomération, l'automobile de M. Anfry heurta et blessa mortellement M. Monnois qui, à pied, traversait la chaussée; que le Fonds de gestion des accidents du travail du port autonome du Havre demanda à M. Anfry le remboursement de ses prestations; que les consorts Monnois sont intervenus à l'instance pour demander la réparation de leur préjudice;

Attendu qu'il est fait grief à l'arrêt d'avoir débouté le Fonds de gestion des accidents du travail du port autonome du Havre et les consorts Monnois alors que, d'une part, en retenant que le fait pour un piéton de traverser de nuit une chaussée mal éclairée, aucun passage protégé ne se trouvant à proximité, constituait une faute inexcusable, la Cour d'Appel avait violé l'art 3, alinéa 1er, de la Loi du 5 juillet 1985 et alors que, d'autre part, tout conducteur tout conducteur devant conserver la maîtrise de son véhicule, en constatant que M. Anfry n'avait freiné que 15m avant le choc et non immédiatement après avoir vu le piéton s'engager sur la chaussée et en ne déduisant pas de cette constatation que l'automobiliste avait, par sa carence, contribué à la réalisation de l'accident, la Cour d'Appel aurait violé à nouveau ledit texte en décidant que la faute du piéton était la cause exclusive de l'accident;

Mais attendu qu'est inexcusable au sens de l'art 3 de la Loi du 5 juillet 1985 la faute volontaire d'une exceptionnelle gravité exposant sans raison valable son auteur à un danger dont il aurait dû avoir conscience;

Et a attendu que l'arrêt, après avoir relevé qu'au lieu de l'accident la chaussée à double sens de circulation est séparé par un terre-plein surmonté d'un muret sur lequel le piéton est monté puis descendu de l'autre côté, retient qu'en s'engageant de nuit sur une voie mal éclairée, après avoir franchi le muret sans s'assurer qu'il pouvait le faire sans danger, et en négligeant au surplus d'emprunter le passage protégé à 75m, M. Monnois n'avait pas pu ne pas avoir conscience du danger auquel il s'exposait et avait accepté de prendre des risques sans nécessité, que l'arrêt ajoute que les traces de freinage laissées par le véhicule ne permettent pas de retenir à l'encontre de l'automobiliste une vitesse excessive ou un défaut d'attention, que M. Anfry, protégé par l'existence du muret contre l'arrivée sur la chaussée de piétons venant de sa droite, ne pouvait prévoir que l'un d'eux escaladerait le muret et s'engagerait immédiatement sur la route, que, surpris, M. Anfry malgré un freinage énergique, n'a pu éviter l'accident; que de ces constatations et énonciations, la Cour d'Appel a pu déduire que la faute de la victime était inexcusable et avait été la cause exclusive de l'accident;

Par ces motifs - Rejette.

MM DEROURE rapp. BOUYSSIC, av. gén. - S.C.P. FORTUNET et MATTEI-DAWANCE, av.

206

# *Cour de cassation*
# (French Supreme Court of Review)

## The Monnois family and another v Anfry

**The Court – giving judgment on the two questions raised within the single ground of application for review:**

According to the judgment in question of the Court of Appeal of Rouen on 29/5/1986, which judgment upheld that of the first instance court, the facts were that at night in a built-up area, Mr Anfry hit and mortally wounded Mr Monnois who was crossing the road on foot. The work accident insurance company of the free port of Le Havre took action against Mr Anfry for reimbursement of the payments it had made. The Monnois family asked to be joined to the proceedings in order to obtain compensation for the loss they had suffered.

It is claimed that the judgment in question was wrong in rejecting the claims of the work accident insurance company of the free port of Le Havre and the Monnois family because:

(a) in finding that for a pedestrian to cross a badly lit road at night when there was no nearby pedestrian crossing was an inexcusable fault, the court had failed properly to apply the provisions of Article 3(1) of the Law of 5 July 1985; and

(b) as every driver must keep control of his vehicle, by finding that Mr Anfry had braked only 15 m from the point of collision and not immediately on seeing the pedestrian step into the road and by failing to infer from this that the driver had, by his failure to take action, contributed to the occurrence of the accident, the court had again failed properly to apply the said provision in coming to the conclusion that the fault of the pedestrian was the sole cause of the accident.

But a fault which is inexcusable within the meaning of Article 3 of the Law of 5 July 1985 is one which is voluntary and of such exceptional gravity that it exposes, without valid reason, the person at fault to a danger which ought to have been foreseen.

Further, having found that at that place where the accident occurred the two sides of the dual carriageway were separated by a central reservation and a low wall over which the pedestrian climbed, the judgment holds that by crossing at night a badly lit road and having climbed over a low wall without ensuring that this could be done without danger to himself and by failing to use the pedestrian crossing 75m away, Mr Monnois could not but have foreseen the danger to which he was exposing himself and had accepted those risks without being required to do so. The judgment adds that the skid marks left by the car did not permit the conclusion that the driver was travelling at an excessive speed or that he had failed to pay proper attention. Mr Anfry, protected by the existence of the wall against the arrival of pedestrians from his right hand side, could not foresee that one would climb the wall and immediately step into the road. In a state of surprise and despite violent braking, Mr Anfry could not have avoided the accident.

From these findings and statements, the Court of Appeal was free to deduce that the fault of the victim was the sole cause of the accident.

For these reasons: the application is dismissed.

Mr. DEROURE, juge rapporteur, Mr. BOUYSSIC, avocat général, Société Civile Professionnelle FORTUNET and MATTEI-DAWANCE, avocats.

## Cour de cassation

### Consorts Duverger c. Verre et autres

**La Cour. – Sur le moyen unique, pris en sa deuxième branche:**

Vu l'art 3, alinéa 1er, de la Loi no. 85-677 du 5 juillet 1985;

Attendu que seule est inexcusable, au sens de ce texte, la faute volontaire d'une exceptionnelle gravité, exposant sans raison valable son auteur à un danger dont il aurait dû avoir conscience;

Attendu, selon l'arrêt infirmatif attaqué, que, de nuit, dans une agglomération, l'automobile de M. Verre heurta et blessa mortellement M. Duverger qui, à pied, traversait la chaussée; que les consorts Duverger demandèrent à M. Verre et à la compagnie Europe la réparation de leur préjudice; que la Caisse primaire d'assurance maladie de Maine et Loire intervint à l'instance;

Attendu que, pour débouter les consorts Duverger en retenant à la charge de la victime une faute inexcusable, l'arrêt énonce qu'à l'approche de plusieurs voitures qu'ill pouvait voir arriver, circulant sur un long boulevard rectiligne, M. Duverger qui était à même de se rendre compte que les feux étaient au vert pour les automobilistes, a commis la très grande imprudence d'effectuer la traversée d'une chaussée à trois voies; qu'en létat de ces énonciations d'où ne résulte pas l'existence d'une faute inexcusable à la charge de la victime, la Cour d'Appel a violé le texte susvisé;

Par ces motifs: Casse,, annule et renvoie devant la Cour de Rennes.

MM. DEROURE, rapp., BOUYSSIC, av. gén., Mes DEFRENOIS, S.C.P. ROUVIERE, LEPITRE et BOUTET, av.

# *Cour de cassation*
# (French Supreme Court of Review)

## The Duverger family v Verre and another

**The Court – Giving judgment on the second question raised in the single ground of application for review:**

Reference having been made to Article 3 of the Law no. 85-677 of 5 July 1985;

Within the meaning of this provision, the only type of fault which is inexcusable is one which is voluntary and of such exceptional gravity that, without valid reason, it exposes the person at fault to a danger which ought to have been foreseen.

According to the judgment in question of the Court of Appeal, which judgment reversed that of the first instance court, the facts were that at night in a built-up area, a car driven by Mr Verre hit and mortally wounded Mr Duverger who was crossing the road on foot.

The Duverger family took action against Mr Verre and the Europe Insurance company for compensation for the loss they had suffered. The sickness insurance fund office of Maine-et-Loire was joined to the proceedings.

In finding against the Duverger family and in holding that it was the inexcusable fault of the victim, the judgment states that at the approach of several vehicles which he could see coming along a long straight road, Mr Duverger, who was in a position to see that the traffic lights were on green, was careless enough to attempt to cross a three lane road. An inexcusable fault on the part of the victim does not follow from these findings and, on that basis, the Court of Appeal has failed properly to apply the above-mentioned provision.

For these reasons:- The application is upheld. The judgment of the Court of Appeal is hereby set aside and the case referred back to the Court of Appeal in Rennes.

Mr. DEROURE, juge rapporteur, Mr. BOUYSSIC, avocat général, Maîtres DEFRENOIS, Société Civile Professionnelle ROUVIERE, LEPITRE and BOUTET, avocats.

# Conseil d'Etat

## Coiffier

**Requête de M. Coiffier tendant à:**

1. l'annulation du jugement du 16 avril 1984 du tribunal admninstratif de Nice rejetant sa demande tendant à l'annulation d'une décision du recteur de l'académie de Nice du 26 août 1983 lui refusant l'autorisation de consulter son dossier administratif accompagné d'un tiers;

2. l'annulation de cette décision;

Vu la loi no. 78-753 du 17 juillet portant diverses mesures d'amélioration des relations entre l'administration et le public; loi no. 83-643 du 13 juillet 1983 portant droits et obligations des fonctionnaires; l'ordonnance du 31 juillet 1945 et le décret du 30 septembre 1953; la loi du 30 décembre 1977;

Considérant qu'en dehors des cas de procédure disciplinaire, les modalités d'accès des fonctionnaires à leur dossier administratif sont régies par la loi susvisée du 17 juillet 1978; que l'article 6 bis de cette loi dispose 'les personnes qui le demandent ont le droit à la communication.....des documents de caractère nominatif les concernant, sans que des motifs tirés du secret de la vie privée, du secret médical portant exclusivement sur des faits qui leur sont personnels puissent leur être opposés';

Considérant que, par la décision attaquée, le recteur de l'académie de Nice, tout en accédant à la demande formulée par M. Coiffier, fonctionnaire au rectorat de Nice, de consulter son dossier administratif, a refusé qu'il se fasse accompagner d'un tiers lors de la consultation;

Considérant que si les dispositions législatives précitées ne prévoient pas expressément que l'intéressé peut se faire accompagner d'une personne de son choix, elles n'y font pas obstacle; que, dès lors, l'administration ne pouvait, en se fondant sur ces seules dispositions et sans invoquer de motif légitime, refusr d'accéder à la demande de M. Coiffier; que M. Coiffier est, dès lors, fondé à demander l'annulation du refus que lui a opposé le recteur de l'académie de Nice et en conséquence, l'annulation du jugement du tribunal administratif de Nice qui a rejeté sa demande dirigée contre ce refus.

# Conseil d'Etat

## Coiffier

**The appeal lodged by Mr Coiffier seeks:**

1) the quashing of the judgment of the administrative court of Nice which rejected his application for the setting aside of a decision of the 26 August 1983 whereby the director of the Nice regional education authority refused to allow him access to his administrative file when accompanied by a third party.

2) the quashing of the director's decision.

Reference has been made to:-

(a) the Law no. 78-753 of the 17 July containing various provisions for the improvement of relations between administrative bodies and members of the public;

(b) the Law no. 83-643 of 13 July 1983 which lays down the rights and duties of civil servants;

(c) the Order of 31 July 1945 and the Decree of the 30 September 1953;

(d) the Law of 30 December 1977

Except in so far as concerns cases of disciplinary proceedings, the procedure whereby civil servants may have access to their administrative files is governed by the above-mentioned Law of 17 July 1978. Article 6(b) provides 'persons who so request shall have a right of access to documents of a referable nature concerning them even if there are arguments based exclusively on personal information relating to private life of medical history put forward against such access.

Whilst acceding to the request of Mr Coiffier, a civil servant within the Nice regional education authority, to be given access to his administrative file, the director refused to allow Mr Coiffier to be accompanied by a third party at the time of access.

Although the above-mentioned provisions do not expressly state that an applicant may be accompanied by a third party of his choice, they do not expressly state otherwise. Thus, in basing his decision solely on these provisions and in not advancing any other legitimate grounds, the director could not refuse Mr Coiffier's request. Thus Mr Coiffier is justified in requesting that the director's refusal be set aside and, in consequence, that the judgment of the administrative court of Nice, which rejected his application in relation to this refusal, also be quashed.

# Appendix 2

## Glossary of legal terminology

Whilst not intended to replace a dictionary, the following summary of words, expressions and phrases is included as a general guide to the special vocabulary used within the French legal system.

| | |
|---|---|
| abroger (abrogation (f)) | to repeal (repeal) |
| accessoirement | in the alternative |
| accord (m) | contract |
| accusé (m) | defendant, accused |
| acte (m) (juridique) | any document having legal significance – an instrument |
| acte authentique | formal (authenticated) agreement |
| acte de commerce | commercial transaction |
| actes de l'état civil | official document relating to civil status (such as birth certificate etc) |
| acte sous seing privé | private (non-authenticated) agreement |
| action (f) en indemnité | action for damages (in tort) |
| action (f) publique | criminal prosecution |
| administration (f) | administration, management |
| adjoint (m) | assistant |
| aide (f) judiciaire | legal aid |
| à juste titre | correctly, properly |
| amende (f) | fine |
| appel (m) | appeal |
| apport (m) | contribution towards a company |
| arrêt (m) | judgment (of a court) |
| arrêt de mise en accusation | judgment in criminal proceedings confirming a *prima facie* case to answer |
| arrêt de non-lieu | judgment of no case to answer |
| arrêt de renvoi | judgment referring a case back to another court |
| arrêté (m) | order, decision, decree (of a minister or other administrative officer |
| arrêter | to decide, to rule (in the case of a court) |
| assemblée générale (f) | general meeting (of company) |
| assemblée plénière (f) | full court, general meeting |

| | |
|---|---|
| assesseur (m) | associate (lay) judge |
| assigner (en justice) | to summon (before a court) |
| association (f) non déclarée | association without legal capacity |
| association déclarée | association with legal capacity |
| association reconnue d'utilité publique | association officially acknowledged to serve public purposes |
| astreinte (f) | penalty |
| attendu que | phrase used to introduce part of a judgment – similar to 'whereas' |
| | |
| autorité judiciaire (f) | ordinary courts |
| audience (f) | court session, hearing |
| aval (m) | guarantee |
| avertissement (m) | summons (in criminal proceedings) |
| avocat (m) | lawyer (whose role is similar to that of a barrister) |
| avoué (m) | lawyer (before the Cour d'Appel) |
| (les) ayant droit (m) | dependants; persons entitled |
| | |
| bail (m) | lease (to tenant) |
| bail commercial | commercial lease |
| bailleur (m) | lessor |
| barreau (m) | bar association |
| bâtonnier (m) | senior member of bar association |
| bénéfice (m) | profit |
| bien-fondé (m) | justification |
| brevet (m) | patent |
| | |
| cadre (m) (dans le cadre de) | framework, context (in the context of) |
| capacité (f) | right to act at law |
| capital social (m) | authorised capital |
| casier (m) judiciaire | criminal record |
| casser | to quash |
| caution (f) | deposit, security |
| cautionnement (m) | bail |
| cession (f) | transfer |
| chambre (f) | chamber (of a court) |
| Chambre d'accusation | investigation section of Court of Appeal |
| charges (f) | expenses |
| chose (f) jugée | *res judicata* |
| circonscription (f) | 1. constituency (public law) |
| | 2. police district (criminal law) |
| citation (f) directe | summons (criminal law) |
| classement (m) sans suite | discharge of a criminal case |

| | |
|---|---|
| cohéritier (m) | joint heir |
| collectivité (f) territoriale | local administrative area |
| commerçant (m) | trader, business man |
| commetant (m) | principal (and agent) |
| Commissaire (m) du Gouvernement | spokesman for the public interest in administrative court proceedings |
| commission (f) rogatoire | delegated authority given by a judge (normally to the police) to conduct the preliminary investigation of a case |
| commissionnaire (m) | agent, broker |
| commune (f) | municipality |
| compensation (f) | set-off, settlement *per contra* |
| compétence (f) (il relève de la compétence de) | jurisdiction (it falls within the jurisdiction of) |
| conclure | to submit |
| conclusion (f) | submission, opinion |
| concurrence (f) | competition |
| concurrence (f) déloyale | unfair competition |
| conjoint (m) | spouse |
| connaître (de) | to hear a case (about) |
| conseil (m) | court, council, advice |
| Conseil d'Etat | supreme court within the administrative legal system |
| conseil juridique | legal executive, in- house lawyer (now merged with the profession of *avocat*) |
| Conseil de Prud'hommes | court dealing with disputes arising out of a contract of employment |
| conseiller (m) | judge, councillor, adviser |
| conseiller délégué | administrative court judge acting alone |
| conseiller rapporteur | administrative court judge responsible for the preliminary investigation of a case |
| considérant que | phrase used to introduce part of a judgment – similar to 'whereas' |
| constat (m) | official report, record |
| constatation (f) | finding, statement, proof |
| constater | to find, to prove, to state |
| contentieux (m) | litigation, court proceedings |
| (procédure (f)) contradictoire | contentious, fully argued (proceedings) |
| contrat (m) | contract |
| contravention (f) | offence of a minor nature, breach |
| contribuable (m) | taxpayer |
| contumace (f) | contempt of court |

215

| | |
|---|---|
| convention (f) | contract, agreement |
| il convient (de) | it is necessary (to) |
| contrôle restreinte (f) | judicial review |
| corps (m. pl) certains | specific goods |
| corps (m) de genre (m) | unascertained goods |
| cour (f) | court |
| Cour administrative d'appel | administrative appeal court |
| Cour (f) d'appel | appeal court |
| Cour (f) d'assises | criminal court dealing with the most serious offences |
| Cour (f) de cassation (f) | supreme court of review within the 'ordinary' legal system |
| Cour (f) de comptes (m) | Court of Auditors |
| courtier (m) | agent, broker |
| créancier (m) | creditor |
| créancier chirographaire (m) | unsecured creditor |
| crime (m) | serious offence; crime |
| décision (f) avant dire droit | interim order |
| décision motivée | reasoned decision |
| déclaration (f) | statement |
| dédommagement (m) | damages |
| dégradation (f) civique | loss of civic rights |
| délai (m) | time limit |
| délai du recours contentieux | time limit for lodging an appeal |
| délibération (f) | decision |
| délit (m) | tort, offence of medium seriousness |
| délivrance (f) | supply, delivery |
| demande (f) | claim, application |
| demande (f) de mise en liberté | bail application |
| dénomination sociale (f) | company name |
| dépens (m. pl) | costs (of the proceedings) |
| déroger (à), dérogation (f) | to depart (from), exception |
| dès | from then, from that time |
| dès lors | thus, hence |
| dès lors que | since (frequently used in court decisions, less in normal parlance) |
| désignation (f) | appointment |
| détention (f) provisoire | remand in custody |
| détenu (m) | prisoner |
| dispositif (m) | operative part of a judgment, its enacting terms – similar to 'held' |
| disposition (f) (d'une loi) | provision (of a law) |

| | |
|---|---|
| doctrine (f) | academic writing/opinion, the 'leading authorities' |
| dol (m) | misrepresentation, fraud |
| domicile (m) | official residence |
| dommages-intérêts (m) | damages, compensation |
| donnée (f) | fact, evidence |
| dossier (m) | (case) file |
| droit (m) | law, right |
| droit (m) commun | ordinary law (not to be confused with the English notion of the common law) |
| droit (m) supplétif | non-binding law |
| élu (m) | elected representative |
| émancipation (f) | premature majority |
| emprunt (m) d'Etat | public loan |
| aux enchères | (sale) by auction |
| engagement (f) | undertaking |
| enquête judiciaire (f) | judicial investigation |
| entreprise (f) | business, commercial undertaking |
| escroquerie (f) | fraud |
| (en l') espèce (f) | (in this) case |
| Etablissement ouvert (m) | open prison |
| Etablissement public (m) | Public corporation, autonomous public body |
| Etat civil (m) | Civil status register |
| évocation (f) | procedure whereby the *Conseil d'Etat* removes a case from a first instance court in order to give a ruling as a court of first and last resort |
| exception (f) | plea, claim |
| exécution (f) | performance |
| exécution forcée | specific performance |
| exécutoire (de plein droit) | enforceable (as of right) |
| expertise (f) | expert evidence |
| faire valoir que | to claim, allege |
| faire droit à | to uphold, grant |
| faire naître (les droits) | to give rise to (rights) |
| fausser (le jeu de concurrence) | to distort (competition) |
| faute (f) personnelle | fault, mistake, error committed by administrative official outside the scope of his duty |

217

| | |
|---|---|
| faute (f) de service | fault, mistake, error committed by administrative official within the scope of his duty |
| flagrant délit (m) | crime where offender is caught in the act |
| fonctionnaire (m) | civil or public servant, official |
| fond (m) | substance (of a case) |
| fonds (m. pl) de commerce | assets of a trader or business |
| forfaitairement | inclusive |
| fusion (f) | merger |
| Garde des Sceaux (m) | Minister of Justice |
| gestion (f) d'affaires (f) | agency of necessity |
| grand tableau (m) | official roll (of *avocats*) |
| greffier (m) | court clerk |
| (à) huis clos (m) | in camera |
| huissier (m) | bailiff, sheriff, process server |
| hypothèque (f) | mortgage |
| s'imposer | to be binding on |
| impôt (m) | tax |
| incompétence (f) | lack of jurisdiction |
| inculpation (f) | criminal charges |
| inculpé (m) | defendant, accused |
| indivision (f) | joint ownership |
| infraction (f) | offence (general term) |
| instance (f) d'arbitrage (m) | arbitration panel |
| instruction (f) | pre-trial investigation |
| intermédiaire (m) | agent |
| irrecevable (irrecevabilité (f)) | inadmissible (inadmissibility) |
| juge (m) | judge, court |
| juge départiteur | judge with casting vote (in the *Conseil de Prud'hommes*) |
| juge du fond | court dealing with law and fact – normally a court of first instance |
| juge rapporteur | judge responsible for the preliminary investigation of a case |
| juge des référés | judge in chambers, court giving an interlocutory ruling |
| juridiction (f) | court |
| juridiction de renvoi | court to which a case has been referred |
| juridictions de droit commun | ordinary (as opposed to administrative) courts with general jurisdiction |

| | |
|---|---|
| juridictions d'exception | court of limited jurisdiction |
| juridictions d'instruction | courts responsible for the preliminary investigation of a case |
| juridictions de jugement | courts responsible for the actual hearing of a case |
| juridictions de l'ordre administratif | administrative (as opposed to ordinary) courts |
| juridictions de l'ordre judiciaire | ordinary (as opposed to administrative) courts |
| juridictions du premier degré | first instance courts |
| juridictions de première instance | first instance courts |
| jurisprudence (f) | case law |
| jurisprudence constante | established case law |
| | |
| libération conditionnelle (f) | release on parole |
| liberté provisoire (f) | release on parole |
| licenciement (m) | dismissal |
| locataire (m) | tenant |
| loi (f) | law (as enacted by Parliament) |
| loi organique | law relating to the Constitution |
| | |
| magistrature (f) assise | branch of the judiciary which hears cases |
| magistrature debout | branch of the judiciary which addresses the court on behalf of the *Ministère public* |
| magistrature du siège | branch of the judiciary which hears cases |
| maison (f) d'arrêt | remand prison |
| maison centrale | central prison |
| mandat (m) | agency |
| mandat (m) d'arrêt | arrest warrant |
| marché ((m) | contract |
| marché de services | contract for services |
| marché de travaux publics | public works contract |
| méconnaître | general term implying that a law has either been wrongly applied, construed, interpreted, understood |
| mémoire (m) écrit | written submission |
| (re)mettre en cause | to call into question |
| mettre en demeure | to summons, order |
| milieu (m) fermé | closed prison |
| ministère public (m) | public prosecutor's department |
| motif (m) | reason (on which a judgment is based) |

motivation (f)    (formal) reasoning

moyen (m) (les moyens tirés de)    ground of (the party's) argument (the arguments based on)

nantissement (m)    security (by way of pledge, bailment, collateral etc) over goods

non-lieu (m)    no case to answer

notaire (m)    lawyer (solicitor)  dealing with non-contentious work

note (f)    annotation

octroi (m), octroyer    grant, to grant

d'office    automatically, officially, on his/her initiative

opposer    to argue, put forward,  claim

opposition (f)    appeal against judgment *in absentia*

ordonnance (f)    order of the court, measure issued by the Government under express delegation from Parliament

ordonnance (f) de renvoi    order refering a case from one court to another

ordre (m) des avocats    bar association

ordre juridique (m)    legal system

ordre public (m)    public policy

organ (m) délibérant    decision making body

ouïr (ouï)    to hear (having heard)

ouï-dire (m)    hearsay

parquet (m)    public prosecutor's department

partie civile (f)    victim of a crime adding civil action to criminal proceedings

perception (f)    collection (of taxes)

personne morale (f)    legal entity

plaidoirie (f)    final speech, summing up

(de) plein droit (m)    automatically

police (f)    police, (insurance) policy

Police (f) Judiciaire    branch of the police force (C.I.D.)

responsible for    investigating offences under the auspices of the *juge d'instruction*

pourvoi (m) (en cassation)    application (to the court of *cassation*)

pouvoir (m), (détournement de, abus de, excès de)    power, authority  (various forms of *ultra vires*)

préalable, au préalable    prior, beforehand

| | |
|---|---|
| Préfecture (f) de police | police station |
| préjudice (m) | loss, damage |
| preneur (m) | tenant, lessee |
| prestation (f) | benefit, payment |
| prétendre | to allege |
| prétendument | allegedly |
| prêter serment (m) | to take an oath |
| se prévaloir de | to rely on |
| prévenu (m) | defendant |
| prévoir, (prévision (f)) | to provide, foresee |
| (provision) privilège (m) | lien |
| procès (m) | trial, law suit |
| procès-verbal (m) | any written report – including a claim form, a statement, a charge sheet |
| propriété foncière (f) | land and buildings |
| puissance (f) publique | public authority |
| | |
| question (f) préjudicielle | preliminary question |
| | |
| recevable (recevabilité (f)) | admissible (admissibility) |
| recevoir délégation (f) | to act on behalf of |
| recours (m) | appeal |
| recueil (m) | (law) report |
| référés (m) (procédure des) | summary proceedings |
| régime (m) | system |
| régime matrimonial (m) | matrimonial property system |
| règlement (m) | regulation (as issued by the government) |
| réglementation (f) | set of regulations |
| réparation (f) | compensation |
| répartition (f) des compétences | allocation of responsibilities |
| requérant (m) -e (f) | plaintiff, applicant |
| requête (f) | application |
| réquisitoire (m) | summing up by public prosecutor |
| résiliation (f) (d'un contrat) | rescision (of a contract) |
| responsabilité (f) | liability (normally tortious or contractual) |
| il ressort de | it emerges from |
| retenir | to find (as a fact) |
| retrait (m) | withdrawal |
| révision (f) | appeal on new evidence |
| | |
| saisie (f) | distraint |
| saisir (un tribunal) de | to refer a matter (to court) |
| section (f) contentieuse | litigation section |

| | |
|---|---|
| sentence arbitrale (f) | arbitration award |
| siège (m) social | registered office (of a company) |
| signification (f) | official notification of a judgment |
| signifier un acte | to serve a document officially |
| société (f) (anonyme) | (limited) company |
| souligner (il y a lieu de souligner) | to emphasise (it must be emphasised) |
| sous la main de justice (f) | in custody |
| soutenir | to maintain, allege, claim |
| stage (m) | work or training placement |
| stagiaire (m-f) | trainee lawyer |
| statuer | to give a ruling, judgment |
| statuts (m.pl) | memorandum and articles of association of a company |
| | |
| subir un préjudice | to suffer loss |
| suffrage (m) | voting |
| surseoir, sursis (m) | to stay, defer, postpone proceedings |
| surveillant (m) | prison warden |
| syndic (m) de la faillite | official receiver |
| | |
| témoin (m) | witness |
| tendre (les dispositions tendent à reprimer) | to seek (the provisions seek to punish) |
| testament (m) | will |
| tiers (m) | third party |
| tirer (de) | to be based (on) |
| trancher (une action) | to decide (a case) |
| (en) vigueur | (in) force |
| tribunal (m) | court |
| Tribunal (m) administratif | first instance administrative court |
| Tribunal des affaires de sécurité sociale | court dealing with social security problems |
| Tribunal de commerce | court dealing with commercial contracts, insolvencies |
| Tribunal des conflits | court with responsibility for deciding which court has jurisdiction to deal with a particular case |
| Tribunal correctionnel | criminal court dealing with offences of medium seriousness |
| Tribunal de grande instance | first instance civil court with general jurisdiction |
| Tribunal d'instance | lower civil court |
| Tribunal paritaire des baux ruraux | court dealing with agricultural leases |
| Tribunal de police | lower criminal court |

| | |
|---|---|
| tutelle (f) (civil law) | guardianship |
| tutelle (f) administrative | supervision of administrative decisions |
| | |
| vice (m) de forme | procedural or formal defect |
| violation (f) | infringement, breach |
| viser (les dispositions visées) | to aim at (the provisions in question) |
| voie (f) de fait | (1) administrative law: an act by an administrative body which is so flagrantly wrong that it ceases to have the quality of an administrative act. |
| | (2) criminal law: assault |
| voie (f) de recours | avenue of appeal |
| vol (m) | theft |

# Bibliography

Ambrosi, C. and Ambrosi, A., *La France*, 1870-1986 (4th edn, 1986, Masson).

Auby, J-M., and Auby, J-B., *Droit public* (Vol 1, 11th edn, 1993, Sirey).

Bot, Y., *Les institutions judiciaires* (1985, Berger-Levrault).

Brown, L.N., and Garner, J.F., *French Administrative Law* (3rd edn, 1983, Butterworths).

Cairns, W.J., 'The Legal Environment', in Nugent, N. and O'Donnel, R. (eds), *The European Business Environment* (1994, MacMillan).

Dadomo, C. and Farrar, S., *The French Legal System* (1993, Butterworths).

David, R., *Les grands systèmes de droit contemporains* (8th edn, 1982, Dalloz).

Dickson, B., *Introduction to French Law* (1994, Pitman).

Duhamel, O., *La constitution française* (in *Que sais-je?* series) (1992, Presses Universitaires de France).

Duverger, M., *Eléments de droit public* (14th edn, 1993, Presses Universitaires de France).

Farrar, J.H. and Dugdale, A.M., *Introduction to Legal Method* (3rd edn, 1990, Sweet & Maxwell).

Flour, J., and Aubert, J-L., *Droit civil – les obligations I. l'acte juridique* (1975, Armand Collin).

Foster, N., *German Law and Legal System* (1993, Blackstone).

Guéry, G., *Droit des affaires* (5th edn, 1991, Dunod).

Giudicelli-Delage, G., *Institutions juridictionnelles* (2nd edn, 1993, Presses Universitaires de France).

Kahn-Freund, O., Lévy, C., and Rudden, B., *A Source-book on French Law* (2nd edn, 1979, Oxford University Press).

Lasok, D. and Bridge, J.W., *Introduction to the Law and Institutions of the European Communities* (5th edn, 1993, Butterworth).

Lawson, F.H., Anton, A.E., Brown, L.N., *Amos & Walton's Introduction to French Law* (3rd edn, 1967, Oxford University Press).

Le Docte, E., *Legal Dictionary in Four Languages* (4th edn, 1989, Maarten Kluwer's Internationale Uitgeversonderneming).

Long, M., Weil, P., Braibant, G., *Les grands arrêts de la jurisprudence administrative* (3rd edn, 1978, Sirey).

Marsh, S.B., and Soulsby, J., *Business Law* (5th edn, 1992, McGraw Hill).

Masclet, J-C., and Maus, D. (eds), *Les constitutions nationales à l'épreuve de l'Europe* (1993, La Documentation Française).

Maurin, *Droit public* (1993, Sirey).

Mueller, G.O.W., *The French Penal Code* (1960, Sweet & Maxwell).

Nicholas, B., *French Law of Contract* (1982, Butterworth).

Pagé, J-P., *Profil économique de la France* (1981, La Documentation Française).

Pearson, E.S., *Law for European Business Students* (1994, Pitman).

Perrot, R., *Institutions judiciaires* (4th edn, 1993, Montchrestien).

Pradel, J. and Leigh, L., 'Le ministère public. Examen comparé des droits anglais et français', *Revue de droit pénal et de criminologie 3* (1989) p. 223 *et seq*.

Robinson, O.F., Fergus, T.D., and Gordon, W.M., *An Introduction to European Legal History* (1985, Professional Books).

Salvage, P., *Droit pénal général* (3rd edn, 1994, Presses Universitaires de Grenoble).

Sourioux, J-L., *Introduction au droit* (2nd edn, 1990, Presses Universitaires de France).

Taisne, J.J., *Institutions judiciaires* (1992, Dalloz).

Trotabas, L., and Isoart, P., *Manuel de droit public et administratif* (1982, LGDJ).

Trouille, H., 'A Look at French Criminal Procedure' (1994) *Criminal Law Review*, p. 735.

Wade, ECS, and Bradley, A.W., *Constitutional and Administrative Law* (11th edn, 1989, Longman).

Walker, D.M., *The Scottish Legal System* (5th edn, 1981, W. Green & Son).

Weil, P., *Le droit administratif* (in *Que sais-je?* series) (15th edn, 1992, Presses Universitaires de France).

Weston, M., *An English Reader's Guide to the French Legal System* (2nd edn, 1993, Berg).

Wright, V., *The Government and Politics of France* (1977, Hutchinson University Library).

# Index